Extreme Values and Financial Risk

Extreme Values and Financial Risk

Special Issue Editors

Stephen Chan

Saralees Nadarajah

MDPI • Basel • Beijing • Wuhan • Barcelona • Belgrade

Special Issue Editors
Stephen Chan
American University of Sharjah
UAE

Saralees Nadarajah
University of Manchester
UK

Editorial Office
MDPI
St. Alban-Anlage 66
4052 Basel, Switzerland

This is a reprint of articles from the Special Issue published online in the open access journal *Journal of Risk and Financial Management* (ISSN 1911-8074) from 2017 to 2018 (available at: https://www.mdpi.com/journal/jrfm/special_issues/extreme_values)

For citation purposes, cite each article independently as indicated on the article page online and as indicated below:

LastName, A.A.; LastName, B.B.; LastName, C.C. Article Title. *Journal Name* **Year**, *Article Number*, Page Range.

ISBN 978-3-03897-439-0 (Pbk)
ISBN 978-3-03897-440-6 (PDF)

Contents

About the Special Issue Editors

Stephen Chan, Assistant Professor, was awarded the EPSRC Doctoral Prize Fellowship in 2016 at the University of Manchester, UK. His research areas include extreme value analysis and distribution theory in analyzing financial commodities data and cryptocurrency data. He co-developed and co-wrote an R package entitled "VaRES" for computing value at risk and expected shortfall. He is a co-author of the book Extreme Events in Finance: A Handbook of Extreme Value Theory and its Applications.

Saralees Nadarajah is a Senior Lecturer in the School of Mathematics, University of Manchester, UK. His research interests include climate modeling, extreme value theory, distribution theory, information theory, sampling and experimental designs, and reliability. He is an author/co-author of four books, and has over 600 papers published or accepted. He has held positions in Florida, California, and Nebraska.

Journal of
Risk and Financial Management

MDPI

Article

Hierarchical Transmuted Log-Logistic Model: A Subjective Bayesian Analysis

Carlos A. dos Santos [1,*,†], Daniele C. T. Granzotto [1,†], Vera L. D. Tomazella [2,†] and Francisco Louzada [3,†]

1 Department of Statistics, State University of Maringá, 87020-900 Maringá-PR, Brazil; dctgranzotto@uem.br
2 Department of Statistics, Federal University of São Carlos, 13565-905 São Carlos-SP, Brazil; vera@ufscar.br
3 Math Science Institute and Computing, University of São Paulo, 13560-970 São Carlos-SP, Brazil; louzada@icmc.usp.br
* Correspondence: casantos@uem.br; Tel.:+55-44-3011-5344
† These authors contributed equally to this work.

Received: 30 December 2017; Accepted: 5 March 2018; Published: 7 March 2018

Abstract: In this study, we propose to apply the transmuted log-logistic (TLL) model which is a generalization of log-logistic model, in a Bayesian context. The log-logistic model has been used it is simple and has a unimodal hazard rate, important characteristic in survival analysis. Also, the TLL model was formulated by using the quadratic transmutation map, that is a simple way of derivating new distributions, and it adds a new parameter λ, which one introduces a skewness in the new distribution and preserves the moments of the baseline model. The Bayesian model was formulated by using the half-Cauchy prior which is an alternative prior to a inverse Gamma distribution. In order to fit the model, a real data set, which consist of the time up to first calving of polled Tabapua race, was used. Finally, after the model was fitted, an influential analysis was made and excluding only 0.1% of observations (influential points), the reestimated model can fit the data better.

Keywords: hierarchical Bayesian model; influential analysis; log-logistic distribution; transmuted map

---

1. Introduction

The genetic prepotency of cows is an important issue since the development of livestock is directly related to the growth of the food production. Brazilians institutes are concerned with the development of a particular race, the Tabapua, which was the first humped cattle developed in the country. Due to the economic results of this particular race, this study is twofold: present the TLL model and fit the times up to the first calving of the cows pointing characteristics of this race.

Proposed by Granzotto and Louzada-Neto (2014), the TLL model presents important characteristics of a good model: it is flexible, tractable, interpretable and simple. Following the Shaw and Buckley (2007) idea, this new distribution incorporates a new third parameter λ that introduces skewness and preserve the moments of the baseline distribution. Several studies can be cited that proposed similar generalizations of survival models, see for example (Aryal and Tsokos 2009; Aryal and Tsokos 2011).

Due to good characteristics of the TTL model along with its simplicity (the main functions are analytically expressed) and the hazard properties (it has a larger range of choices for the shape of the hazard function most commonly observed in the survival analysis field), this paper present an application of the model in a Bayesian context.

In order to fit this new model, the subjective Bayesian analysis was used. For that, the half-Cauchy prior distribution, cited by several authors such as (Polson and Scott 2012; Gelman 2006), as an alternative prior to a inverse Gamma distribution, was used. Specially, Gelman (2006) made use of this particular prior for variance parameters in hierarchical models which is our case.

Furthermore, in order to provide an indication of bad model fitting or influential observations, an influential analysis was made, see for example (Ortega et al. 2003; Fachini et al. 2008).

The paper is organized as follows. The hierarchical log-logistic model built by using the half-Cauchy prior distribution is presented in Section 2. In Section 3 we presented an application by using a real data set on a polled Tabapua race time up to first calving data. An influence diagnostic was presented in Section 4 and the data set was re-analyzed refitting the model. Final remarks and conclusions are presented in Section 5.

2. Hierarchical TLL Model

Proposed by Granzotto and Louzada-Neto (2014), the TLL is a generalization of the log-logistic model containing the baseline model as a particular case (for log-logistic distribution see (Bennett 1983; Chen et al. 2001)). Tractable, Interpretable and flexible enough, the new construction can be used to analyze more complex dataset, introducing skew to a base distribution and preserving its moments. Let X be a nonnegative random variable denoting the lifetime of an individual in some population then, the probability density function (pdf) and the cumulative function of the TLL distribution are respectively given by

$$f(x) \quad = \quad \frac{e^{\mu}\beta x^{\beta-1}\left[\left(1+e^{\mu}x^{\beta}\right)-\lambda\left(e^{\mu}x^{\beta}-1\right)\right]}{\left(1+e^{\mu}x^{\beta}\right)^{3}}. \tag{1}$$

and

$$F(x) \quad = \quad \frac{e^{\mu}x^{\beta}}{\left(1+e^{\mu}x^{\beta}\right)^{2}}\left(1+e^{\mu}x^{\beta}+\lambda\right). \tag{2}$$

where $\beta > 0$, $\mu \in \mathbb{R}$ and $-1 \leq \lambda \leq 1$. Since the distribution was proposed to model experiments in reliability analysis, Figure 1 presents several examples of survival, probability density and hazard rate functions for different values of the parameters.

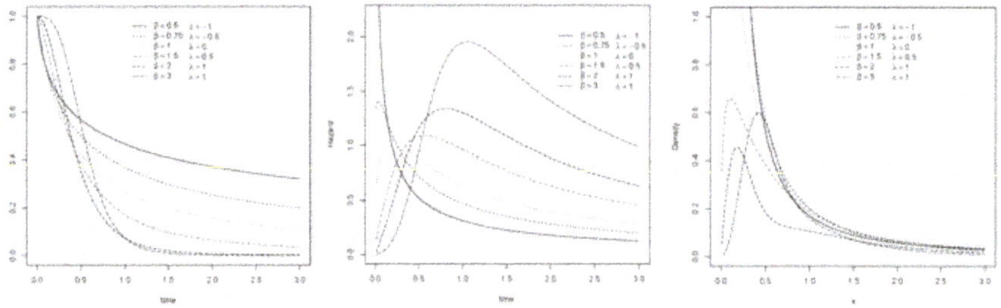

(a) (b) (c)

Figure 1. Transmuted model curves: (**a**) Survival, (**b**) hazard and (**c**) probability density function.

According to Chen and Ibrahim (2006), one of most common ways of combining several sources of information is though hierarchical modeling. Thus, the authors show us the relationship between the power prior and hierarchical models using as example the regression models.

Also, Gelman (2006) show us that several studies by using multilevel models are central to modern Bayesian statistics for both conceptual and practical reasons. The authors suggest to use the half-t family as a prior distribution for variance parameters such the half-Cauchy distribution, that is a special conditionally-conjugate folded-noncentral-t family case of prior distributions for parameters that represent the discrepancy. Even though several studies use the half-Cauchy prior for scale parameter (see for example Polson and Scott 2012), Gelman (2006) used this prior not for scale but for variance parameters and illustrated serious problems with the inverse-Gamma prior which is the most commonly used prior for variance component, see Daniels and Daniels (1998).

In this paper we proposed to use the hierarchical models in two levels, for that, suppose the hierarchical model given as $[X|\mu,\beta,\lambda] \sim f(x|\mu,\beta,\lambda)$, $\mu|\sigma^2 \sim \pi_\mu(\mu|\sigma^2)$, $\beta|\theta \sim \pi_\beta(\beta|\theta)$, $\lambda \sim \pi_\lambda(\lambda)$, $\sigma^2 \sim \psi_\sigma(\sigma^2)$ and $\theta \sim \psi_\theta(\theta)$. The posterior distribution can be constructed as following.

Proposition 1. *Let us suppose that, in the first stage, we considered a class Γ of priors that led to following*

$$\begin{aligned} \Gamma &= \Big\{\pi(\mu,\beta,\lambda|\sigma^2,\theta) : \pi(\mu,\beta,\lambda|\sigma^2,\theta) = \pi_\mu(\mu|\sigma^2)\pi_\beta(\beta|\theta)\pi_\lambda(\lambda)\Big| \\ &\quad \pi_\mu \text{ being } \mathrm{N}(\tau,\sigma^2), (\tau,\sigma^2) \in \mathbb{R}\times\mathbb{R}^+; \quad \pi_\beta \text{ being } \mathrm{HC}(\theta), \theta \in \mathbb{R}^+; \\ &\quad \pi_\lambda \text{ being } \mathrm{U}(a,b), (a,b) \in \mathbb{R}\times\mathbb{R}, a<b\Big\}. \end{aligned}$$

Also, the second stage (sometimes called a hyperprior), would consist of putting a prior distribution $\psi_k(\cdot)$ on the hyperparameters σ^2 and θ where

$$\begin{aligned} \Psi &= \Big\{\psi(\sigma^2,\theta) : \psi(\sigma^2,\theta) = \psi_{\sigma^2}(\sigma^2)\psi_\theta(\theta) \quad \psi_{\sigma^2} \text{ being } \mathrm{Gamma}(\alpha,\zeta), \\ &\quad (\alpha,\zeta) \in \mathbb{R}^+\times\mathbb{R}^+; \quad \psi_\beta \text{ being } \mathrm{Gamma}(\eta,\vartheta), (\eta,\vartheta) \in \mathbb{R}^+\times\mathbb{R}^+; \\ &\quad \alpha,\zeta,\eta,\vartheta \text{ are known and does not depend on any other hyperparameter}\Big\}. \end{aligned}$$

Thus, the hyerarchical log-logistic posterior distribution is written as

$$\begin{aligned} \pi(\mu,\beta,\lambda|\mathbf{x}) &\propto \frac{e^\mu\beta\theta}{\sigma}\left[x^{\beta+\alpha+\eta-3}\frac{[(1+e^\mu x^\beta)-\lambda(e^\mu x^\beta-1)]}{(1+e^\mu x^\beta)^3}\right] \\ &\quad \times \exp\left\{-\left(\zeta+\vartheta+\frac{x}{2\sigma^2}\right)\right\}. \end{aligned} \tag{3}$$

Proof. The demonstration is direct.

Note that, the β parameter is supposed to be a half-Cauchy distribution which probability density function given by

$$f(x) = \frac{2\theta}{\pi\,(x^2+\theta^2)}, \qquad x>0, \theta>0, \tag{4}$$

where θ is a scale parameter which has a broad peak at zero and, in limit, $\theta \to \infty$ this becomes a uniform prior density. However, large finite values for θ represent prior distributions which we call "weakly informative". For example, Gelman (2006) show us that, for $\theta = 25$, the half-Cauchy is nearly flat although it is not completely. □

3. Application to Real Data

Founded in 70's, the Brazilian Agricultural Research Corporation (Embrapa) is under the aegis of the Brazilian Ministry of Agriculture, Livestock, and Food Supply. Since the foundation, they have taken on the challenge to develop a genuinely Brazilian model of tropical livestock (and agriculture as well), to keep increasing the production of food. As a result of the intense research work, the beef and pork supply were quadrupled, helping the Brazilian food to one of the world's largest food producers and exporters.

One of the special research is related to the genetic prepotency of cows whereas the economic results is directly related to beef cattle, see for example Pereira (2000). Granzotto and Louzada-Neto (2014) study the Tabapua race time up to first calving of 17,026 animals observed from 1983 to 2007, held at Embrapa. Firstly, as the minimum observed calving was 721 days, we subtract this amount of the observed times and the distribution of the first calving times can be observed in the Figure 2b.

Also, the TTT plot, presented in Figure 2a shows the possible unimodal hazard rate as it is concave, convex and then concave again, see for example Barlow and Campo (1975).

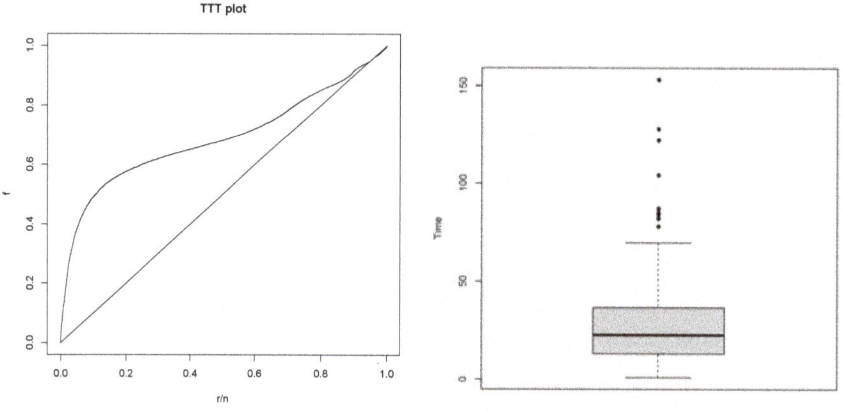

(a) (b)

Figure 2. (**a**) TTT Plot and (**b**) boxplot of times.

After initial analysis, we are considering the hierarchical TLL model, as we specify in Section 2, to fit the data. The posterior samples were generated by the Metropolis-Hastings technique. Three chains of the dimension 100,000 was considered for each parameter, discarding the first 10,000 iterations (in order to eliminate the effect of the initial values), a lag size 10 was used to avoid the correlation problems, resulting in a final sample size 10,000. The posterior summaries for $\mu, \beta, \lambda, \sigma^2$ and θ are present in Table 1 and the 95% credible intervals by considering the priors above-mentioned can be seem in Table 2.

Table 1. Posterior model summary of the hierarchical TLL model parameters.

Parameter	Mean	Standard Deviation	Percentiles		
			25%	50%	75%
μ	−17.865	0.138	−17.958	−17.871	−17.775
β	3.043	0.022	3.029	3.044	3.058
λ	−0.815	0.012	−0.823	−0.815	−0.807
σ^2	900.100	822.500	333.800	640.400	1208.100
θ	198.800	195.100	60.171	139.800	273.400

Table 2. 95% Credible Interval of parameters estimated.

Parameter	Equal-Tail Interval		HPD Interval	
μ	−18.123	−17.576	−18.118	−17.571
β	2.997	3.085	2.997	3.084
λ	−0.838	−0.791	−0.838	−0.790
σ^2	96.474	3044.600	37.837	2516.300
θ	5.395	733.800	0.008	594.800

The convergence of the chain was verified by Gelman and Rubin's convergence diagnostic criterion, see for example (Gelman and Rubin 1992), which demonstrate that these criteria is satisfied (Table 3). Also, the convergence can be seem in Figure 3a–j.

Table 3. Gelman and Rubin's criterion to verify the parameters convergence of the hierarchical TLL distribution.

Parameter	Estimate	Upper Bound
μ	1.0085	1.0060
β	1.0082	1.0057
λ	1.0020	1.0017
σ^2	1.0016	1.0019
θ	1.0004	1.0009

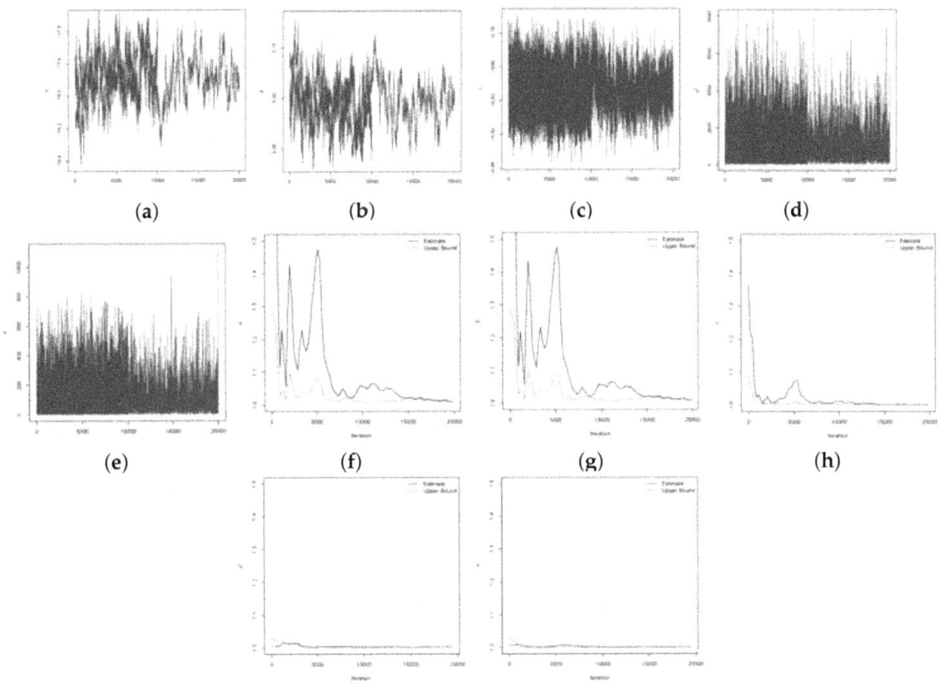

(a) (b) (c) (d)

(e) (f) (g) (h)

(i) (j)

Figure 3. Traceplots and convergence plots, respectively, for: (**a**,**f**): μ; (**b**,**g**): β; (**c**,**h**): λ; (**d**,**i**): σ^2 and; (**e**,**j**): θ.

Also, the marginal posterior densities for μ, β and λ, respectively, can be analyzed by the Figure 4a–e. After estimate and analyze the convergence of the model, Figure 5a,b show us, respectively, the hazard estimate curve, with the $\hat{T}_{\max}$ and the $T_{\max}$ 95% confidence interval; the survival curves estimated vs empirical and the histograma which are possible to see how well it fits a set of observations.

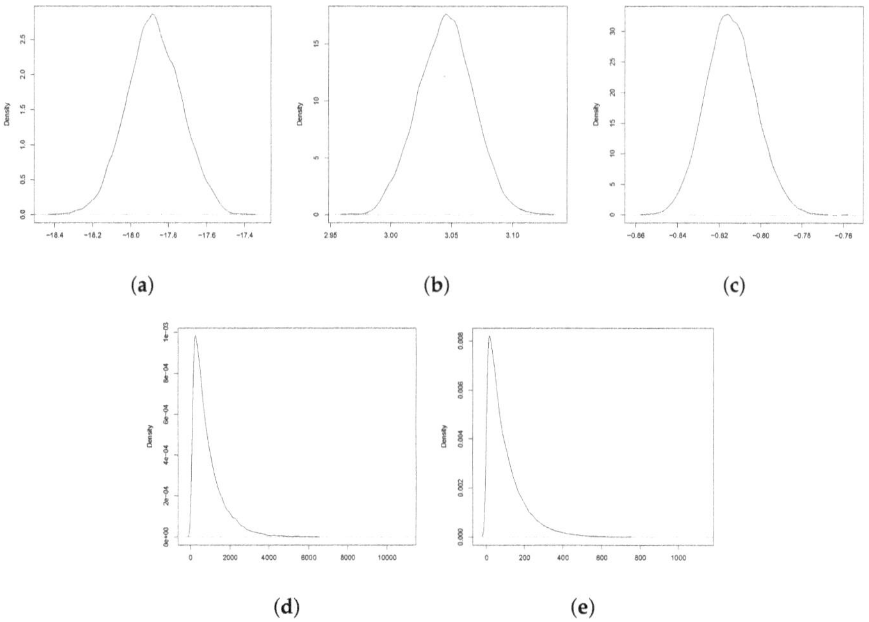

Figure 4. Marginal posteriors densities for: (**a**) μ, (**b**) β, (**c**) λ, (**d**) σ^2 and (**e**) θ.

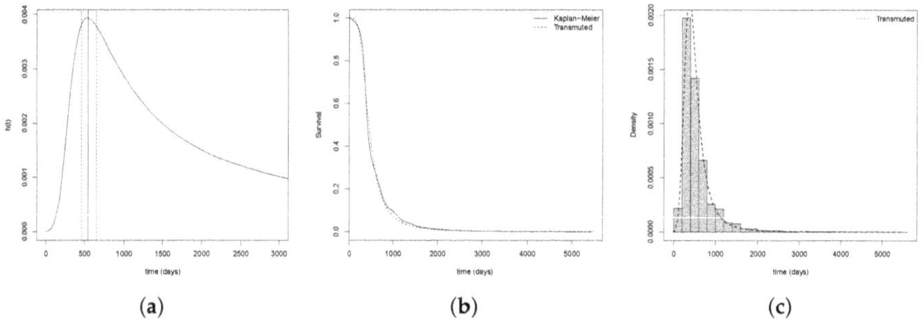

Figure 5. (**a**) hazard estimate curve, with the $\hat{T}_{\max}$ and the $T_{\max}$ 95% confidence interval, (**b**) survival curves and (**c**) histogram.

Considering the hyerarchical TLL fitting, the $\hat{T}_{\max}$ is equals to 546.77 days (18.23 months) and its 95% confidence interval is given by $IC[T_{\max}, 95\%] = (460.04; 652.86)$ days (see Figure 5a). Furthermore, the median time up to first calving is equals to 452.48 days (or approximately 15.08 months), and the mean of time is 540.13 days (or approximately 18 months), with standard deviation equals to 13.34 months.

4. Influence Analysis

In this section we present an analysis of global influence for the data set given, using the TLL model in a bayesian context.

In few words, the influence analysis is a case-deletion, that we study the effect of withdraw of the *i*th element sampled. Several measures of global influence analysis are presented in the literature.

In this study we are considering two: the generalized Cook's distance (CD) and the likelihood difference (LD). The first one, CD, defined as the standard norm of $\zeta_i = (\mu_i, \beta_i, \lambda_i, \sigma_i^2, \theta_i)$ and $\hat{\zeta} = (\hat{\mu}, \hat{\beta}, \hat{\lambda}, \hat{\sigma}^2, \hat{\theta})$, and the LD are given, respectively, by

$$CD_i(\zeta) = \left[\ \zeta_i - \hat{\zeta}\ \right]^T [-\ddot{L}(\zeta)] \left[\ \zeta_i - \hat{\zeta}\ \right], \tag{5}$$

and

$$LD_i(\zeta) = 2\left\{l(\hat{\zeta}) - l(\zeta_i)\right\}. \tag{6}$$

According to Lee et al. (2006), $\ddot{L}(\zeta)$ can be approximated by the estimated covariance and variance matrix. Some possible influence points are identified in the LD plot, Figure 6.

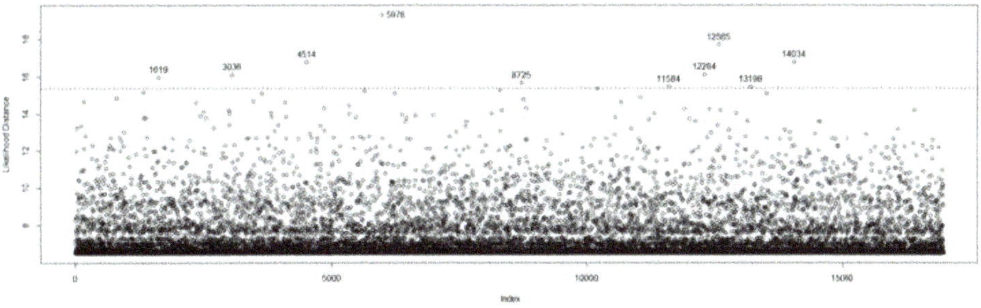

Figure 6. Likelihood distance.

Furthermore, the impact of the identified influential points should be measured. For that, we consider the relative changes that can be measured as $RC_{\zeta_j} = \left|\frac{\hat{\zeta}_j - \hat{\zeta}_{j(I)}}{\hat{\zeta}_j}\right| \times 100\%$, $j = 1, \ldots, p+1$, where $\hat{\zeta}_{j(I)}$ denotes the MLE of ζ_j after the set I of observations has been removed.

Three measures of influential observations are considered: TRC is the total relative changes, MRC the maximum relative changes and LD the likelihood displacement, see for example (Lee et al. 2006; Granzotto and Louzada-Neto 2014). Table 4 presents the values when we withdrew from 0.01% to 5% of the outstand identified points in Figure 6.

By considering the RC's, 10 most influential points were withdrew and the model was re-fitted. Again, by using the Metropolis-Hastings technique we generated a chain of 100,000 observations, burn in of 10,000 and lag 10, resulting in a final sample size 10,000. Tables 5 and 6 shows the posterior summaries and the 95% credible intervals.

Clearly, the most affected estimate parameter was λ if we compare to the parameters estimated by using the original dataset. Further, withdrawing 0.1% of sample, i.e., just 17 observations, we do not lose much information and also improve the fitted model, see Figure 7a–c, that show us the fitted model.

Table 4. RC (in %) and the corresponding TRC, MRC and $LD_{(I)}$.

Removed Case	Parameter	RC	TRC	MRC	$LD_{(I)}$
Identify Points	μ	8.271			
	β	5.142			
	λ	68.336	86.438	68.336	142
	σ_2	2.877			
	θ	1.811			
0.1%	μ	0.844			
	β	0.818			
	λ	0.123	3.598	1.358	217
	σ_2	0.456			
	θ	1.358			
0.5%	μ	2.098			
	β	2.073			
	λ	0.098	8.634	3.219	949
	σ_2	1.144			
	θ	3.219			
1%	μ	3.257			
	β	3.250			
	λ	0.368	9.782	3.257	1821
	σ_2	1.700			
	θ	1.207			
2%	μ	5.843			
	β	5.855			
	λ	0.393	17.064	5.855	3519
	σ_2	2.911			
	θ	2.062			
3%	μ	8.096			
	β	8.162			
	λ	1.460	22.086	8.162	5178
	σ_2	3.111			
	θ	1.258			
4%	μ	10.458			
	β	10.547			
	λ	0.785	28.558	10.547	6775
	σ_2	6.566			
	θ	0.201			
5%	μ	12.463			
	β	12.627			
	λ	2.160	34.232	12.627	8383
	σ_2	6.277			
	θ	0.704			

Table 5. Posterior model summary of the hierarchical TLL model parameters.

Removed Case	Parameter	Mean	Standard Deviation	Percentiles		
				25%	50%	75%
Identify Points	μ	−19.343	1.269	−20.522	−20.327	−17.975
	β	3.200	0.130	3.062	3.285	3.319
	λ	−0.258	0.519	−0.813	0.153	0.232
	σ^2	926.00	840.30	348.70	664.10	1224.00
	θ	202.40	204.70	59.08	139.20	282.00
0.1%	μ	−18.016	0.129	−18.098	−18.015	−17.933
	β	3.068	0.021	3.055	3.068	3.082
	λ	−0.814	0.012	−0.822	−0.814	−0.806
	σ^2	904.20	826.40	334.50	651.90	1207.20
	θ	196.10	194.80	56.84	137.20	270.50
0.5%	μ	−18.240	0.135	−18.336	−18.238	−18.146
	β	3.107	0.022	3.091	3.106	3.122
	λ	−0.816	0.012	−0.824	−0.816	−0.808
	σ^2	910.40	842.80	339.00	643.80	1203.30
	θ	205.20	203.70	61.83	142.40	284.10
1%	μ	−18.447	0.131	−18.536	−18.441	−18.352
	β	3.142	0.021	3.127	3.142	3.157
	λ	−0.818	0.012	−0.826	−0.818	−0.810
	σ^2	915.40	853.70	337.50	647.80	1221.70
	θ	196.40	195.20	56.19	136.90	273.10
2%	μ	−18.909	0.144	−19.007	−18.907	−18.811
	β	3.222	0.023	3.206	3.221	3.238
	λ	−0.818	0.013	−0.827	−0.818	−0.810
	σ^2	926.30	826.60	353.60	667.40	1235.00
	θ	202.90	199.40	60.53	143.40	279.70
3%	μ	−19.312	0.142	−19.410	−19.304	−19.222
	β	3.292	0.023	3.277	3.291	3.308
	λ	−0.827	0.012	−0.835	−0.827	−0.819
	σ^2	928.10	849.10	352.20	668.20	1215.20
	θ	196.30	193.30	56.37	139.00	275.50
4%	μ	−19.734	0.154	−19.834	−19.737	−19.641
	β	3.364	0.025	3.350	3.365	3.381
	λ	−0.821	0.013	−0.830	−0.821	−0.813
	σ^2	959.20	858.50	365.20	698.70	1267.90
	θ	198.40	195.60	58.00	137.50	277.00
5%	μ	−20.092	0.175	−20.221	−20.093	−19.967
	β	3.428	0.028	3.407	3.428	3.448
	λ	−0.832	0.013	−0.842	−0.833	−0.824
	σ^2	956.60	854.00	372.90	704.10	1259.10
	θ	200.20	198.30	59.91	141.00	273.20

Table 6. 95% Credible Interval of parameters estimated.

Removed Case	Parameter	Equal-Tail Interval		HPD Interval	
Identify Points	μ	−20.709	−17.754	−20.713	−17.760
	β	3.026	3.351	3.027	3.352
	λ	−0.833	0.293	−0.837	0.284
	σ^2	104.300	3096.600	43.226	2603.000
	θ	5.211	746.000	0.143	601.600
0.1%	μ	−18.2762	−17.7678	−18.2845	−17.7776
	β	3.0289	3.11	3.0283	3.1093
	λ	−0.8365	−0.7896	−0.8372	−0.7906
	σ^2	94.0797	3151.6	40.6435	2574.8
	θ	5.2045	728.6	0.1098	586.3
0.5%	μ	−18.4967	−17.9843	−18.4981	−17.9863
	β	3.0654	3.1476	3.0664	3.1483
	λ	−0.8391	−0.7905	−0.84	−0.7918
	σ^2	98.81	3143.7	28.4125	2605.9
	θ	5.1449	745.1	0.0156	613.7
1%	μ	−18.7121	−18.205	−18.7066	−18.2029
	β	3.103	3.1855	3.1015	3.1829
	λ	−0.8407	−0.793	−0.8421	−0.7948
	σ^2	102.2	3172.8	34.7775	2578.2
	θ	4.6184	727.6	0.0235	591.8
2%	μ	−19.1832	−18.6319	−19.184	−18.6338
	β	3.1769	3.266	3.1779	3.2663
	λ	−0.8415	−0.7927	−0.8428	−0.7944
	σ^2	106.2	3111.3	39.5096	2606.1
	θ	5.4845	729.9	0.0306	600.2
3%	μ	−19.5917	−19.0343	−19.5817	−19.0259
	β	3.247	3.3364	3.2482	3.3373
	λ	−0.8504	−0.8013	−0.851	−0.8023
	σ^2	107.5	3224.1	30.9968	2597.3
	θ	4.8582	710.8	0.0153	578.9
4%	μ	−20.0252	−19.4068	−20.0321	−19.4161
	β	3.312	3.4113	3.3143	3.4124
	λ	−0.8458	−0.7955	−0.8459	−0.7958
	σ^2	111	3307.1	50.2358	2671.5
	θ	5.2325	734.3	0.0631	604.8
5%	μ	−20.4078	−19.7676	−20.418	−19.7839
	β	3.3762	3.4789	3.3778	3.4802
	λ	−0.8572	−0.8055	−0.8581	−0.8066
	σ^2	119	3273.2	56.2007	2652.8
	θ	5.0109	743.8	0.0992	605.8

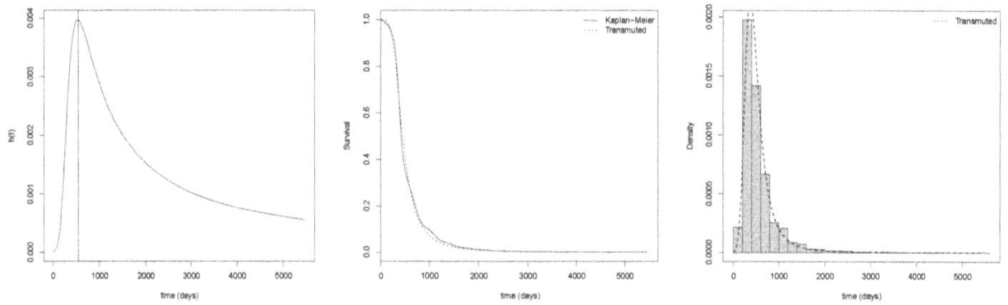

(a) (b) (c)

Figure 7. (**a**) Hazard estimate curve, with the $\hat{T}_{\max}$, (**b**) survival curves and (**c**) histogram.

5. Concluding Remarks

In this paper study the model propose by Granzotto and Louzada-Neto (2014), the TLL distribution, in a Bayesian context. The two levels hierarchical TLL model was formulated by using the half-Cauchy as a prior to the parameter of discrepancy.

Techniques of influential analysis were used to identify and measure the influence of the outstanding observed points. It is important to observe that the re-fitted model presents a reduction in the estimated likelihood value plus a reduction in the estimated standard deviation, which shortens the range of the confidence interval obtained for the most probable time up to first calving.

Finally, considering the final fitted model, the $\hat{T}_{\max}$ changes to 547.71 against 546.77 days (18.26 months) and its 95% confidence interval is given by $\text{IC}[T_{\max}, 95\%] = (15.56; 21.47)$ months. The median time up to first calving is equals to 452.41 days (or approximately 15.08 months), and the mean of time is 538.54 days (or approximately 17.95 months), with standard deviation equals to 13.11 months.

Author Contributions: All authors contributed equally to this manuscript insomuch that Francisco Louzada and Vera L. D. Tomazella worked in the theoretical part and Carlos A. dos Santos and Daniele C. T. Granzotto provided the simulation and application.

Conflicts of Interest: The authors declare no conflict of interest.

References

Aryal, Gokarna R., and Chris P. Tsokos. 2009. On the transmuted extreme value distribution with applications. *Nonlinear Analysis* 71: 1401–7.

Aryal, Gokarna R., and Chris P. Tsokos. 2011. Transmuted Weibull distribution: A generalization of the Weibull probability distribution. *European Journal of Pure and Applied Mathematics* 4: 89–102.

Barlow, Richard E., and Rafael A. Campo. 1975. *Total Time on Test Processes and Applications to Failure Data Analysis*. Berkeley: California University Berkeley Operations Research Center.

Bennett, Steve. 1983. Log-logistic regression models for survival data. *Journal of the Royal Statistical Society Series C: Applied Statistics* 32: 165–71.

Chen, Ming-Hui, Joseph G. Ibrahim, and Debajyoti Sinha. 2001. *Bayesian Survival Analysis*. Springer Series in Statistics. New York: Springer.

Chen, Ming-Hui, and Joseph G. Ibrahim. 2006. The relationship between the power prior and hierarchical models. *Bayesian Analysis* 1: 551–74.

Daniels, Michael J. 1998. A prior for the variance in hierarchical models. *The Canadian Journal of Statistics/La Revue Canadienne de Statistique* 27: 567–78.

Fachini, B. Juliana, Edwin M. M. Ortega, and Francisco Louzada. 2008. Influence diagnostics for polyhazard models in the presence of covariates. *Statistical Methods and Applications* 17: 413–33.

Gelman, Andrew. 2006. Prior distributions for variance parameters in hierarchical models. *Communications in Statistics. Theory and Methods* 1: 515–33.

Gelman, Andrew, and Donald B. Rubin. 1992. Inference from iterative simulation using multiple sequences. *Statistical Science* 7: 457–511.

Granzotto, Daniele Cristina Tita, and Louzada-Neto Francisco. 2014. The Transmuted Log-Logistic distribution: modeling, inference and an application to a polled tabapua race time up to first calving data. *Communications in Statistics—Theory and Methods* 44: 3387–402.

Lee, Sik-Yum, Bin Lu, and Xin-Yuan Song. 2006. Assessing local influence for nonlinear structural equation models with ignorable missing data. *Computational Statistics & Data Analysis* 50: 1356–77.

Ortega, Edwin M. M., Heleno Bolfarine, and Gilberto A. Paula. 2003. Influence diagnostics in generalized log-gamma regression models. *Computational Statistics and Data Analysis* 42: 165–86.

Pereira, Jonas C. C. 2000. Contribuição genética do Zebu na pecuária bovina do Brasil. *Informe Agropecuário* 21: 30–38.

Polson, Nicholas G., and James G. Scott. 2012. On the half-Cauchy prior for a global scale parameter. *Bayesian Analysis* 7: 887–902.
Shaw, William T., and Ian R. C. Buckley. 2007. The alchemy of probability distributions: Beyond Gram-Charlier expansions, and a skew-kurtotic-normal distribution from a rank transmutation map. *arXiv*. arXiv:0901.0434.

Journal of
Risk and Financial Management

MDPI

Article

A New Generalization of the Pareto Distribution and Its Application to Insurance Data

Mohamed E. Ghitany [1,*], Emilio Gómez-Déniz [2] and Saralees Nadarajah [3]

[1] Department of Statistics and Operations Research, Faculty of Science, Kuwait University, Safat 13060, Kuwait
[2] Department of Quantitative Methods and T*i*DES Institute, University of Las Palmas de Gran Canaria, 35017 Gran Canaria, Spain; emilio.gomez-deniz@ulpgc.es
[3] School of Mathematics, University of Manchester, Manchester M13 9PL, UK; Saralees.Nadarajah@manchester.ac.uk
* Correspondence: meghitany@yahoo.com

Received: 26 November 2017; Accepted: 2 February 2018; Published: 7 February 2018

Abstract: The Pareto classical distribution is one of the most attractive in statistics and particularly in the scenario of actuarial statistics and finance. For example, it is widely used when calculating reinsurance premiums. In the last years, many alternative distributions have been proposed to obtain better adjustments especially when the tail of the empirical distribution of the data is very long. In this work, an alternative generalization of the Pareto distribution is proposed and its properties are studied. Finally, application of the proposed model to the earthquake insurance data set is presented.

Keywords: gamma distribution; estimation; financial risk; fit; pareto distribution

MSC: 62E10; 62F10; 62F15; 62P05

1. Introduction

In general insurance, only a few large claims arising in the portfolio represent the largest part of the payments made by the insurance company. Appropriate estimation of these extreme events is crucial for the practitioner to correctly assess insurance and reinsurance premiums. On this subject, the single parameter Pareto distribution (Arnold 1983; Brazauskas and Serfling 2003; Rytgaard 1990), among others has been traditionally considered as a suitable claim size distribution in relation to rating problems. Concerning this, the single parameter Pareto distribution, apart from its favourable properties, provides a good depiction of the random behaviour of large losses (e.g., the right tail of the distribution). Particularly, when calculating deductibles and excess–of–loss levels for reinsurance, the simple Pareto distribution has been demonstrated convenient, see for instance (Boyd 1988; Mata 2000; Klugman et al. 2008), among others.

In this work, an alternative to the Pareto distribution will be carried out. Properties and applications of this distribution will be studied here. As far as we know, these properties have not been studied for this distribution. In particular, we concentrate our attention to results connected with financial risk and insurance.

The paper is organized as follows. In Section 2, the new proposed distribution is shown, including some of its more relevant properties. Section 3 presents some interesting results connecting with financial risk and insurance. Next, Section 4 deals with parameter estimation, paying special attention to the maximum likelihood method. In Section 5, numerical application by using real insurance data is considered. Finally, some conclusions are given in the last section.

2. The Proposed Distribution

2.1. Probability Density Function

A continuous random variable X is said to have a generalized truncated log-gamma (GTLG) distribution if its probability density function (p.d.f.) is given by

$$f(x) = \frac{\theta^{\lambda}}{\alpha\Gamma(\lambda)}\left(\frac{x}{\alpha}\right)^{-\theta-1}\left(\log\frac{x}{\alpha}\right)^{\lambda-1}, \qquad x \geq \alpha, \quad \alpha, \theta, \lambda > 0, \tag{1}$$

where $\Gamma(z) = \int_0^{\infty} t^{z-1}\exp(-t)\,dt$ is the Euler gamma function. Note that, for all $\alpha, \theta > 0$, we have

$$f(\alpha) = \begin{cases} \infty, & \text{if } 0 < \lambda < 1, \\ \theta/\alpha, & \text{if } \lambda = 1, \\ 0, & \text{if } \lambda > 1, \end{cases} \qquad f(\infty) = 0.$$

As it can be easily seen, the parameter α marks a lower bound on the possible values that (1) can take on. When $\alpha = 1$, the GTLG distribution reduced to the log-gamma distribution proposed by Consul and Jain (1971) with p.d.f.

$$fz(z) = \frac{\theta^{\lambda}}{\Gamma(\lambda)} z^{-\theta-1}(\log z)^{\lambda-1}, \qquad z > 1, \quad \theta, \lambda > 0.$$

Note that Consul and Jain (1971) considered only the case $\lambda \geq 1$. For this case, they derived the raw moments and the distribution of the product of two independent log-gamma random variables. The p.d.f. (1) can now be obtained by the transformation $X = \alpha Z$.

Expression (1) is a particular case of the generalized truncated log–gamma distribution proposed in Amini et al. (2014) and related with the family proposed by Zografos and Balakrishnan (2009). When $\lambda = 1$, we obtain the famous Pareto distribution. In addition, when $\lambda = 2$, we obtain a distribution reminiscent of the distribution proposed in Gómez-Déniz and Calderín (2014). Properties and applications of this distribution will be studied here. In particular, we concentrate attention to results connecting with financial risk and insurance.

Theorem 1. *For all $\alpha, \theta > 0$, $f(x)$ is decreasing (increasing-decreasing) if $0 < \lambda \leq 1$ ($\lambda > 1$).*

Proof. The first derivative of $f(x)$ given by

$$f'(x) = \left[-(\theta+1) + \frac{\lambda-1}{\log(x/\alpha)}\right]\frac{f(x)}{x},$$

which can be seen to be strictly negative if $0 < \lambda \leq 1$ and has a unique zero at $x_m = \alpha\exp\left[(\lambda-1)/(\theta+1)\right]$, if $\lambda > 1$. □

Note that the mode of $f(x)$ is given by α if $0 < \lambda \leq 1$ (x_m if $\lambda > 1$).

Figure 1 shows the p.d.f. (1) for selected values of λ and θ when $\alpha = 1$.

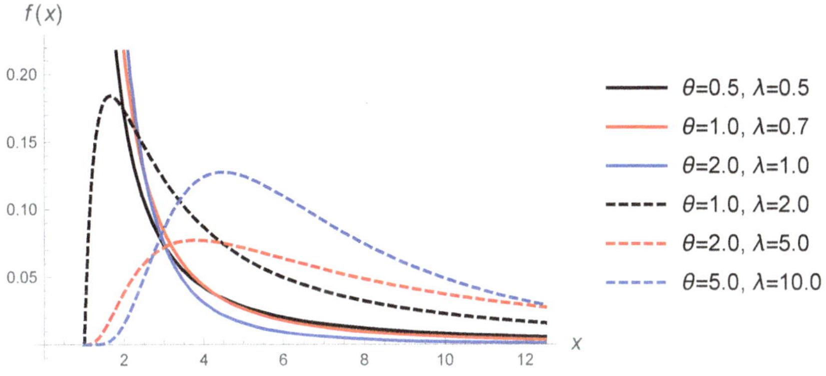

Figure 1. Probability density function of GTLG distribution for selected values of θ and λ when $\alpha = 1$.

2.2. Hazard Rate Function

The survival function (s.f.) of the GTLG distribution is given by

$$\overline{F}(x) = P(X > x) = \frac{\Gamma\left(\lambda, \theta \log\left(\frac{x}{\alpha}\right)\right)}{\Gamma(\lambda)}, \quad x \geq \alpha. \tag{2}$$

where $\Gamma(a, z) = \int_z^\infty t^{a-1} \exp(-t)\, dt$ is the incomplete gamma function. When λ is a positive integer, we have

$$\overline{F}(x) = (x/\alpha)^{-\theta} \sum_{k=0}^{\lambda-1} \frac{[\theta \log(x/\alpha)]^k}{k!}, \quad x \geq \alpha.$$

The hazard rate function (h.r.f.) of the GTLG distribution is given by

$$h(x) = \frac{f(x)}{\overline{F}(x)} = \frac{\theta^\lambda}{\alpha \Gamma\left(\lambda, \theta \log\left(\frac{x}{\alpha}\right)\right)} \left(\frac{x}{\alpha}\right)^{-\theta-1} \left(\log \frac{x}{\alpha}\right)^{\lambda-1}, \quad x \geq \alpha, \quad \alpha, \theta, \lambda > 0. \tag{3}$$

Note that, $h(\alpha) = f(\alpha)$ and $h(\infty) = 0$.

Theorem 2. *For all $\alpha, \theta > 0$, $h(x)$ is decreasing (increasing-decreasing) if $0 < \lambda \leq 1$ ($\lambda > 1$).*

Proof. Let

$$\eta(x) = -\frac{f'(x)}{f(x)} = \left[(\theta + 1) - \frac{\lambda - 1}{\log(x/\alpha)}\right] \frac{1}{x}.$$

It is straightforward to show that $\eta(x)$ is decreasing if $0 < \lambda \leq 1$ and $\eta(x)$ is increasing-decreasing if $\lambda > 1$. Now by Glaser (1980), $h(x)$ is decreasing if $\lambda \leq 1$ and increasing-decreasing if $\lambda > 1$, since $f(\alpha) = h(\alpha) = 0$ when $\lambda > 1$. □

Figure 2 shows the h.r.f. (3) for selected values of λ and θ when $\alpha = 1$.

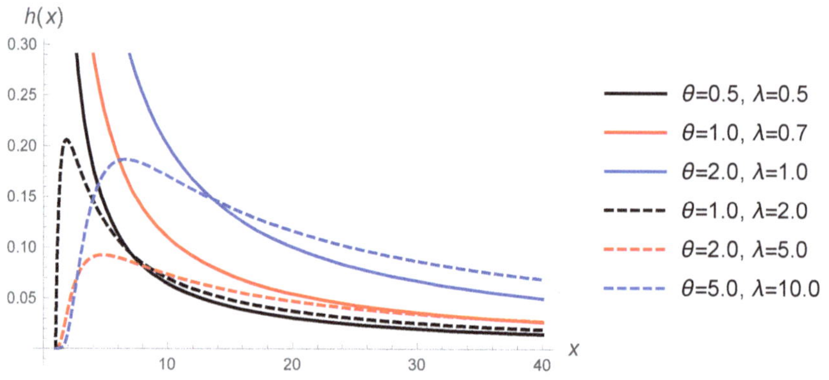

Figure 2. Hazard rate function of GTLG distribution for selected values of θ and λ when $\alpha = 1$.

2.3. Mean Residual Life Function

For the GTLG$(\alpha, \lambda, \theta)$, we have

$$\int_x^\infty y f(y) dy = \mu \int_x^\infty f_{\theta-1}(y) dy = \mu \, \overline{F}_{\theta-1}(x), \qquad x > \alpha, \quad \theta > 1.$$

where, for $\theta > 1$, $\mu = E(X) = \alpha \left(1 - \frac{1}{\theta}\right)^{-\lambda}$ is the mean of the GTLG distribution, and $f_{\theta-1}(x)$ ($\overline{F}_{\theta-1}(x)$) is the p.d.f. (1) (s.f. (2)) when θ is replaced by $\theta - 1$.

The mean residual life function (m.r.l.f.) of the GTLG distribution is given by

$$\begin{aligned} e(x) &= E(X - x | X > x) \\ &= \frac{1}{\overline{F}(x)} \int_x^\infty y f(y)\, dy \; - \; x \\ &= \mu \, \frac{\overline{F}_{\theta-1}(x)}{\overline{F}_\theta(x)} \; - \; x, \qquad x > \alpha, \quad \theta > 1. \end{aligned} \tag{4}$$

Theorem 3. *For all $\alpha > 0, \theta > 1$, the m.r.l.f. $e(x)$ is increasing (decreasing-increasing) if $0 < \lambda \leq 1$ ($\lambda > 1$).*

Proof. Since $h(x)$ is decreasing for $0 < \lambda \leq 1$, it follows that, in this case, $e(x)$ is increasing. In addition, since $h(x)$ is increasing-decreasing for $\lambda > 1$ and $f(\alpha)e(\alpha) = 0$, it follows that, in this case, $e(x)$ is decreasing-increasing, by Gupta and Akman (1995). □

From the point of view of a risk manager, the expression $e(x) + x = E(X|X > x)$ is the so-called *Expected Shortfall*, that is the conditional mean of X given X exceeds a given quantile value x. This is a risk measurement appropriate to evaluate the market risk or credit risk of a portfolio.

Figure 3 shows the m.r.l.f. (4) for selected values of λ and θ when $\alpha = 1$.

It is noted that, unlike the classical Pareto distribution, this expression is not a linear function of x.

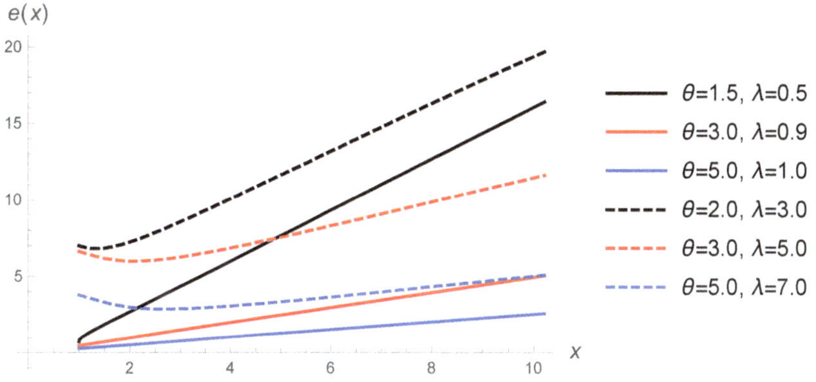

Figure 3. Mean residual life function of GTLG distribution for selected values of θ and λ when $\alpha = 1$.

2.4. Moments

The GTLG distribution with p.d.f. (1) can be obtained from a monotonic transformation of the gamma distribution, as it can be seen in the next result.

Theorem 4. *Let us assume that Y follows a Gamma(λ, θ) distribution with p.d.f. $f(y) \propto y^{\lambda-1}\exp(-\theta y)$, where $\lambda > 0$ and $\theta > 0$. Then the random variable*

$$X = \alpha\, e^{Y} \tag{5}$$

has p.d.f. (1).

Proof. The proof follows after a simple change of variable. □

Note that $Z = e^Y$ has a log-gamma distribution over $(1, \infty)$. That is $X = \alpha Z$ as indicated before.

Now, by using representation (5) and the moments of the Gamma distribution, the expression for the r-th moment about zero of distribution (1) is easily obtained,

$$\mu_r' = E(X^r) = \alpha^r\, M_Y(r) = \alpha^r \left(1 - \frac{r}{\theta}\right)^{-\lambda}, \qquad r = 1, 2, \ldots,$$

provided $\theta > r$ and $\lambda > 0$.

In particular, the mean is given by

$$\mu = \alpha \left(1 - \frac{1}{\theta}\right)^{-\lambda}, \qquad \theta > 1, \tag{6}$$

and the variance is given by

$$\sigma^2 = \alpha^2 \left[\left(1 - \frac{2}{\theta}\right)^{-\lambda} - \left(1 - \frac{1}{\theta}\right)^{-2\lambda}\right], \qquad \theta > 2, \tag{7}$$

Furthermore, by using the representation given by (5) the following result is obtained

$$E\left[\log\left(\frac{X}{\alpha}\right)\right]^r = E(Y^r) = \frac{\Gamma(\lambda + r)}{\theta^r \Gamma(\lambda)}, \qquad r = 1, 2, \ldots. \tag{8}$$

Solving the equation

$$\mu = \alpha \left(1 - \frac{1}{\theta}\right)^{-\lambda},$$

in θ, we obtain

$$\theta = \frac{(\mu/\alpha)^{1/\lambda}}{(\mu/\alpha)^{1/\lambda} - 1}, \qquad \mu > \alpha.$$

This implies that the covariates can be introduced into the model in a simple way.

2.5. Conjugate Distributions

The following results show that both the inverse Gaussian distribution and the gamma distribution are conjugate with respect to the distribution proposed in this work.

Theorem 5. *Let X_i, $i = 1, 2, \ldots, n$ independent and identically distributed random variables following the p.d.f. (1). Let us suppose that θ follows a prior inverse Gaussian distribution $\pi(\theta)$ with parameters τ and ϕ, i.e., $\pi(\theta) \propto \theta^{-3/2} \exp\left[-\frac{1}{2}\left(\frac{\phi}{\tau^2}\theta + \frac{\phi}{\theta}\right)\right]$. Then the posterior distribution of θ given the sample information $(X_1, \ldots, X_n)$ is a generalized inverse Gaussian distribution $GIG(\lambda^*, \tau^*, \phi^*)$, where*

$$\begin{aligned} \lambda^* &= n\lambda - \frac{1}{2}, \\ \tau^* &= \tau\sqrt{1 + \frac{2\tau^2}{\phi}\sum_{i=1}^{n} \log(x_i/\alpha)}, \\ \phi^* &= \phi. \end{aligned}$$

Proof. The result follows after some computations by applying Bayes' Theorem and arranging parameters. □

Theorem 6. *Let X_i, $i = 1, 2, \ldots, n$ independent and identically distributed random variables following the p.d.f. (1). Let us suppose that θ follows a prior gamma distribution $\pi(\theta)$ with a shape parameter $\tau > 0$ and a scale parameter $\sigma > 0$, i.e., $\pi(\theta) \propto \theta^{\tau-1} \exp(-\sigma\theta)$. Then the posterior distribution of θ given the sample information $(X_1, \ldots, X_n)$ is again a gamma distribution with shape parameter $\tau + n\lambda$ and scale parameter $\sigma + \log(x_i/\alpha)$.*

Proof. Again, the result follows after some algebra by using Bayes' Theorem and arranging parameters. □

2.6. Stochastic Ordering

Stochastic ordering of positive continuous random variables is an important tool for judging the comparative behavior. We will recall some basic definitions, see (Shaked and Shanthikumar 2007).

Let X and Y be random variables with p.d.f.s $f(x)$ and $g(y)$ (s.f.s $\overline{F}(x)$ and $\overline{G}(y)$) (h.r.f.s $h(x)$ and $r(y)$), respectively.

A random variable X is said to be smaller than a random variable Y in the

(i) stochastic order (denoted by $X \preceq_{ST} Y$) if $\overline{F}(x) \leq \overline{G}(x)$ for all x,
(ii) hazard rate order (denoted by $X \preceq_{HR} Y$) if $h(x) \geq r(x)$ for all x,
(iii) likelihood ratio order (denoted by $X \preceq_{LR} Y$) if $\frac{f(x)}{g(x)}$ decreases for all x.

The following implications are well known:

$$X \preceq_{LR} Y \Rightarrow X \preceq_{HR} Y \Rightarrow X \preceq_{ST} Y.$$

Members of the family of distributions with p.d.f. (1) are ordered with respect to the strongest "likelihood ratio" ordering, as shown in the following theorem.

Theorem 7. *Let X and Y be two continuous random variables distributed according to (1) with p.d.f.'s given by* $f(x) = f(x; \alpha, \theta_1, \lambda)$ *and* $g(x) = f(x; \alpha, \theta_2, \lambda)$*, respectively. If* $\theta_1 \geq \theta_2 > 0$*, then* $X \preceq_{LR} Y$ $(X \preceq_{HR} Y)$ $(X \preceq_{ST} Y)$

Proof. Firstly, let us observe that the ratio

$$\frac{f(x)}{g(x)} = \left(\frac{\theta_1}{\theta_2}\right)^{\lambda} \alpha^{\theta_1 - \theta_2} x^{\theta_2 - \theta_1}$$

wih derivative

$$\left(\frac{f(x)}{g(x)}\right)' = \left(\frac{\theta_1}{\theta_2}\right)^{\lambda} \alpha^{\theta_1 - \theta_2} (\theta_2 - \theta_1) x^{\theta_2 - \theta_1 - 1} \leq 0,$$

for all $\theta_1 \geq \theta_2 > 0$, proving the theorem. □

Properties for higher-order stochastic dominance in financial economics can be obtained following the line of the work of (Guo and Wong 2016). In this regard, let X and Y be random variables defined on $[a, b]$ with p.d.f.'s $f(x), g(y)$ and s.f.'s $\overline{F}(x), \overline{G}(y)$, respectively, satisfying

$$F_j^D(x) = \int_x^b F_{j-1}^D(y) dy, \qquad G_j^D(x) = \int_x^b G_{j-1}^D(y) dy, \qquad j \geq 1,$$

where $F_0^D(x) = f(x)$, $G_0^D(x) = g(x)$, $F_1^D(x) = \overline{F}(x)$, and $G_1^D(x) = \overline{G}(x)$.

A random variable X is said to be smaller than a random variable Y

(i) in the *first-order* descending stochastic dominance (denoted by $X \preceq^1 Y$) iff $F_1^D(x) \leq G_1^D(x)$ for each $x \in [a, b]$.
(ii) in the *second-order* descending stochastic dominance (denoted by $X \preceq^2 Y$) iff $F_2^D(x) \leq G_2^D(x)$ for each $x \in [a, b]$.
(iii) in the *N-order* descending stochastic dominance (denoted by $X \preceq^N Y$) iff $F_N^D(x) \leq G_N^D(x)$ for each $x \in [a, b]$ and $F_k^D(a) \leq G_k^D(a)$ for $2 \leq k \leq N-1$, $N \geq 3$.

Theorem 8. *Let X and Y be two continuous random variables distributed according to (1) with p.d.f.'s given by* $f(x) = f(x; \alpha, \theta_1, \lambda)$ *and* $g(y) = f(y; \alpha, \theta_2, \lambda)$*, respectively.*

(i) If $\theta_1 \geq \theta_2 > 0$*, then* $X \preceq^1 Y$.

(ii) If $\theta_1 \geq \theta_2 > 0$*, then* $X \preceq^2 Y$.

(iii) If $\theta_1 \geq \theta_2 > 1$*, then* $X \preceq^N Y$ *for* $N \geq 3$.

Proof. (i) For $\theta_1 \geq \theta_2 > 0$, we have

$$F_1^D(x) = \overline{F}_{\theta_1}(x) = \frac{\Gamma(\lambda, \theta_1 \log(x/\alpha))}{\Gamma(\lambda)} \leq \frac{\Gamma(\lambda, \theta_2 \log(x/\alpha))}{\Gamma(\lambda)} = \overline{G}_{\theta_2}(x) = G_1^D(x).$$

Therefore, for $\theta_1 \geq \theta_2 > 0$, $X \preceq^1 Y$.

(ii) For $\theta_1 \geq \theta_2 > 0$, we have

$$F_2^D(x) = \int_x^{\infty} F_1^D(y) dy \leq \int_x^{\infty} G_1^D(y) dy = G_2^D(x).$$

Therefore, for $\theta_1 \geq \theta_2 > 0$, $X \preceq^2 Y$.

(iii) For $\theta_1 \geq \theta_2 > 1$, we have

$$F_3^D(x) = \int_x^\infty F_2^D(y)dy \leq \int_x^\infty G_2^D(y)dy = G_3^D(x).$$

Also, for $\theta_1 \geq \theta_2 > 1$, we have

$$F_2^D(\alpha) = \int_\alpha^\infty \overline{F}_{\theta_1}(y)dy = \mu_{\theta_1} \leq \mu_{\theta_2} = \int_\alpha^\infty \overline{G}_{\theta_2}(y)dy = G_2^D(\alpha).$$

Therefore, for $\theta_1 \geq \theta_2 > 1$, $X \preceq^3 Y$.

Now assume that, for $\theta_1 \geq \theta_2 > 1$, $X \preceq^N Y$ for some $N \geq 3$, i.e., $F_N^D(x) \leq G_N^D(x)$ for each $x \in [a,b]$ and $F_k^D(a) \leq G_k^D(a)$ for $2 \leq k \leq N-1$, $N \geq 3$.

Now for $\theta_1 \geq \theta_2 > 1$, we have

$$F_{N+1}^D(x) = \int_x^\infty F_N^D(y)dy \leq \int_x^\infty G_N^D(y)dy = G_{N+1}^D(x).$$

Also, for $\theta_1 \geq \theta_2 > 1$, we have

$$F_N^D(\alpha) = \int_\alpha^\infty F_{N-1}^D(y)dy \leq \mu_{\theta_2} = \int_\alpha^\infty G_{N-1}^D(y)dy = G_N^D(\alpha).$$

Therefore, for $\theta_1 \geq \theta_2 > 1$, $X \preceq^N Y$ for all $N \geq 3$. □

3. Some Theoretical Financial Results

The integrated tail distribution function (also known as equilibrium distribution function):

$$F_I(x) = \frac{1}{E(X)} \int_\alpha^x \overline{F}(y)\, dy, \qquad x > \alpha.$$

is an important probability model that often appears in insurance and many other applied fields (see for example Yang 2004).

For the GTLG$(\alpha, \lambda, \theta)$, we have

$$\int_\alpha^x y f(y)dy = \mu \int_\alpha^x f_{\theta-1}(y)dy = \mu\, F_{\theta-1}(x), \qquad x > \alpha, \quad \theta > 1.$$

The integrated tail distribution of the GTLG $(\alpha, \lambda, \theta)$ is given by

$$\begin{aligned} F_I(x) &= \frac{1}{\mu} \int_\alpha^x \overline{F}_\theta(y)dy \\ &= \frac{1}{\mu} \left\{ x\, \overline{F}_\theta(x) - \alpha + \mu \int_\alpha^x f_{\theta-1}(y)dy \right\} \\ &= \frac{1}{\mu} \left\{ x\, \overline{F}_\theta(x) - \alpha + \mu\, F_{\theta-1}(x) \right\}, \qquad x > \alpha, \quad \theta > 1. \end{aligned} \tag{9}$$

Under the classical model (see Yang 2004) and assuming a positive security loading, ρ, for the claim size distributions with regularly varying tails we have that, by using (3), it is possible to obtain an approximation of the probability of ruin, $\Psi(u)$, when $u \to \infty$. In this case the asymptotic approximations of the ruin function is given by

$$\Psi(u) \quad \sim \quad \frac{1}{\rho}\overline{F}_I(u), \quad u \to \infty.$$

where $\overline{F}_I(u) = 1 - F_I(u)$.

The use of heavy right-tailed distribution is of vital importance in general insurance. In this regard, Pareto and log-normal distributions have been employed to model losses in motor third liability insurance, fire insurance or catastrophe insurance. It is already known that any probability distribution, that is specified through its cumulative distribution function $F(x)$ on the real line, is heavy right-tailed if and only if for every $t > 0$, $e^{tx}\overline{F}(x)$ has an infinite limit as x tends to infinity. On this particular subject, (1) decays to zero slower than any exponential distribution and it is long-tailed since for any fixed $t > 0$ (see Rytgaard 1990) it is verified that

$$\overline{F}(x+t) \sim \overline{F}(x), \quad x \to \infty.$$

Therefore, as a long-tailed distribution is also heavy right-tailed, the distribution introduced in this manuscript is also heavy right–tailed.

Another important issue in extreme value theory is the regular variation (see Bingham 1987; Rytgaard 1990). A distribution function is called regular varying at infinity with index $-\beta$ if

$$\lim_{x \to \infty} \frac{\overline{F}(tx)}{\overline{F}(x)} = t^{-\beta},$$

where the parameter $\beta \geq 0$ is called the tail index.

Theorem 9. *The GTLG distribution is regularly varying at infinity with index* $-\theta$.

Proof. Using L'Hospital rule, we have

$$\begin{aligned}
\lim_{x \to \infty} \frac{\overline{F}(tx)}{\overline{F}(x)} &= \lim_{x \to \infty} \frac{\Gamma(\lambda, \theta \log \frac{tx}{\alpha})}{\Gamma(\lambda, \theta \log \frac{x}{\alpha})} = \lim_{x \to \infty} \frac{-\left(\theta \log \frac{tx}{\alpha}\right)^{\lambda-1} e^{-\theta \log \frac{tx}{\alpha}} \left(\frac{\theta}{x}\right)}{-\left(\theta \log \frac{x}{\alpha}\right)^{\lambda-1} e^{-\theta \log \frac{x}{\alpha}} \left(\frac{\theta}{x}\right)} \\
&= \lim_{x \to \infty} \left(1 + \frac{\log t}{\log \frac{x}{\alpha}}\right)^{\lambda-1} t^{-\theta} = t^{-\theta},
\end{aligned}$$

for all $\alpha, \theta, \lambda > 0$. □

As a consequence of this result we have that if $X, X_1, \ldots, X_n$ are i.i.d. random variables with common s.f. (2) and $S_n = \sum_{i=1}^{n} X_i$, $n \geq 1$, then

$$\Pr(S_n > x) \sim \Pr(X > x) \quad \text{as} \quad x \to \infty.$$

Therefore, if $P_n = \max_{i=1,\ldots,n} X_i$, $n \geq 1$, we have that

$$\Pr(S_n > x) \sim n \Pr(X > x) \sim \Pr(P_n > x).$$

This means that for large x the event $\{S_n > x\}$ is due to the event $\{P_n > x\}$. Therefore, exceedance of high thresholds by the sum S_n are due to the exceedance of this threshold by the largest value in the sample.

On the other hand, let the random variable X represent either a policy limit or reinsurance deductible (from an insurer's perspective); then the limited expected value function L of X with cdf $F(x)$, is defined by

$$\begin{aligned}
L(x) &= E[\min(X, x)] \\
&= \int_{\alpha}^{x} y\, f_\theta(y)\, dy + x\, \overline{F}_\theta(x) \qquad (10) \\
&= \mu\, F_{\theta-1}(x) + x\, \overline{F}_\theta(x), \qquad x > \alpha, \quad \theta > 1.
\end{aligned}$$

Note that $L(x)$ represents the expected amount per claim retained by the insured on a policy with a fixed amount deductible of x.

Figure 4 shows the limited expected value function (10) for selected values of λ and θ when $\alpha = 1$.

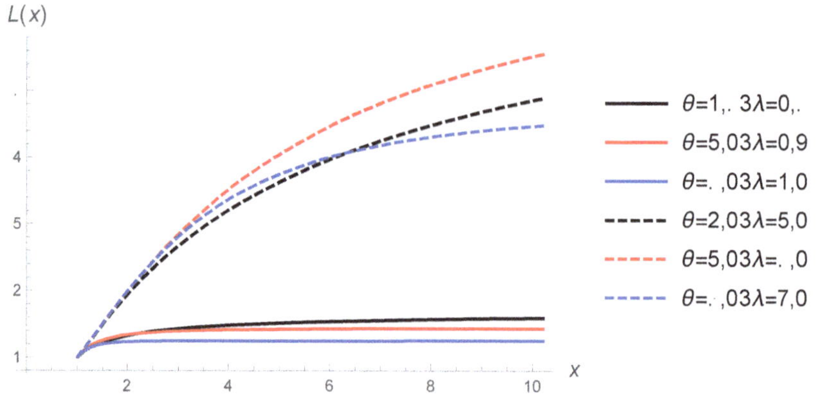

Figure 4. Limited expected value function of GTLG distribution for selected values of θ and λ when $\alpha = 1$.

On the other hand, the new distribution can also be applied in rating excess–of–loss reinsurance as it can be seen in the next result.

Theorem 10. *Let X be a random variable denoting the individual claim size taking values only for individual claims greater than d. Let us also assumed that X follows the pdf (1), then the expected cost per claim to the reinsurance layer when the losses excess of m subject to a maximum of l is given by*

$$\begin{aligned} E[\min(l, \max(0, X - m))] &= \frac{\theta^\lambda}{\Gamma(\lambda)} \left[m \left(R(\lambda, \theta, m+l) - R(\lambda, \theta, m)\right)\right. \\ &\quad \left. + \alpha \left(R(\lambda, \theta - 1, m) - R(\lambda, \theta - 1, m + 1)\right)\right] \\ &\quad + l\overline{F}(m+l), \end{aligned}$$

where $R(a, b, z) = \log^\lambda(z/\alpha) E_{1-a}(b \log(z/\alpha))$*, being* $E_n(z) = \int_1^\infty t^{-n} \exp(-zt)\, dt$ *the exponential integral function.*

Proof. The result follows by having into account that

$$E[\min(l, \max(0, X - m))] = \int_m^{m+l} (x - m) f(x)\, dx + l\overline{F}(m+l),$$

from which we get the result after some tedious algebra. □

4. Maximum Likelihood Estimation

In the following it will be assumed that $\mathbf{x} = (x_1, x_2, \ldots, x_n)$ is a random sample selected from the GTLG distribution with known parameter α and unknown parameters $\nu = (\theta, \lambda)$ from the p.d.f. (1). Then, the log–likelihood function is given by

$$\ell(\nu; \mathbf{x}) = n \left[\lambda \log \theta - \log \alpha \Gamma(\lambda)\right] + \sum_{i=1}^n \left[-(\theta+1) \log\left(\frac{x_i}{\alpha}\right) + (\lambda - 1) \log \log\left(\frac{x_i}{\alpha}\right)\right]. \tag{11}$$

The maximum likelihood estimates (MLEs) $\widehat{v} = (\widehat{\theta}, \widehat{\lambda})$, of the parameters $v = (\theta, \lambda)$ are obtained by solving the score equations:

$$\begin{aligned} \frac{\partial \ell}{\partial \theta} &= \frac{n\lambda}{\theta} - \sum_{i=1}^{n} \log(x_i/\alpha) = 0, \\ \frac{\partial \ell}{\partial \lambda} &= n\left[\log\theta - \psi(\lambda)\right] + \sum_{i=1}^{n} \log\log(x_i/\alpha) = 0, \end{aligned}$$

where $\psi(\cdot)$ is the digamma function. Therefore,

$$\widehat{\theta} = \frac{n\widehat{\lambda}}{\sum_{i=1}^{n} \log(x_i/\alpha)},$$

where $\widehat{\lambda}$ is the solution of the equation:

$$\log(\widehat{\lambda}) - \psi(\widehat{\lambda}) - \log\left[\frac{1}{n}\sum_{i=1}^{n} \log(x_i/\alpha)\right] + \frac{1}{n}\sum_{i=1}^{n} \log\log(x_i/\alpha) = 0.$$

The second partial derivatives are given by

$$\begin{aligned} \frac{\partial^2 \ell}{\partial \theta^2} &= -\frac{n\lambda}{\theta^2}, \\ \frac{\partial^2 \ell}{\partial \theta \partial \lambda} &= \frac{n}{\theta}, \\ \frac{\partial^2 \ell}{\partial \lambda^2} &= -n\psi'(\lambda). \end{aligned}$$

The expected Fisher's information matrix is given by

$$\mathcal{I}(v) = \begin{bmatrix} \frac{n\lambda}{\theta^2} & -\frac{n}{\theta} \\ -\frac{n}{\theta} & n\psi'(\lambda) \end{bmatrix}. \tag{12}$$

Now the estimated variance-covariance matrix of the MLEs $\widehat{v}$ is given by the inverse matrix $\mathcal{I}^{-1}(\widehat{v})$.

It is known that under certain regularity conditions, the maximum likelihood estimator $\widehat{v}$ converges in distribution to a bivariate normal distribution with mean equal to the true parameter value and variance-covariance matrix given by the inverse of the information matrix. That is, $\widehat{v} \xrightarrow{D} \mathcal{N}(v, \mathcal{I}^{-1}(v))$, which provides a basis for constructing tests of hypotheses and confidence regions. The regularity conditions are verified by taking into account that the Fisher's information matrix exists and is non-singular and that the parameter space is a subset of the real line and the range of x is independent of v. Furthermore, additional computations provides that $E\left(\frac{\partial f(x)}{\partial v}\right) = \mathbf{0}$ and that $\frac{\partial^3 f(x)}{\partial v^3}$ is bounded.

5. Numerical Application

Because the main application of the heavy tail distributions is the so-called extreme value theory, we consider a data set coming from catastrophic events. The data set represents loss ratios (yearly data in billion of dollars) for earthquake insurance in California from 1971 through 1993 for values larger than zero. The data are given in Embrechts et al. (1999).

For comparison with other heavy tail distributions, we consider the following models:

(1) Pareto distribution:

$$f(x) = \frac{\theta}{x}\left(\frac{\alpha}{x}\right)^{\theta}, \qquad x \geq \alpha, \quad \alpha, \theta > 0.$$

(2) Shifted log-normal (SLN):

$$f(x) = \frac{\theta\sqrt{2\pi}}{x-\alpha} \exp\left[-\frac{1}{2\theta^2}(\log(x-\alpha)-\lambda)^2\right], \qquad x \geq \alpha, \quad \alpha, \theta > 0, \lambda \in \mathbb{R}.$$

(3) Burr distribution:

$$f(x) = \frac{\theta\lambda(x-\alpha)^{\theta-1}}{\left[1-(x-\alpha)^{\theta}\right]^{\lambda+1}}, \qquad x \geq \alpha, \quad \alpha, \theta, \lambda > 0.$$

(4) Stoppa distribution:

$$f(x) = \frac{\lambda\theta}{x}\left(\frac{\alpha}{x}\right)^{\theta}\left[1-\left(\frac{\alpha}{x}\right)^{\theta}\right]^{\lambda-1}, \qquad x \geq \alpha, \quad \alpha, \theta, \lambda > 0.$$

(5) Log-gamma distribution (LG):

$$f(x) = \frac{(1+x-\alpha)^{-1-1/\theta}}{\theta^{\lambda}\Gamma(\lambda)} \log^{\lambda-1}(1+x-\alpha), \qquad x \geq \alpha, \quad \alpha, \theta, \lambda > 0.$$

Table 1 provides parameter estimates together with standard errors (in brackets) using the maximum likelihood estimation method of the parameters θ and λ when $\alpha = 0.1$. This table also gives the negative log-likelihood (NLL), Akaike's Information Criteria (AIC), Bayesian information criterion (BIC), and Consistent Akaike's Information Criteria (CAIC).

A lower value of these measures is desirable. These results show that the proposed GTLG distribution provides better fit than the considered competing distributions. Table 2 shows three goodness-of-fit tests for all considered models and that the classical Pareto model is rejected for this data set.

Table 1. Estimated values of the considered models when $\alpha = 0.1$.

Distribution	Estimates (S.E.)	NLL	AIC	BIC	CAIC
Pareto	$\theta = 0.249\ (0.057)$	77.939	157.878	158.822	159.822
SLN	$\theta = 1.477\ (0.239)$ $\lambda = 1.668\ (0.339)$	66.080	136.161	138.05	140.05
Burr	$\theta = 2.287\ (0.895)$ $\lambda = 0.243\ (0.106)$	67.352	138.703	140.592	142.592
Stoppa	$\theta = 0.768\ (0.159)$ $\lambda = 12.013\ (6.065)$	66.321	136.643	138.532	140.532
LG	$\theta = 0.802\ (0.271)$ $\lambda = 2.474\ (0.755)$	66.273	136.547	138.435	140.435
GTLG	$\theta = 1.845\ (0.606)$ $\lambda = 7.401\ (2.352)$	65.987	135.974	137.863	139.863

Table 2. Test statistics (p-values) of goodness-of-fit tests of the considered models when $\alpha = 0.1$.

Distribution	Kolmogorov-Smirnov	Cramér-Von Misses	Anderson-Darling
Pareto	0.360 (0.010)	0.706 (0.012)	3.574 (0.014)
SLN	0.116 (0.933)	0.031 (0.970)	0.205 (0.989)
Burr	0.182 (0.500)	0.090 (0.633)	0.483 (0.761)
Stoppa	0.148 (0.746)	0.040 (0.933)	0.242 (0.974)
LN	0.149 (0.731)	0.043 (0.918)	0.257 (0.966)
GTLG	0.148 (0.745)	0.040 (0.932)	0.242 (0.974)

6. Conclusions

In this paper, a continuous probability distribution function with positive support suitable for fitting insurance data has been introduced. The distribution, that arises from a monotonic transformation of the classical Gamma distribution, can be considered as a generalization of the log-gamma distribution. This new development, which has a promising approach for data modeling in the actuarial field, may be very useful for practitioners who handle large claims. For that reason, it can be deemed as an alternative to the classical Pareto distribution. Besides, an extensive analysis of its mathematical properties has been provided.

Acknowledgments: The authors would like to express their gratitude to two anonymous referees for their relevant and useful comments. Emilio Gómez-Déniz was partially funded by grant ECO2013-47092 (Ministerio de Economía y Competitividad, Spain and ECO2017-85577-P (Ministerio de Economía, Industria y Competitividad, Agencia Estatal de Investigación)).

Author Contributions: Mohamed E. Ghitany, Emilio Gómez-Déniz and Saralees Nadarajah have contributed jointly to all of the sections of the paper.

Conflicts of Interest: The authors declare no conflict of interest.

Amini, Morteza, S. M. T. K. MirMostafaee, and Jafar Ahmadi. 2014. Log-gamma-generated families of distributions. *Statistics* 48: 913–32.

Arnold, Barry C. 1983. *Pareto Distributions*. Silver Spring: International Cooperative Publishing House.

Bingham, Nicholas H. 1987. *Regular Variation*. Cambridge: Cambridge University Press.

Boyd, Albert V. 1988. Fitting the truncated Pareto distribution to loss distributions. *Journal of the Staple Inn Actuarial Society* 31: 151–58.

Brazauskas, Vytaras, and Robert Serfling. 2003. Favorable estimator for fitting Pareto models: A study using goodness-of-fit measures with actual data. *ASTIN Bulletin* 33: 365–81.

Consul, Prem C., and Gaurav C. Jain. 1971. On the log-Gamma distribution and its properties. *Statistische Hefte* 12: 100–6.

Embrechts, Paul, Sidney I. Resnick, and Gennady Samorodnitsky. 1999. Extreme value theory as a risk management tool. *North American Actuarial Journal* 3: 30–41.

Glaser, Ronald E. 1980. Bathtub and related failure rate characterizations. *Journal of the American Statistical Association* 75: 667–72.

Gómez-Déniz, Emilio, and Enrique Calderín. 2014. A suitable alternative to the Pareto distribution. *Hacettepe Journal of Mathematics and Statistics* 43: 843–60.

Guo, Xu, and Wing-Keung Wong. 2016. Multivariate stochastic dominance for risk averters and risk seekers. *RAIRO-Operations Research* 50: 575–86.

Gupta, Ramesh C., and Akman, H. Olcay. 1995. Mean residual life function for certain types of non-monotonic ageing. *Communications in Statistics-Stochastic Models* 11: 219–25.

Klugman, Stuart A., Harry H. Panjer, and Gordon E. Willmot. 2008. *Loss Models: From Data to Decisions*, 3rd ed. Hoboken: Wiley.

Mata, Ana J. 2000. Princing excess of loss reinsurance with reinstatements. *ASTIN Bulletin* 30: 349–68.

Rytgaard, Mette. 1990. Estimation in the Pareto distribution. *ASTIN Bulletin* 20: 201–16.

Shaked, Moshe, and Jeyaveerasingam G. Shanthikumar. 2007. *Stochastic Orders*. Series: Springer Series in Statistics. New York: Springer.

Yang, Hailiang. 2004. Crámer-Lundberg asymptotics. In *Encyclopedia of Actuarial Science*. New York: Wiley, pp. 1–6.

Zografos, Konstantinos, and Narayanaswamy Balakrishnan. 2009. On families of beta and generalized gamma-generated distributions and associated inference. *Statistical Methodology* 6: 344–62.

Journal of
Risk and Financial Management

MDPI

Article

Does the Assumption on Innovation Process Play an Important Role for Filtered Historical Simulation Model?

Emrah Altun [1,*], Huseyin Tatlidil [1], Gamze Ozel [1] and Saralees Nadarajah [2]

[1] Department of Statistics, Hacettepe University, 06800 Ankara, Turkey; tatlidil@hacettepe.edu.tr (H.T.); gamzeozl@hacettepe.edu.tr (G.O.)
[2] School of Mathematics, University of Manchester, Manchester M13 9PL, UK; Saralees.Nadarajah@manchester.ac.uk
* Correspondence: emrahaltun@hacettepe.edu.tr

Received: 30 November 2017; Accepted: 22 January 2018; Published: 23 January 2018

Abstract: Most of the financial institutions compute the Value-at-Risk (*VaR*) of their trading portfolios using historical simulation-based methods. In this paper, we examine the Filtered Historical Simulation (FHS) model introduced by Barone-Adesi et al. (1999) theoretically and empirically. The main goal of this study is to find an answer for the following question: "Does the assumption on innovation process play an important role for the Filtered Historical Simulation model?". For this goal, we investigate the performance of FHS model with skewed and fat-tailed innovations distributions such as normal, skew normal, Student's-t, skew-T, generalized error, and skewed generalized error distributions. The performances of FHS models are evaluated by means of unconditional and conditional likelihood ratio tests and loss functions. Based on the empirical results, we conclude that the FHS models with generalized error and skew-T distributions produce more accurate *VaR* forecasts.

Keywords: Filtered Historical Simulation Model; Value-at-Risk; volatility; backtesting

1. Introduction

The most well known risk measure, Value-at-Risk (*VaR*), is used to measure and quantify the level of financial risk within a firm or investment portfolio over a specific holding period. The *VaR* measures the potential loss of risky asset or portfolio over a defined period and for a given confidence level. The *VaR* is defined as

$$VaR_p = F^{-1}(1-p), \tag{1}$$

where F is the cumulative distribution function (cdf) of financial losses, F^{-1} denotes the inverse of F and p is the quantile at which *VaR* is calculated. The approaches to *VaR* could be investigated in three categories: (i) fully parametric models approach based on a volatility models; (ii) non-parametric approaches based on the Historical Simulation (HS) methods and (iii) Extreme Value Theory approach based on modeling the tails of the return distribution.

In this paper, we focus on the non-parametric HS models. The HS model is based on the assumption that historical distribution of returns will remain the same over the next periods. The HS model assumes that price change behaviour repeats itself over the time. Thus, future distribution of asset returns could be described by the empirical one. The one-day-ahead *VaR* R forecast for HS model is given by

$$VaR_{t+1} = Quantile\left\{\{X_t\}_{t=1}^{n}, p\right\}, \tag{2}$$

where p is the quantile at which *VaR* is calculated. Mögel and Auer (2017) compared the performance of HS model with several competitive *VaR* models and stated that HS model produces the similar *VaR* forecasts with unconditional generalized Pareto distribution.

The HS model has several advantages. For instance, it is easy to understand and implement. It is a nonparametric model and does not require any distributional assumption. However, the HS model has also several shortcomings. The HS model ignores the time-varying volatility dynamics. In order to remove lack of HS model, Hull and White (1998) and Barone-Adesi et al. (1999) introduced the FHS model. This approach can be viewed as mixture of the HS and the Generalized Autoregressive Conditional Heteroskedasticity (GARCH) models. Specifically, it does not make any distributional assumption about the standardized returns, while it forecasts the variance through a volatility model. Hence, it is mixture of parametric and non-parametric statistical procedures. Barone-Adesi and Giannopoulos (2001) demonstrated the usefulness of the FHS model over the historical one. Kuester et al. (2006) compared the forecasting performance of several advanced *VaR* models. Kuester et al. (2006) concluded that GARCH-Skew-T, Extreme Value Theory (EVT) approach with normal and Skew-T innovations and FHS model with normal and Skew-T innovations perform the best. Angelidis et al. (2007) compared the FHS model with GARCH models specified under different innovation distributions such as normal, Student's-t and Skewed-T. Roy (2011) estimated the *VaR* of the daily return of Indian capital market using FHS model. Omari (2017) compared FHS, Exponentially Weighted Moving Average (EWMA), GARCH-normal, GARCH-Student's-t, GJR-GARCH-normal and GJR-GARCH-Student's-t models in terms of accuracy of *VAR* forecasts. Omari (2017) demonstrated that GJR-GARCH-Stundet's-t approach and Filtered Historical Simulation method with GARCH volatility specification perform competitively accurate in estimating *VaR* forecasts for both standard and more extreme quantiles thereby generally out-performing all the other models under consideration.

The goal of this paper is to investigate the *VaR* forecasting performance of the FHS model specified under skewed and fat-tailed innovations distributions. For this goal, the comprehensive introduction to the FHS and GARCH models is given. The FHS model under six innovation distributions are introduced. Rolling window estimation produce is used to obtain both unknown parameters of GARCH models and *VaR* forecasts. The performance of the FHS models, in terms of accuracy of *VaR* forecasts, are evaluated by means of backtesting methods and loss functions.

The rest of the paper is organized as follows: Section 2 is devoted to theoretical properties of the FHS and GARCH models under normal, Student's-t, skew-normal, skew-T, generalized error and skewed generalized error innovation distributions. Backtesting methodology is given in Section 3. Empirical findings and model comparisons are presented in Section 4. Concluding remarks are given in Section 5.

2. Filtered Historical Simulation Models

In this section, the FHS model is defined. Then, the log-likelihood functions of GARCH model specified under normal, skew-normal, Student's-t, skew-T, generalized error and skewed genealized error innovation distributions are presented.

FHS model can be summarized as follows:

√ Let R_t denotes the daily log-returns. The benchmark GARCH(1,1) model, introduced by Bollerslev (1986), is defined by

$$\begin{aligned} R_t &= \mu + e_t, \\ e_t &= \varepsilon_t h_t, \ \varepsilon_t \sim i.i.d. \\ h_t^2 &= \omega + \gamma_1 e_{t-1}^2 + \gamma_2 h_{t-1}^2, \end{aligned} \tag{3}$$

where $\omega > 0$, $\gamma_1 > 0$,$\gamma_2 > 0$, μ_t and h_t^2 are the conditional mean and variance, respectively, and ε_t is the innovation distribution with zero mean and unit variance. Maximum Likelihood Estimation (MLE) method is widely used to estimate parameters of GARCH models. Under the assumption of independently and identically distributed (iid) innovations with $f(\varepsilon_t;\tau)$ density function, the log-likelihood function of r_t for a sample of T observations is given by

$$\ell(\psi) = \sum_{t=1}^{T} \left[\ln\left(f(\varepsilon_t;\tau)\right) - \frac{1}{2}\ln\left(h_t^2\right) \right] \tag{4}$$

where $\psi = (\mu, \omega, \gamma_1, \gamma_2, \tau)$ is the parameter vector of GARCH model, τ is the shape parameter(s) of $f(\varepsilon_t;\tau)$ and $\varepsilon_t = \frac{e_t}{h_t}$.
The standardized residuals of estimated GARCH(1,1) model are extracted as follows:

$$\varepsilon_t = \frac{\hat{e}_t}{\hat{h}_t}, \tag{5}$$

where $\hat{e}_t$ is the estimated residual and $\hat{h}_t$ is the corresponding daily estimated volatility.
Now, we can generate the first simulated residual by randomly (with replacement) draw standardized residuals from the dataset with multiplying the one-day ahead volatility forecast:

$$z_{t+1}^* = e_1^* h_{t+1}. \tag{6}$$

The first simulated return for period $t+1$ can be obtained as follows:

$$R_{t+1}^* = \mu_{t+1} + z_{t+1}^*, \tag{7}$$

where z_{t+1}^* is the first simulated residual for period $t+1$.

This procedure is repeated B times of length T. Here, B represents the number of bootstrapped samples and T represents the each of bootstrapped sample size. Then, VaR for period $t+1$ can be forecasted as follows:

$$VaR_{t+1} = \frac{\sum_{b=1}^{B} Quantile\left\{\{R_t^*\}_{t=1}^{T}, 100p\right\}}{B}. \tag{8}$$

The rest of this section is devoted to present the log-likelihood functions of GARCH model under normal, skew-normal, Student's-t, skew-T, generalized error and skewed generalized error distributions.

2.1. Normal Distribution

The log-likelihood function of the GARCH model specified under normal innovations is given by

$$\ell(\psi) = -0.5\left(T\ln 2\pi + \sum_{t=1}^{T}\ln h_t^2 + \sum_{t=1}^{T}\varepsilon_t^2\right), \tag{9}$$

where $\psi = (\mu, \omega, \gamma_1, \gamma_2)$ denotes the parameter vector of the GARCH-normal (GARCH-N) model and $h_t^2 = \omega + \gamma_1 e_{t-1}^2 + \gamma_2 h_{t-1}^2$.

2.2. Skew-Normal Distribution

The first skew extension of normal distribution was proposed by Azzalini (1985). The probability density function (pdf) of skew-normal (SN) distribution is given by

$$\phi(z;\lambda) = 2\phi(z)\,\Phi(z\lambda),z \in \Re, \lambda \in \Re, \tag{10}$$

where λ is an additional parameter that controls the skewness. When $\lambda < 0$, the SN distribution is left skewed, otherwise, it is right skewed. If $\lambda = 0$, the SN distribution reduces to standard normal distribution. The k*th* moment of SN distribution is given by

$$E\left(Z^{2k+1}\right) = \sqrt{\frac{2}{\pi}}\frac{(2k+1)!}{2^k k!}\sum_{i=0}^{k}(-1)^i\binom{k}{i}\frac{\delta^{2i+1}}{2i+1}. \tag{11}$$

here, $k = 0, 1, 2, \ldots, n$ and $\delta = \lambda\Big/\sqrt{1+\lambda^2}$. Note that the even moments of the SN distribution are equal to standard normal distribution. The mean and variance of SN distribution is, respectively, given by,

$$\begin{aligned} \mu &= b\delta \\ \sigma^2 &= 1-(b\delta)^2 \end{aligned} \tag{12}$$

where $b = \sqrt{\frac{2}{\pi}}$. The standardized SN distribution is obtained using the transformed random variable $\varepsilon = (z-\mu)/\sigma$ where $E(\varepsilon) = 0$ and $\text{var}(\varepsilon) = 1$. The random variable z can be expressed as $z = \varepsilon\sigma + \mu$ and $\partial z/\partial\varepsilon = \sigma$. Thus, the pdf of the standardized SN distribution is given by

$$f(\varepsilon;\lambda) = 2\sigma\phi\left((\varepsilon\sigma+\mu)\right)\Phi\left((\varepsilon\sigma+\mu)\lambda\right) \tag{13}$$

Hereafter, using the standardized SN distribution, the log-likelihood function of GARCH model with SN innovation distribution is given by

$$\ell(\psi) = \sum_{t=1}^{T}\ln\left[2\sigma\phi\left(\varepsilon_t\sigma+\mu\right)\right] + \sum_{t=1}^{T}\ln\left[\Phi\left(\left(\varepsilon_t\sigma+\mu\right)\lambda\right)\right] - \frac{1}{2}\sum_{t=1}^{T}\ln\left(h_t^2\right), \tag{14}$$

where $\psi = (\mu, \omega, \gamma_1, \gamma_2, \lambda)$ is the parameter vector.

2.3. Student's-t Distribution

Since financial return series has fatter tails than normal distribution, Bollerslev (1986, 1987) proposed the GARCH model with the Student's-t innovations. GARCH model with the Student's-t innovations enables to model both fat-tail and excess kurtosis observed in financial return series. The log-likelihood function of the GARCH-Student's-t (GARCH-T) model is given by

$$\begin{aligned} \ell(\psi) = {} & T\left[\ln\Gamma\left(\tfrac{v+1}{2}\right) - \ln\Gamma\left(\tfrac{v}{2}\right) - \tfrac{1}{2}\ln\left[\pi(v-2)\right]\right] \\ & -\tfrac{1}{2}\sum_{t=1}^{T}\left[\ln h_t^2 + (1+v)\ln\left(1+\tfrac{\varepsilon_t^2}{v-2}\right)\right] \end{aligned}, \tag{15}$$

where $\psi = (\mu, \omega, \gamma_1, \gamma_2, v)$ is the parameter vector, $\Gamma(v)$ is the gamma function and parameter v controls the tails of the distribution.

2.4. Skew-T Distribution

The pdf of skew-T distribution obtained by Azzalini and Capitanio (2003) is given by

$$f(x;\lambda,v) = 2t(x;v)\,T\left(\sqrt{\frac{1+v}{x^2+v}}\lambda t; v+1\right), x \in \Re, \tag{16}$$

where $t(\cdot)$ and $T(\cdot)$ are pdf and cdf of Student's-t distribution, respectively, and λ controls the skewness. When $\lambda = 0$, ST distribution reduces to Student's-t distribution in Equation (16). The moments of ST distribution are given by

$$E\left(X^k\right) = \frac{\left(\frac{v}{2}\right)^{\frac{k}{2}}\Gamma\left(\frac{(v-k)}{2}\right)}{\Gamma\left(\frac{v}{2}\right)}E\left(Z^k\right), \tag{17}$$

The mean and variance of ST distribution are, respectively, given by

$$\begin{aligned} \mu &= \frac{\left(\frac{v}{\pi}\right)^{\frac{1}{2}}\Gamma\left(\frac{(v-1)}{2}\right)}{\Gamma\left(\frac{v}{2}\right)}\frac{\lambda}{\sqrt{1+\lambda^2}}, \\ \sigma^2 &= \left(\frac{v}{v-2} - \mu^2\right). \end{aligned} \tag{18}$$

The standardized ST distribution is obtained using the transformed random variable $\varepsilon = (z-\mu)/\sigma$, where $E(\varepsilon) = 0$ and $\mathrm{var}(\varepsilon) = 1$. The random variable z can be expressed as $z = \varepsilon\sigma + \mu$ and $\partial z/\partial\varepsilon = \sigma$. Thus, the pdf of standardized ST distribution is given by

$$f(\varepsilon;\lambda,v) = 2\sigma t\left((\varepsilon\sigma+\mu);v\right)T\left(\sqrt{\frac{1+v}{(\varepsilon\sigma+\mu)^2+v}}\lambda(\varepsilon\sigma+\mu);v+1\right), v>2 \tag{19}$$

where μ and σ are mean and standard deviation of ST distribution, respectively. The log-likelihood function of GARCH model with the ST innovation distribution is given by

$$\begin{aligned} \ell(\psi) &= T\ln(2) + T\ln(\sigma) + \sum_{t=1}^{T}\ln\left[t\left((\varepsilon_t\sigma+\mu);v\right)\right] \\ &+ \sum_{t=1}^{T}\ln\left[T\left(\sqrt{\frac{1+v}{(\varepsilon_t\sigma+\mu)^2+v}}\lambda(\varepsilon_t\sigma+\mu);v+1\right)\right] - \frac{1}{2}\sum_{t=1}^{T}\ln\left(h_t^2\right) \end{aligned} \tag{20}$$

where $\psi = (\mu,\omega,\gamma_1,\gamma_2,\lambda,v)$ is the parameter vector.

2.5. Generalized Error Distribution

Nelson (1991) introduced the GARCH volatility model of generalized error distribution (GED). The log-likelihood function of GARCH-GED model is given by

$$\ell(\psi) = \sum_{t=1}^{T}\left[\ln\left(\frac{v}{2}\right) - \frac{1}{2}\left|\frac{\varepsilon_t}{\lambda}\right|^v - \left(1+v^{-1}\right)\ln(2) - \ln\Gamma\left(\frac{1}{2}\right) - \frac{1}{2}\ln\left(h_t^2\right)\right] \tag{21}$$

where $\psi = (\mu,\omega,\gamma_1,\gamma_2,v)$ is the parameter vector, v is tail-thickness parameter and

$$\lambda = \left(\frac{\Gamma\left(\frac{1}{v}\right)}{2^{\frac{2}{v}}\Gamma\left(\frac{3}{v}\right)}\right)^{\frac{1}{2}}. \tag{22}$$

Note that the normal distribution is a special case of the GED when $v = 2$. If $v < 2$, the GED has heavier tails than the Gaussian distribution.

2.6. Skewed Generalized Error Distribution

Skewed Generalized Error Distribution (SGED) provides an opportunity to model skewness and excess kurtosis observed in financial return series. Lee et al. (2008) introduced the GARCH-SGED model and concluded that GARCH model with SGED innovation process outperformed the GARCH-N model for all confidence levels.

The pdf of standardized SGED is given by,

$$f(\varepsilon_t) = C\exp\left(-\frac{|\varepsilon_t+\delta|^{\kappa}}{[1+sign(\varepsilon_t+\delta)\lambda]^{\kappa}\theta^{\kappa}}\right) \tag{23}$$

where

$$\begin{aligned} C &= \tfrac{\kappa}{2\theta}\Gamma\left(\tfrac{1}{\kappa}\right)^{-1}, \theta = \Gamma\left(\tfrac{1}{\kappa}\right)^{0.5}\Gamma\left(\tfrac{3}{\kappa}\right)^{0.5}S(\lambda)^{-1} \\ S(\lambda) &= \sqrt{1+3\lambda^2-4A^2\lambda^2}, \delta = \tfrac{2\lambda A}{S(\lambda)} \\ A &= \Gamma\left(\tfrac{2}{\kappa}\right)\Gamma\left(\tfrac{1}{\kappa}\right)^{-0.5}\Gamma\left(\tfrac{3}{\kappa}\right)^{-0.5}, \end{aligned} \tag{24}$$

where $\kappa > 0$ is the shape parameter, $-1 < \lambda < 1$ is skewness parameter. The SGED turns out to be the standard normal distribution when $\kappa = 2$ and $\lambda = 0$. The log-likelihood function of GARCH-SGED model is given by

$$\ell(\psi) = -\sum_{t=1}^{T}\left(\frac{|\varepsilon_t+\delta|^{\kappa}}{[1+sign\,(\varepsilon_t+\delta)\,\lambda]^{\kappa}\theta^{\kappa}}\right) + T\ln(c) - \sum_{t=1}^{T}\ln(h_t) \tag{25}$$

where $\psi = (\mu, \omega, \gamma_1, \gamma_2, \lambda, \kappa)$ is the parameter vector.

3. Evaluation of *VaR* Forecasts

Now, we introduce backtesting methodology that is used to compare *VaR* forecast accuracy of the models. Statistical accuracy of the models is evaluated by backtests of Kupiec (1995), Christoffersen (1998), Engle and Manganelli (2004) and Sarma et al. (2003). Recently, some alternative backtesting methods for VaR forecasts were proposed by Ziggel et al. (2014) and Dumitrescu et al. (2012).

Kupiec (1995) proposed a likelihood ratio (LR) test of unconditional coverage (LR_{uc}) to evaluate the model accuracy. The test examines whether the failure rate is equal to the expected value. The LR test statistic is given by

$$LR = -2\ln\left[\frac{p^{n_1}(1-p)^{n_0}}{\hat{\pi}^{n_1}(1-\pi)^{n_0}}\right] \sim \chi_1^2, \tag{26}$$

where $\hat{\pi} = n_1/(n_0+n_1)$ is the MLE of p, n_1 represents the total violation and n_0 represents the total non-violations forecasts. Violation means that if $VaR_t > r_t$, violation occurs, opposite case indicates the non-violation. Under the null hypothesis $(H_0 : p = \hat{\pi})$, the LR statistic follows a chi-square distribution with one degree of freedom.

The LR_{uc} test fails to detect if violations are not randomly distributed. Christoffersen (1998) proposed a LR test of conditional coverage LR_{cc} to remove the lack of Kupiec (1995) test. The LR_{cc} test investigates both equality of failure rate and expected one and also independently distributed violations. The LR_{cc} test statistic under the null hypothesis shows that the failures are independent and equal to the expected one. It is given by

$$LR_{cc} = -2\ln\left[\frac{(1-\alpha)^{n_0}\alpha^{n_1}}{(1-\pi_{01})^{n_{00}}\pi_{01}{}^{n_{01}}(1-\pi_{11})^{n_{10}}\pi_{11}{}^{n_{11}}}\right] \sim \chi_2^2, \tag{27}$$

where n_{ij} is the number of observations with value i followed by j for $i,j = 0,1$ and $\pi_{ij} = n_{ij}/\sum_j n_{ij}$ is the probability, for $i,j = 1$. It denotes that the violation occurred, otherwise indicates the opposite case. The LR_{cc} statistic follows a chi-square distribution with two degrees of freedom.

The Dynamic Quantile (DQ) test, proposed by Engle and Manganelli (2004), examines if the violations is uncorrelated with any variable that belongs to information set Ω_{t+1} when the *VaR* is calculated. The main idea of DQ test is to regress the current violations on past violations in order to test for different restrictions on the parameters of the model. The estimated linear regression model is given by

$$I_t = \beta_0 + \sum_{i=1}^{p} \beta_i I_{t-i} + \sum_{i=1}^{q} \mu_j X_j + \varepsilon_t \tag{28}$$

where

$$I_t = \begin{cases} 1, \mathrm{r_t} < \mathrm{VaR_t} \\ 0, \mathrm{r_t} \geq \mathrm{VaR_t} \end{cases} \tag{29}$$

This regression model tests whether the probability of violation depends on the level of the *VaR*. Here, p and q are used as 5 and 1, respectively, for illustrative purpose.

In most instances, evaluating the performance of *VaR* models by means of LR_{uc}, LR_{cc} and DC tests may not be sufficient to decide the most adequate model among others. For instance, some models may have the same violation number with different forecast errors. Sarma et al. (2003) defined a test on the basis of *regulator's loss function* (RLF) to take into account differences between realized returns and *VaR* forecasts. The RLF is given by

$$RLF_{t+1} = \begin{cases} (r_{t+1} - VaR_{t+1})^2, \text{if } r_{t+1} < VaR_{t+1} \\ 0, \qquad\qquad\qquad\quad \text{if } r_{t+1} \geq VaR_{t+1} \end{cases} \tag{30}$$

where VaR_{t+1} represents the one-day-ahead *VaR* forecast for a long position.

The unexpected loss (UL) is equal to average value of differences between realized return and VaR forecasts. The one-day-ahead magnitude of the violation for long position is given by

$$\mathrm{UL}_{t+1} = \begin{cases} (r_{t+1} - VaR_{t+1}), \text{if } r_{t+1} < VaR_{t+1} \\ 0, \qquad\qquad\qquad\quad \text{if } r_{t+1} \geq VaR_{t+1} \end{cases} \tag{31}$$

The QLF and UL loss functions do not consider the case in which the realized returns exceed the *VaR* forecast. The appropriate loss function should take into consideration the cost of excess capital. Because, overestimated *VaR* forecasts yield firms to hold much more capital value than required one. The main objective of any firm is to maximize the their profits. For this reason, Sarma et al. (2003) is proposed the new loss function, called Firm's Loss Function (FLF). The FLF is given by

$$FLF_{t+1} = \begin{cases} (r_{t+1} - VaR_{t+1})^2, \text{if } r_{t+1} < VaR_{t+1} \\ -\beta VaR_{t+1}, \qquad\quad \text{if } r_{t+1} \geq VaR_{t+1} \end{cases} \tag{32}$$

where β is the cost of excess capital.

4. Empirical Results

4.1. Data Description

To evaluate the performance of FHS models in terms of accuracy of *VaR* forecasts, ISE-100 index of Turkey is used. The used time series data contains 1092 daily log-returns from 3 January 2013 to 4 May 2017. The descriptive statistics of the log-returns of ISE-100 index are given in Table 1.

Table 1. Summary statistics for the ISE-100 index.

ISE-100	
Number of observations	1092
Minimum	−0.048
Maximum	0.027
Mean	6.6×10^{-5}
Median	2×10^{-4}
Std. Deviation	0.006
Skewness	−0.603
Kurtosis	4.957
Jarque-Bera	1190.970 (p <0.001)

Table 1 shows that the mean return is closed to 0. The results of the Jarque-Bera test prove that the null hypothesis of normality is rejected at any level of significance. It shows strong evidence for high excess kurtosis and negative skewness. Thus, it is clear that log return of ISE-100 index has non-normal characteristics, excess kurtosis, and fat tails. Figure 1 displays the daily log-returns of ISE-100 index.

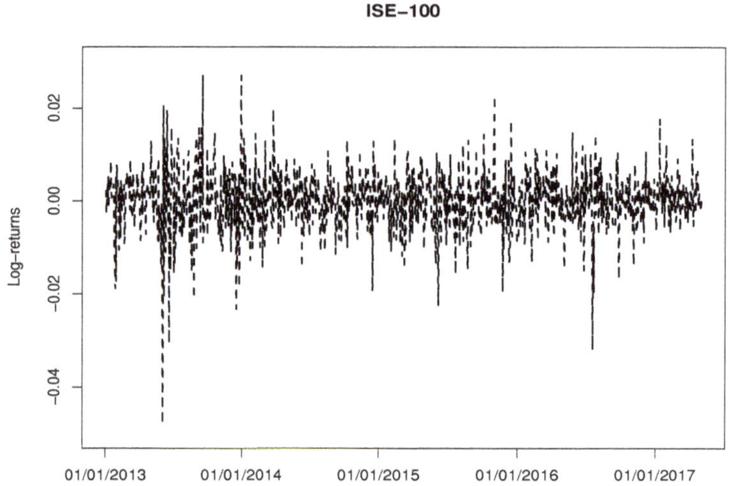

Figure 1. Daily log-returns of the ISE-100 index.

Figure 2 displays the time-varying skewness and kurtosis of ISE-100. For Figure 2, window length is determined as 392 and the rolling window procedure is used. Based on Figure 2, it is clear that skewness and kurtosis of ISE-100 index exhibit great variability across the time.

The benchmark model, GARCH(1,1), is estimated with six different innovation distributions: Normal, SN, Student's-t, ST, GED and SGED. Table 2 shows the estimated parameters of GARCH models. The **rugarch** package in R software is used to obtain parameter estimation of normal, Student's-t, GED and SGED models. The **constrOptim** function in R software is used to minimize negative log-likelihood functions of GARCH-ST and GARCH-SN models.

Based on Table 2, we conclude that GARCH-T and GARCH-SGED models have the lower log-likelihood value among others. Since GARCH-T model has the lowest log-likelihood value, it could be chosen as best model for in-sample period. Table 2 also shows that the conditional variance parameters γ_2 are highly significant for all GARCH models.

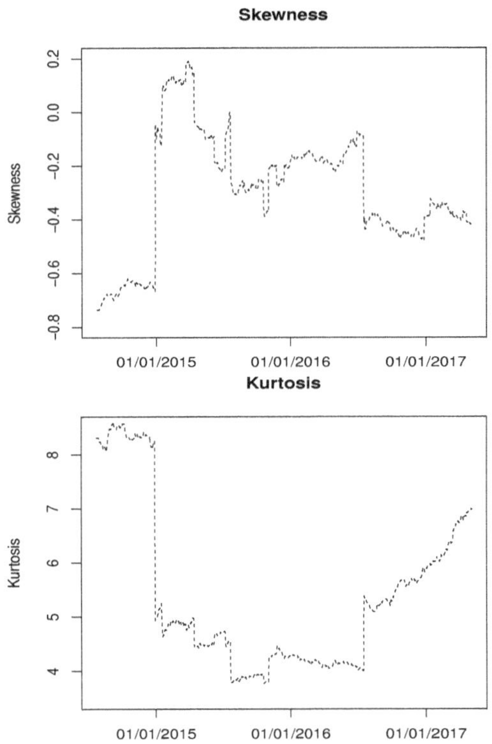

Figure 2. Time varying skewness and kurtosis plots of ISE-100 index.

Table 2. In-sample performance of GARCH models under skewed and fat-tailed innovation distributions.

Parameters	Normal	Student-T	ST	SN	GED	SGED
μ	5.24×10^{-4}	5.67×10^{-4}	8.56×10^{-4}	4.05×10^{-4}	5.67×10^{-4}	3.51×10^{-4}
	3.41×10^{-4}	3.04×10^{-4}	3.60×10^{-4}	3.34×10^{-4}	3.77×10^{-4}	3.26×10^{-4}
ω	3.69×10^{-6}	2.01×10^{-6}	2.27×10^{-6}	3.65×10^{-6}	2.72×10^{-6}	2.63×10^{-6}
	1.50×10^{-6}	1.53×10^{-6}	6.71×10^{-6}	1.73×10^{-6}	1.66×10^{-6}	1.57×10^{-6}
γ_1	0.1194	0.0759	0.1510	0.1460	0.0930	0.0873
	0.0413	0.0336	0.2940	0.0560	0.0393	0.0353
γ_2	0.8234	0.8908	0.8240	0.7950	0.8600	0.8650
	0.0449	0.0485	0.3130	0.0662	0.0518	0.0486
v	-	4.7490	4.8760	-	1.2020	-
	-	1.1600	0.5620	-	0.1040	-
λ	-	-	−0.2750	−1.5050	-	0.8860
	-	-	2.4260	0.2630	-	0.0440
κ	-	-	-	-	-	1.2200
	-	-	-	-	-	0.1093
$-\ell$	−1381.1100	−1405.003	−1402.2630	−1388.1800	−1401.0600	−1402.7300

4.2. Backtesting Results

In this subsection, rolling window estimation procedure is used to estimate parameters of GARCH models. Then, *VaR* forecasts of FHS models are obtained by using estimated parameters of GARCH models, one-day-ahead forecasts of conditional mean and conditional variance and standardized residuals extracted from estimated GARCH models. Rolling window estimation produce allows us to capture time-varying characteristics of the time series in different time periods. Window length is determined as 392 and next 700 daily returns are used to evaluate the out of sample performance of *VaR* models.

Table 3 shows the backtesting results for FHS-N, FHS-T, FHS-ST, FHS-SN, FHS-GED and FHS-SGED models. The two step decision making procedure is applied to decide the best *VaR* model. In first step, the performance of *VaR* models are evaluated according to results of LR_uc, LR_cc and *DC* tests. In second step, the models, achieved to pass these three backtest, considered as accurate model and obtained the results of loss functions of these *VaR* models. Finally, the lowest values of loss functions indicate the best VaR models.

Table 4 shows that all FHS models perform well based on the results of LR_{uc}, LR_{cc} and *DC* tests results at $p = 0.05$ ad $p = 0.025$ levels. However, FHS model with Student's-t and ST innovation distributions provide better *VaR* forecasts than other competitive models at $p = 0.01$ level based on the result of *DC* test. Therefore, it can be concluded that FHS model specified under skewed and fat-tailed innovation distributions provides more accurate VaR forecasts especially for high quantiles.

Even if FHS models have similar results in view of LR_{uc}, LR_{cc} and *DC* results, they have different failure rates and forecast errors. Loss functions are useful to compare *VaR* models with their forecast errors. Based on the ARLF, UL and FLF results, we conclude following results: (i) FHS-SN is the best performed model at $p = 0.05$ and $p = 0.025$ levels according to ARLF and UL criteria. Based on the FLF results, FHS-GED model has the lowest excess capital value than other models at $p = 0.05$ and $p = 0.025$ levels. Therefore, FHS-GED model could be chosen as best model for $p = 0.05$ and $p = 0.025$ levels; (ii) Based on the three backtesting results, FHS-T and FHS-ST models provide the most accurate *VaR* forecasts among others at $p = 0.01$ level. According to loss functions results, it is easy to see that FHS-ST model has lower values of ARLF, UL and FLF results than FHS-T model. Therefore, FHS-ST model could be chosen as the best model for $p = 0.01$ model.

Figures 3 displays the *VaR* forecasts of FHS models specified under six innovation distributions. As seen in Figure 3, the assumption on innovation process does not affect the *VaR* forecasts of FHS model soulfully. However, the GED and ST distributions could be preferable to reduce the forecast error of the FHS model.

Table 3. Backtesting results of FHS models for long position ($p = 0.05$, $p = 0.025$, and $p = 0.01$).

			$p = 0.05$			
Models	**Mean *VaR* (%)**	**N. Of Vio.**	**Failure Rate**	**LR-uc**	**LR-cc**	**DQ**
FSH-N	−0.910	29	0.041	1.146 (0.284)	1.186 (0.552)	4.586 (0.710)
FSH-SN	−0.911	29	0.041	1.146 (0.284)	1.186 (0.552)	4.545 (0.715)
FSH-T	−0.897	32	0.046	0.278 (0.597)	0.459 (0.794)	2.996 (0.885)
FSH-GED	−0.899	30	0.043	0.788 (0.374)	0.863 (0.649)	4.041 (0.775)
FSH-SGED	−0.904	30	0.043	0.788 (0.374)	0.863 (0.649)	4.255 (0.749)
FSH-ST	−0.897	32	0.046	0.278 (0.597)	0.459 (0.794)	3.187 (0.867)
			$p = 0.025$			
Models	**Mean *VaR* (%)**	**N. Of Vio.**	**Failure Rate**	**LR-uc**	**LR-cc**	**DQ**
FSH-N	−1.193	20	0.029	0.350 (0.554)	0.630 (0.729)	6.820 (0.448)
FSH-SN	−1.196	20	0.029	0.350 (0.554)	0.630 (0.729)	6.805 (0.449)
FSH-T	−1.177	20	0.029	0.350 (0.554)	0.630 (0.729)	4.056 (0.773)
FSH-GED	−1.179	20	0.029	0.350 (0.554)	0.630 (0.729)	4.579 (0.711)
FSH-SGED	−1.187	20	0.029	0.350 (0.554)	0.630 (0.729)	5.102 (0.647)
FSH-ST	−1.177	20	0.029	0.350 (0.554)	0.630 (0.729)	4.051 (0.774)

Table 3. *Cont.*

			p = 0.01			
Models	**Mean *VaR* (%)**	**N. Of Vio.**	**Failure Rate**	**LR-uc**	**LR-cc**	**DQ**
FSH-N	−1.546	9	0.013	0.529 (0.466)	0.764 (0.682)	15.479 (0.030)
FSH-SN	−1.549	9	0.013	0.529 (0.466)	0.764 (0.682)	16.338 (0.022)
FSH-T	−1.526	9	0.013	0.529 (0.466)	0.764 (0.682)	13.185 (0.067)
FSH-GED	−1.530	8	0.011	0.137 (0.710)	0.323 (0.851)	16.115 (0.024)
FSH-SGED	−1.538	9	0.013	0.529 (0.466)	0.764 (0.682)	14.620 (0.041)
FSH-ST	−1.526	9	0.013	0.529 (0.466)	0.764 (0.682)	12.893 (0.075)

p values of LR-uc, LR-cc and DC tests are presented in parentheses.

Table 4. Loss functions results of FHS models for long position ($p = 0.05$, $p = 0.025$, and $p = 0.01$).

			p = 0.05			
Models	**ARLF**	**Min.-Max. ARLF**	**UL**	**Min.-Max. UL**	**FLF**	**Min.-Max. FLF**
FSH-N	0.0172063	$(1 \times 10^{-4}, 5.133)$	−0.0179110	(−2.265, −0.010)	0.0283988	$(1 \times 10^{-4}, 5.133)$
FSH-SN	0.0171900	$(1 \times 10^{-4}, 5.121)$	−0.0178643	(−2.263, −0.011)	0.0283877	$(1.37 \times 10^{-4}, 5.121)$
FSH-T	0.0173740	$(5.84 \times 10^{-8}, 5.150)$	−0.0181385	$(-2.269, -2 \times 10^{-4})$	0.0284271	$(5.84 \times 10^{-8}, 5.150)$
FSH-GED	0.0172983	$(1.89 \times 10^{-6}, 5.135)$	−0.0180858	(−2.266, −0.001)	0.0283820	$(1.89 \times 10^{-6}, 5.135)$
FSH-SGED	0.0173162	$(2.05 \times 10^{-5}, 5.145)$	−0.0179867	(−2.268, −0.004)	0.0284463	$(2.05 \times 10^{-5}, 5.145)$
FSH-ST	0.0173437	$(9.28 \times 10^{-6}, 5.127)$	−0.0181591	(−2.264, −0.003)	0.0283897	$(9.28 \times 10^{-6}, 5.127)$
			p = 0.025			
Models	**ARLF**	**Min.-Max. ARLF**	**UL**	**Min.-Max. UL**	**FLF**	**Min.-Max. FLF**
FSH-N	0.0097984	(0.003, 3.896)	−0.0108364	(−1.974, −0.058)	0.0228029	(0.003, 3.896)
FSH-SN	0.0097622	(0.001, 3.863)	−0.0107498	(−1.965, −0.033)	0.0227883	(0.001, 3.863)
FSH-T	0.0098350	(0.002, 3.886)	−0.0108600	(−1.971, −0.049)	0.0226889	(0.002, 3.886)
FSH-GED	0.0097898	(0.004, 3.876)	−0.0108694	(−1.968, −0.063)	0.0226529	(0.004, 3.876)
FSH-SGED	0.0098099	(0.002, 3.893)	−0.0107848	(−1.973, −0.040)	0.0227502	(0.002, 3.893)
FSH-ST	0.0098287	(0.002, 3.884)	−0.0108752	(−1.971, −0.049)	0.0226755	(0.002, 3.884)
			p = 0.01			
Models	**ARLF**	**Min.-Max. ARLF**	**UL**	**Min.-Max. UL**	**FLF**	**Min.-Max. FLF**
FSH-N	0.0052475	$(7.17 \times 10^{-5}, 2.885)$	−0.0051635	(−1.698, −0.008)	0.0212668	$(7.17 \times 10^{-5}, 2.885)$
FSH-SN	0.0052483	$(8.22 \times 10^{-5}, 2.893)$	−0.0051776	(−1.700, −0.009)	0.0213011	$(8.22 \times 10^{-5}, 2.893)$
FSH-T	0.0052399	$(1 \times 10^{-4}, 2.914)$	−0.0051979	(−1.707, −0.011)	0.0210625	$(1.15 \times 10^{-4}, 2.914)$
FSH-GED	0.0052125	$(3 \times 10^{-4}, 2.882)$	−0.0051546	(−1.697, −0.017)	0.0210964	$(2.81 \times 10^{-4}, 2.882)$
FSH-SGED	0.0052148	$(4 \times 10^{-4}, 2.883)$	−0.0051849	(−1.697, −0.019)	0.0211543	$(3.98 \times 10^{-4}, 2.883)$
FSH-ST	0.0052135	$(3.32 \times 10^{-5}, 2.895)$	−0.0051634	(−1.701, −0.006)	0.0210319	$(3.32 \times 10^{-5}, 2.895)$

p values of LR-uc and LR-cc tests are presented in parentheses.

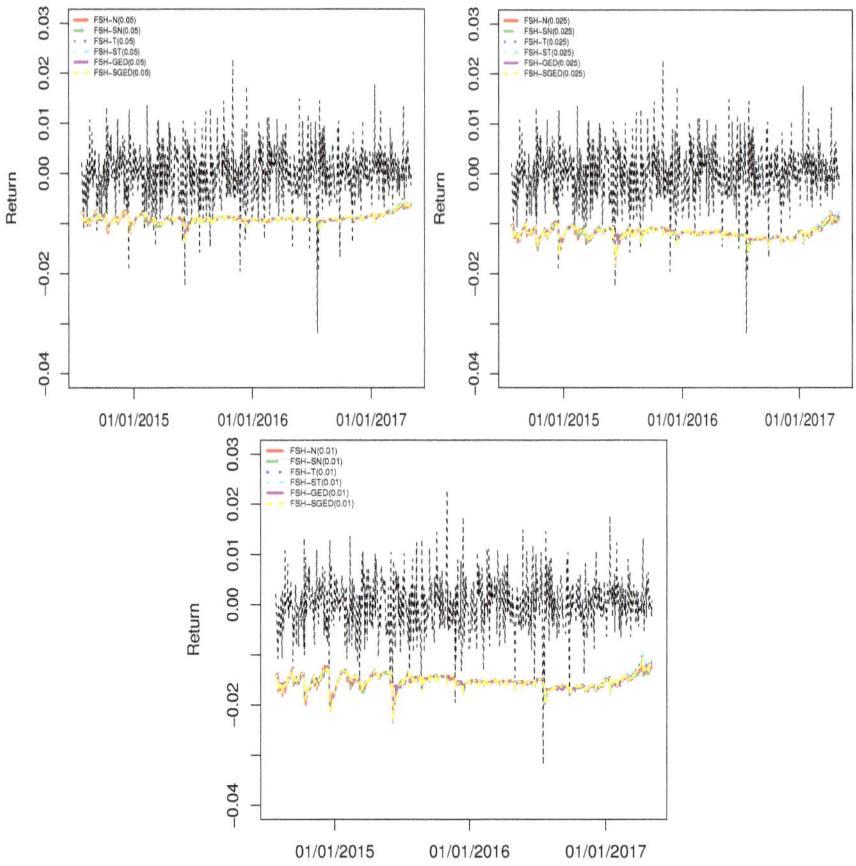

Figure 3. Daily *VaR* forecast of GARCH models with different innovation distributions for 97.5% and 99% confidence levels.

5. Conclusions

In this study, we investigate FHS models with skewed and fat-tailed innovation distributions both theoretically and empirically. For this aim, we use Normal, Student's-t, ST, SN, GED and SGED as the innovation distributions. The empirical findings show that all of FHS models perform well based on the LR_{uc}, LR_{cc} and DC results at $p = 0.05$ and $p = 0.025$ levels. However, only two FHS model, FHS-T and FHS-ST models achieve to pass LR_{uc}, LR_{cc} and DC tests at $p = 0.01$ level. Based on the results of loss functions, FHS-GED is the best performed model at $p = 0.05$ and $p = 0.025$ levels and FHS-ST model is the best performed model at $p = 0.01$ level. We conclude that skewed and fat-tailed distributions are preferable to reduce the *VaR* forecast error of FHS models. We hope that the results given in this study will be useful for both researchers and practitioners.

Author Contributions: Emrah Altun, Huseyin Tatlidil, Gamze Ozel and Saralees Nadarajah have contributed jointly to all of the sections of the paper.

Conflicts of Interest: The authors declare no conflict of interest.

Angelidis, Timotheos, Alexandros Benos, and Stavros Degiannakis. 2007. A robust VaR model under different time periods and weighting schemes. *Review of Quantitative Finance and Accounting* 28: 187–201.

Azzalini, Adelchi. 1985. A class of distributions which includes the normal ones. *Scandinavian Journal of Statistics* 12: 171–78.

Azzalini, Adelchi, and Antonella Capitanio. 2003. Distributions generated by perturbation of symmetry with emphasis on a multivariate skew t-distribution. *Journal of the Royal Statistical Society: Series B (Statistical Methodology)* 65: 367–89.

Barone-Adesi, Giovanni, Kostas Giannopoulos, and Les Vosper. 1999. VaR without correlations for nonlinear portfolios. *Journal of Futures Markets* 19: 583–602.

Barone-Adesi, Giovanni, and Kostas Giannopoulos. 2001. Non parametric var techniques. myths and realities. *Economic Notes* 30: 167–81.

Bollerslev, Tim. 1986. Generalized autoregressive conditional heteroskedasticity. *Journal of Econometrics* 31: 307–27.

Bollerslev, Tim. 1987. A conditionally heteroskedastic time series model for speculative prices and rates of return. *The Review of Economics and Statistics* 69: 542–47.

Christoffersen, Peter F. 1998. Evaluating interval forecasts. *International Economic Review* 39: 841–62.

Dumitrescu, Elena-Ivona, Christophe Hurlin, and Vinson Pham. 2012. Backtesting value-at-risk: from dynamic quantile to dynamic binary tests. *Finance* 33: 79–112.

Engle, Robert F., and Simone Manganelli. 2004. CAViaR: Conditional autoregressive value at risk by regression quantiles. *Journal of Business & Economic Statistics* 22: 367–81.

Hull, John, and Alan White. 1998. Incorporating volatility updating into the historical simulation method for value-at-risk. *Journal of Risk* 1: 5–19.

Kupiec, Paul H. 1995. Techniques for verifying the accuracy of risk measurement models. *The Journal of Derivatives* 3: 73–84.

Kuester, Keith, Stefan Mittnik, and Marc S. Paolella. 2006. Value-at-risk prediction: A comparison of alternative strategies. *Journal of Financial Econometrics* 4: 53–89.

Lee, Ming-Chih, Jung-Bin Su, and Hung-Chun Liu. 2008. Value-at-risk in US stock indices with skewed generalized error distribution. *Applied Financial Economics Letters* 4: 425–31.

Mögel, Benjamin, and Benjamin R. Auer. 2017. How accurate are modern Value-at-Risk estimators derived from extreme value theory? *Review of Quantitative Finance and Accounting*, 1–52.

Nelson, Daniel B. 1991. Conditional heteroscedasticity in asset returns: A new approach. *Econometrica* 59: 347–70.

Omari, Cyprian Ondieki. 2017. A Comparative Performance of Conventional Methods for Estimating Market Risk Using Value at Risk. *International Journal of Econometrics and Financial Management* 5: 22–32.

Roy, Indrajit. 2011. Estimating Value at Risk (VaR) using Filtered Historical Simulation in the Indian capital market. *Reserve Bank of India Occasional Papers* 32: 81–98.

Sarma, Mandira, Susan Thomas, and Ajay Shah. 2003. Selection of Value-at-Risk models. *Journal of Forecasting* 22: 337–58.

Ziggel, Daniel, Tobias Berens, Gregor N. F. Weiß, and Dominik Wied. 2014. A new set of improved Value-at-Risk backtests. *Journal of Banking & Finance* 48: 29–41.

Journal of
Risk and Financial Management

MDPI

Article

Negative Binomial Kumaraswamy-G Cure Rate Regression Model

Amanda D'Andrea [1,2,*], Ricardo Rocha [3], Vera Tomazella [1] and Francisco Louzada [2]

[1] Department of Statistics, Federal University of São Carlos, São Carlos, SP 13565-905, Brazil; veratomazella@gmail.com
[2] Institute of Mathematical Science and Computing, University of São Paulo, São Carlos, SP 13565-905, Brazil; louzadaneto@gmail.com
[3] Department of Statistics, Institute of Mathematics and Statistics, Federal University of Bahia, Salvador, BA 40170-115, Brazil; ricardorocha23@hotmail.com
[*] Correspondence: amanda_eudes@hotmail.com; Tel.: +55-16-991-448-646

Received: 8 December 2017; Accepted: 16 January 2018; Published: 19 January 2018

Abstract: In survival analysis, the presence of elements not susceptible to the event of interest is very common. These elements lead to what is called a fraction cure, cure rate, or even long-term survivors. In this paper, we propose a unified approach using the negative binomial distribution for modeling cure rates under the Kumaraswamy family of distributions. The estimation is made by maximum likelihood. We checked the maximum likelihood asymptotic properties through some simulation setups. Furthermore, we propose an estimation strategy based on the Negative Binomial Kumaraswamy-G generalized linear model. Finally, we illustrate the distributions proposed using a real data set related to health risk.

Keywords: long-term survivors; Kumaraswamy family; survival analysis; negative binomial distribution; generalized linear model

---

1. Introduction

In survival analysis, the study is based on data relating to the time until the occurrence of a particular event of interest, also known as time to failure. This data can come from the time until there is a failure in an electronic component; time until a particular disease occurs in a patient; time for a particular drug to have the desired effect, among others. The behavior of such data can be verified empirically; this approach is said to not be parametric. If the data follows a probability distribution, then this approach is called parametric; this is the most used form in this work.

The survival and hazard functions, the objects of greatest interest in survival analysis, allow the study of such behavior. The survival function is the probability of an individual or component surviving after a preset time and the hazard function is the instantaneous failure rate, which graphically can take various forms, such as constant, increasing, decreasing, unimodal or bathtub shaped. However, when the behavior of the hazard function is not monotonous, the most commonly known distributions, such as exponential and Weibull, cannot accommodate this kind of behavior.

This is because a disadvantage of these models is that they are very limited due to the small number of parameters and therefore the conclusions drawn from the models cannot be sufficiently robust to accommodate deviations from the data. There are some distributions that accommodate the non-monotonic hazard function, but they are usually very complicated and with many parameters.

We can model real survival data using almost any continuous distribution and with positive values; the simplest and most common models, such as exponential and Weibull distribution, may not be appropriate. Therefore, to find a distribution that accommodates non-monotone hazard functions is a known issue in survival analysis. Therefore, it is desirable to consider other approaches to achieve greater flexibility, and this is what has motivated studies to find distributions that accommodate these types of function.

Kumaraswamy (1980) proposed the Kumaraswamy distribution, which was widely used in hydrology and, based on this, Cordeiro and de Castro (2011) proposed a new family of generalized distributions, called Kumaraswamy generalized (Kum-G). It is flexible and contains distributions with unimodal and bathtub-shaped hazard functions, as shown by De Pascoa et al. (2011), and has, as special cases, any distribution that is normal, exponential, Weibull, Gamma, Gumbel and inverse Gaussian. The domain of the distribution is the range in which the particular cases are set. Other examples of generalized distributions are the Generalized exponential distribution (Gupta and Kundu 1999) and the Stoppa (or Generalized Pareto) distribution (Stoppa 1990) and (Calderín-Ojeda and Kwok 2016).

In a population, there may be individuals who have not experienced the event of interest until the end of the study; this is called censorship. When there are a large number of censored individuals, we have an indication that in this population there are individuals who are not subjected to the event; they are considered immune, cured or not susceptible to the event of interest.

From the traditional models of survival, it is not possible to estimate the cured fraction of the population, or the percentage of individuals who are considered cured. Thus, statistical models are needed to incorporate such fractions and these are termed long-term or cure rate models. Because of this capability, different fit methods have been proposed in several areas such as biomedical studies, financial, criminology, demography and industrial reliability, among others. For example, in biomedical data, an event of interest may be the death of the patient due to tumor recurrence, but there may be patients who are cured and do not die due to cancer. When the financial data is studied, an event of interest may be the customer's closing of a bank account by default, but there may be customers who will never close their account. In criminology data, the event of interest may be a repeat offence and there may be people who do not repeat an offence. In industrial reliability, long duration models are used to verify the proportion of components that are not tested at zero time and are exposed to various voltage regimes or uses. In market research areas, individuals who will never buy a particular product are considered immune. See, for example, (Anscombe 1961; Farewell 1977; Goldman 1984; Broadhurst and Maller 1991; Meeker and Escobar 1998).

Many authors have contributed to the theory of long-term models. Boag (1949) was the pioneer; the maximum likelihood method was used to estimate the proportion of survivors in a population of 121 women with breast cancer, in an experiment that lasted 14 years. Based on Boag's idea, Berkson and Gage (1952) proposed a mixture model in order to estimate the proportion of cured patients in a population subjected to a treatment of stomach cancer. More complex long-term models, such as Yakovlev and Tsodikov (1996), Chen et al. (1999) among others, have emerged in order to better explain the biological effects involved. More recently, Rodrigues et al. (2009) proposed a unified theory of long duration, considering different competitive causes. In this context, most long-term models make use of this proposal, among which are (Sy and Taylor 2000; Castro et al. 2009; Cancho et al. 2011; Gu et al. 2011), besides (Ibrahim et al. 2005; Cooner et al. 2007; Ortega et al. 2008, 2009; Cancho et al. 2009).

A very important point in survival analysis is the study of covariates, because many factors can influence the survival time of an individual. Therefore, incorporate covariates enable us to have a much more complete model, full of valuable information. For example, if we are interested in studying the life time of patients with a particular disease who are receiving a certain treatment, other factors may influence the patient's healing, so we can find new ways to treat the disease from covariates. One real situation is the study of patients that were observed for recurrence after the removal of a malignant melanoma; it is desired to know if the nodule category or the age of the patient may influence the recurrence of melanoma. We will analyze this clinical study latter.

This paper presents the unified long-term model using, as a distribution of the number of competing causes, the negative binomial distribution, as studied in Cordeiro et al. (2015), where the authors use the Birnbaum–Saunders distribution of times. However, our contribution is proposing the use of a different distribution of times, i.e., the family of Kum-G distributions, which were studied only in the usual models of survival analysis, as in De Pascoa et al. (2011), De Santana et al. (2012) and Bourguignon et al. (2013). In this new model, we propose the incorporation of covariates influencing the survival time. In addition, we performed a simulation study to see how this model would behave with different sample sizes, as well as an application to a data set to demonstrate the applicability of this model.

The paper is organized as follows: in Section 2, we have the methodology, in which we present the family of Kumaraswamy generalized distributions, the unified cure rate model and a distribution used in this model, i.e., the negative binomial distribution; then, we propose a unified model Kumaraswamy-G cure rate as well as a regression approach, using the distribution Kumaraswamy exponential and its inferential methods. Section 2.7 presents some simulation studies. Application to a real data set is presented in Section 3. Finally, in Section 4, we conclude the paper with some final remarks.

2. Methodology

2.1. Kumaraswamy Family of Distributions

The time until the occurrence of some event of interest can be generally accommodated by a probability distribution. In the literature, various distributions have been used to describe survival times but most commonly used distributions do not have the flexibility to model non-monotone hazard functions, such as unimodal and bathtub-shaped hazard functions, which are very common in biological studies. Thus, in this section, we will study the Kumaraswamy generalized distribution because it is a flexible but simple distribution.

The Kumaraswamy generalized distribution (Kum-G) presented by Cordeiro and de Castro (2011) has the flexibility to accommodate different shapes for the hazard function, which can be used in a variety of problems for modeling survival data. It is a generalization of the Kumaraswamy distribution with the addition of a distribution function $G(t)$ of a family of continuous distributions.

Definition. *Let $G(t)$ be a cumulative distribution function (cdf) of any continuous random variable. The cdf of the Kum-G distribution is given by*

$$F(t) = 1 - \left[1 - G\left(t\right)^{\lambda}\right]^{\varphi},$$

where $\lambda > 0$ and $\varphi > 0$. Let $g(t) = \frac{dG(t)}{dt}$ be the probability density function (pdf) of the distribution of $G(t)$, then the pdf of Kum-G is

$$f(t) = \lambda\varphi g(t)G(t)^{\lambda-1}\left[1 - G(t)^{\lambda}\right]^{\varphi-1}.$$

Thus, we obtain the survival and hazard functions, given respectively by

$$S(t) = \left[1 - G(t)^{\lambda}\right]^{\varphi}$$

and

$$h(t) = \frac{\lambda\varphi g(t)G(t)^{\lambda-1}}{1 - G(t)^{\lambda}}.$$

In the literature, there are different generalized distributions, one of which is the beta distribution. The pdf of beta generalizations uses the beta function, which is difficult to handle. On the other hand, the Kum-G distribution is a generalization that shows no complicated function in its pdf, and it is more advantageous than many generalizations.

As the Kum-G distribution depends on a $G(t)$ distribution function, for each continuous distribution, we have a case of Kum-G with the number of parameters of $G(t)$ over the two parameters

λ and φ. For example, if we take the cumulative distribution function of an exponential distribution as $G(t)$, then in this case we have the Kumaraswamy exponential distribution. In the literature, many cases of this distribution were studied, some of which are Kumaraswamy normal (Correa et al. 2012), Kumaraswamy log-logistic (De Santana et al. 2012), Kumaraswamy pareto (Bourguignon et al. 2013), Kumaraswamy pareto generalized (Nadarajah and Eljabri 2013), Kumaraswamy gamma generalized (De Pascoa et al. 2011), Kumaraswamy *half*-normal generalized (Cordeiro et al. 2012), Kumaraswamy Weibull inverse (Shahbaz et al. 2012) and Kumaraswamy Rayleigh inverse (Hussian and A Amin 2014).

2.2. The Unified Cure Rate Model

The unified model of the cured fraction of Rodrigues et al. (2009) is a statistical model capable of estimating the proportion of a cured population, that is, in data sets in which many individuals do not experience the event of interest, even if observed over a long period of time, part of the population is cured or immune to the event of interest; we can estimate the cured fraction. Several authors have worked with this modeling, for example, (Rodrigues et al. 2009, Peng and Xu 2012; Balakrishnan and Pal 2012, 2013a, 2013b, 2015), and others.

In general, the basic idea of the unified model of the cured fraction is based on the notion of occurrence of the event of interest in a process in two stages:

Initiation stage. Let N be a random variable representing the number of causes or competitive risks of occurrence of an event of interest. The cause of the occurrence of the event is unknown, and the variable N is not observed, with probability distribution p_n and its tail given respectively by $p_n = P(N = n)$ e $q_n = P(N > n)$ with $n = 0, 1, 2, \ldots$.

Maturation stage. Given that $N = n$ equal Z_k, $k = 1, \ldots, n$, continuous random variables (non-negative), independent of a cumulative distribution function $F(z) = 1 - S(z)$ and independent of N, represent the time of occurrence of an event of interest because of the k-th cause.

In order to include individuals who are not susceptible to the event of interest, its time of occurrence is defined as

$$T = \min\left(Z_0, Z_1, Z_2, \ldots, Z_N\right),$$

where $P(Z_0 = \infty) = 1$, admitting the possibility that a proportion p_0 of the population lacks the occurrence of an event of interest, T is an observable or censored random variable, and Z_j and N are latent variables.

Let $\{a_n\}$ be a sequence of real numbers. $A(s)$ is defined as a function of the sequence $\{a_n\}$ as follows

$$A(s) = a_0 + a_1 s + a_2 s^2 + \cdots,$$

where s belongs to the interval $[0, 1]$.

The survival function of the random variable T (population survival function) will be indicated by

$$\begin{aligned} S_{pop}(t) &= P(N = 0) + P(Z_1 > t, Z_2 > t, \ldots, Z_N > t, N \geq 1) \\ &= P(N = 0) + \sum_{n=1}^{\infty} P(N = n) P(Z_1 > t, Z_2 > t, \ldots, Z_N > t) \\ &= p_0 + \sum_{n=1}^{\infty} p_n S(t)^n \\ &= A\left[S(t)\right], \end{aligned}$$

where $A(\cdot)$ corresponds to a genuine generating function of the sequence p_n. That is, in the survival function of the random variable T, corresponding to a long-term model in two stages, the composition is a probability-generating function and survival function. The long-term survival function, in two stages $S_{pop}(t)$, is not a survival function.

Note that for the survival function, $\lim_{t\to 0} S(t) = 1$ and $\lim_{t\to\infty} S(t) = 0$. As for the improper survival function, $\lim_{t\to 0} S(t) = 1$ and $\lim_{t\to\infty} S_{pop}(t) = P(N=0) = p_0$. Thus, p_0 is the proportion of non-event occurrences in a population of interest, that is, the cured fraction.

The population survival function has the following properties:

- If $p_0 = 1$, then $S_{pop}(t) = S(t)$;
- $S_{pop}(0) = 1$;
- $S_{pop}(t)$ it is not increasing;
- $\lim_{t\to\infty} S_{pop}(t) = p_0$.

The density and hazard functions associated with long-term survival function are given respectively by

$$f_{pop}(t) = f(t)\frac{dA(s)}{ds}|_{s=S(t)}$$

and

$$h_{pop}(t) = \frac{f_{pop}(t)}{S_{pop}(t)} = f(t)\frac{\frac{dA(s)}{ds}|_{s=S(t)}}{S_{pop}(t)}.$$

Any discrete distribution can be used to model N, such as Bernoulli, binomial, Poisson, negative binomial and Geometric. What follows is the negative binomial distribution, which will be used because it is a very flexible distribution with various special cases, including those resulting in the standard model mix.

2.3. Negative Binomial Distribution

Assuming the number of competitive causes N following a negative binomial distribution, N has the probability function defined by

$$P(N=n) = \frac{\Gamma(n+\eta^{-1})}{n!\Gamma(\eta^{-1})}\left(\frac{\eta\theta}{1+\eta\theta}\right)^n (1+\eta\theta)^{-1/\eta},$$

where $n = 0, 1, 2, \ldots, \theta > 0$ e $1+\eta\theta > 0$, and then $\mathrm{E}(N) = \theta$ and $\mathrm{Var}(N) = \theta + \eta\theta^2$.

The probability generating function is given by

$$A(s) = \sum_{n=0}^{\infty} p_n s^n = [1+\eta\theta(1-s)]^{-1/\eta}, \quad 0 \le s \le 1.$$

Thus, the long-term survival function for the negative binomial model is given by

$$S_{pop}(t) = [1+\eta\theta F(t)]^{-1/\eta}, \tag{1}$$

where $F(t)$ is the cumulative distribution function of the random variable T and the cured fraction of the population is

$$p_0 = \lim_{t\to\infty} S_{pop}(t) = (1+\eta\theta)^{-1/\eta}.$$

The density function of the model (1) is

$$f_{pop}(t) = -\frac{dS_{pop}(t)}{dt} = \theta f(t)\,[1+\eta\theta F(t)]^{-1-1/\eta},$$

where $f(t) = -S'(t)$. Furthermore, the corresponding hazard function is given by

$$h_{pop}(t) = \theta f(t)\left[1 + \eta\theta F(t)\right]^{-1}.$$

We observed some particular cases in this model: from the Equation (1), when $\eta \to 0$, we obtain the density function of the Poisson distribution, resulting in the promotion time model; if $\eta = -1$, we fall into the Bernoulli distribution, where we have the model of the standard mixture; if $\eta = 1$, we have the geometric distribution; when $\eta = 1/m$ (m integer), we have a binomial distribution (m, θ/m), where $0 \le \theta/m \le 1$. We also observed, from expressions of expectation and the variance of the model, that the variance of the number of competing causes is very flexible. If $-1/\theta < \eta < 0$, there is an underdispersion relative to the Poisson distribution; if $\eta > 0$, there is an overdispersion.

Table 1 presents the long-term survival function, improper density and cure rate corresponding to negative binomials and their particular cases.

Table 1. Survival function $S_{pop}(t)$, density function $f_{pop}(t)$, and cured fraction of different distributions of latent causes.

Distribution	$S_{pop}(t)$	$f_{pop}(t)$	p_0	$A(s)$
Bernoulli(θ)	$1-\theta+\theta S(t)$	$\theta f(t)$	$1-\theta$	$1-\theta+\theta s$
Binomial(K, θ^*)	$[1-\theta^*+\theta^* S(t)]^K$	$K\theta^* f(t)\,[1-\theta^*+\theta^* S(t)]^{K-1}$	$(1-\theta^*)^K$	$(1-\theta^*+\theta^* s)^K$
Poisson(θ)	$\exp[-\theta F(t)]$	$\theta f(t)\exp[-\theta F(t)]$	$e^{-\theta}$	$\exp[\theta(1-s)]$
Geometric(θ)	$[1+\theta F(t)]^{-1}$	$\theta f(t)\,[1+\theta F(t)]^{-2}$	$1/(1+\theta)$	$[1+\theta(1-s)]^{-1}$
Negative Binomial(η, θ)	$[1+\eta\theta F(t)]^{-1/\eta}$	$\theta f(t)\,[1+\eta\theta F(t)]^{-1-1/\eta}$	$(1+\eta\theta)^{-1/\eta}$	$[1+\eta\theta(1-s)]^{-1/\eta}$

2.4. Negative Binomial Kumaraswamy-G Cure Rate Model

Considering the negative binomial distribution for the number of competing causes and the time following the Kumaraswamy-G distribution, we obtain a family of long-term distributions, wherein the population survival function of the model is given by

$$S_{pop}(t) = \left[1 + \eta\theta F(t)\right]^{-1/\eta} = \left\{1 + \eta\theta\left\{1 - \left[1 - G(t)^{\lambda}\right]^{\varphi}\right\}\right\}^{-1/\eta}, \tag{2}$$

with the cured fraction of the population given by

$$p_0 = (1 + \eta\theta)^{-1/\eta}.$$

So, by replacing the function $G(t)$ by the cumulative distribution function of some distribution, one obtains a negative binomial Kumaraswamy-G model of long-term survival.

The population density function is

$$f_{pop}(t) = \theta\lambda\varphi g(t)G(t)^{\lambda-1}\left[1 - G(t)^{\lambda}\right]^{\varphi-1}\left\{1 + \eta\theta\left\{1 - \left[1 - G(t)^{\lambda}\right]^{\varphi}\right\}\right\}^{-1-1/\eta}$$

and the population hazard function is given by

$$h_{pop}(t) = \theta\lambda\varphi g(t)G(t)^{\lambda-1}\left[1 - G(t)^{\lambda}\right]^{\varphi-1}\left\{1 + \eta\theta\left\{1 - \left[1 - G(t)^{\lambda}\right]^{\varphi}\right\}\right\}^{-1}.$$

Table 2 shows the particular cases of this model. It is noteworthy that for every $G(t)$, we will have different distributions.

Table 2. $S_{pop}(t)$, $f_{pop}(t)$ and the cured fraction for different distributions of N.

Parametrization	Model	$S_{pop}(t)$
$\eta \to 0$	Poisson	$\exp\left\{-\theta\left\{1-\left[1-G(t)^{\lambda}\right]^{\varphi}\right\}\right\}$
$\eta = -1$	Bernoulli	$1-\theta+\theta\left[1-G(t)^{\lambda}\right]^{\varphi}$
$\eta = -1/m$	Binomial	$\left\{1-\frac{\theta}{m}+\frac{\theta}{m}\left[1-G(t)^{\lambda}\right]^{\varphi}\right\}^{m}$
$\eta = 1$	geometric	$\left\{1+\theta\left\{1-\left[1-G(t)^{\lambda}\right]^{\varphi}\right\}\right\}^{-1}$

Negative Binomial Kumaraswamy Exponential Cure Rate Model

Considering $G(t)$, following an Exponential(α) distribution and substituting in (2), we have the NegBinKumExp($\alpha, \lambda, \varphi, \eta, \theta$), i.e., a family of cure rate models where their population survival function is given by

$$S_{pop}(t) = \left\{1+\eta\theta\left\{1-\left[1-\left(1-e^{-\alpha t}\right)^{\lambda}\right]^{\varphi}\right\}\right\}^{-1/\eta}.$$

The population density and hazard function of this model are, respectively,

$$f_{pop}(t) = \theta\varphi\lambda\alpha e^{-\alpha t}\left(1-e^{-\alpha t}\right)^{\lambda-1}\left[1-\left(1-e^{-\alpha t}\right)^{\lambda}\right]^{\varphi-1}\left\{1+\eta\theta\left\{1-\left[1-\left(1-e^{-\alpha t}\right)^{\lambda}\right]^{\varphi}\right\}\right\}^{-1-1/\eta}, \quad (3)$$

and

$$h_{pop}(t) = \theta\varphi\lambda\alpha e^{-\alpha t}\left(1-e^{-\alpha t}\right)^{\lambda-1}\left[1-\left(1-e^{-\alpha t}\right)^{\lambda}\right]^{\varphi-1}\left\{1+\eta\theta\left\{1-\left[1-\left(1-e^{-\alpha t}\right)^{\lambda}\right]^{\varphi}\right\}\right\}^{-1}.$$

2.5. *Negative Binomial Kumaraswamy-G Regression Cure Rate Model*

The use of covariate information is essential when analyzing survival data. Here, we discuss an approach to including covariate information for the proposed models.

Suppose that $\boldsymbol{x}' = (1, x_1, \ldots, x_k)$ is a vector of covariates from a data set and $\boldsymbol{\beta}' = (\beta_0, \beta_1, \ldots, \beta_k)$ is a vector of regression coefficients. We are going to set $\theta(\boldsymbol{x}) = \exp(\boldsymbol{\beta}'\boldsymbol{x})$ to link the cure rate to the covariates. The only two parameters that link the cure rate to the covariates are θ and η. Since θ has a positive domain, we can use it to simply model the covariates through the exponential function.

This way, the Negative Binomial Kumaraswamy-G generalized linear model is given by

$$S(t|\boldsymbol{x}) = \left\{1+\eta\theta\left\{1-\left[1-G(t)^{\lambda}\right]^{\varphi}\right\}\right\}^{-1/\eta} = \left\{1+\eta\exp(\boldsymbol{\beta}'\boldsymbol{x})\left\{1-\left[1-G(t)^{\lambda}\right]^{\varphi}\right\}\right\}^{-1/\eta}, \quad (4)$$

for $t > 0$. The cure rate p is given by

$$p = (1+\eta\theta)^{-1/\eta} = [1+\eta\exp(\boldsymbol{\beta}'\boldsymbol{x})]^{-1/\eta}. \quad (5)$$

This way, the cured fraction does not depend on the parameters of the Kumaraswamy family or the baseline distribution, but on the parameters η and θ. They are estimated differently for each baseline distribution and then they are incorporated into the cure rate.

Other particular cure rate models can be obtained. The Bernoulli Kumaraswamy-G generalized linear model and its respective cure rate is given by

$$\begin{aligned} S(t|\boldsymbol{x}) &= 1+\exp(\boldsymbol{\beta}'\boldsymbol{x})\left\{1-\left[1-G(t)^{\lambda}\right]^{\varphi}\right\} \\ p &= 1-\exp(\boldsymbol{\beta}'\boldsymbol{x}). \end{aligned} \quad (6)$$

The Poisson Kumaraswamy-G generalized linear model is given by

$$\begin{aligned} S(t|x) &= \exp\left(-\exp\left(\beta' x\right)\left\{1-\left[1-G(t)^{\lambda}\right]^{\varphi}\right\}\right). \\ p &= \exp\left[-\exp\left(\beta' x\right)\right] \end{aligned} \tag{7}$$

The Geometric Kumaraswamy-G generalized linear model is given by

$$\begin{aligned} S(t|x) &= \left\{1+\exp\left(\beta' x\right)\left\{1-\left[1-G(t)^{\lambda}\right]^{\varphi}\right\}\right\}^{-1}, \\ p &= 1/\left[1+\exp\left(\beta' x\right)\right]. \end{aligned} \tag{8}$$

In Section 2.6, we discuss the estimation procedures of the NegBinKum-G cure rate generalized linear model. An application of these models is presented in Section 3.

2.6. Inference

Here, we present a procedure to obtain maximum likelihood estimates for the Negative Binomial Kumaraswamy Exponential generalized linear model. We consider data with right-censored information. Let $\mathbf{D} = (\mathbf{t}, \boldsymbol{\delta}, \mathbf{x})$, where $\boldsymbol{t} = (t_1, \ldots, t_n)'$ are the observed failure times, $\boldsymbol{\delta} = (\delta_1, \ldots, \delta_n)'$ are the right-censored times and $\boldsymbol{x}$ is the covariates information. The δ_i is equal to 1 if a failure is observed and 0 otherwise. Suppose that the sample data is independently and identically distributed and comes from a distribution with density and survival functions specified by $f(\cdot, \boldsymbol{v})$ and $S(\cdot, \boldsymbol{v})$, respectively, where $\boldsymbol{v} = (\alpha, \lambda, \varphi, \eta, \boldsymbol{\beta})'$ denotes a vector of $4 + (k+1)$ parameters, with $\theta = \exp(\boldsymbol{\beta}'\boldsymbol{x})$, as described in Section 2.5. By combining (4) and the expression (3), the log-likelihood function of $\boldsymbol{v}$ for the NegBinKumExp distribution is

$$\begin{aligned} \ell(\boldsymbol{v}, \mathbf{D}) &= \log L(\boldsymbol{v}, \mathbf{D}) = \text{const} + \textstyle\sum_{i=1}^{n} \delta_i \log f(t_i, \boldsymbol{v}) + (1-\delta_i) \log S(t_i, \boldsymbol{v}). \\ &= \text{const} + \textstyle\sum_{i=1}^{n} \delta_i \log \Big\{ \exp(\boldsymbol{\beta}'\boldsymbol{x}) \varphi \lambda \alpha e^{-\alpha t_i} \left(1-e^{-\alpha t_i}\right)^{\lambda-1} \left[1-\left(1-e^{-\alpha t_i}\right)^{\lambda}\right]^{\varphi-1} \\ &\quad \left\{1+\eta \exp(\boldsymbol{\beta}'\boldsymbol{x}) \left\{1-\left[1-\left(1-e^{-\alpha t_i}\right)^{\lambda}\right]^{\varphi}\right\}\right\}^{-1} \Big\} \\ &\quad -\tfrac{1}{\eta} \textstyle\sum_{i=1}^{n} \log\left\{1+\eta \exp(\boldsymbol{\beta}'\boldsymbol{x}) \left\{1-\left[1-\left(1-e^{-\alpha t_i}\right)^{\lambda}\right]^{\varphi}\right\}\right\}. \end{aligned} \tag{9}$$

The maximum likelihood estimates are the simultaneous solutions of

$$\frac{\partial l(\boldsymbol{v}, \mathbf{D})}{\partial v_i} = 0.$$

The estimates are obtained using the BFGS algorithm of maximization, which is an option for the `optim` function in R (R Core Team 2013).

If $\widehat{\boldsymbol{v}}$ denotes the maximum likelihood estimator of $\boldsymbol{v}$, then it is well known that the distribution of $\widehat{\boldsymbol{v}} - \boldsymbol{v}$ can be approximated by a $(k+5)$-variate normal distribution with zero means and a covariance matrix $\boldsymbol{I}^{-1}(\widehat{\boldsymbol{v}})$, where $\mathbf{I}(\boldsymbol{v})$ denotes the observed information matrix defined by

$$\mathbf{I}(\boldsymbol{v}) = -\left(\frac{\partial^2 l(\boldsymbol{v}, \mathbf{D})}{\partial v_i \partial v_j}\right)$$

for i and j in $1, \ldots, k+5$. This approximation can be used to deduce confidence intervals and tests of hypotheses. For example, an approximate $100(1-\gamma)$ percent confidence interval for v_i is $\left(\widehat{v} - z_{\gamma/2}\sqrt{I^{ii}}, \widehat{v} + z_{\gamma/2}\sqrt{I^{ii}}\right)$, where I^{ii} denotes the ith diagonal element of the inverse of $\mathbf{I}$ and z_{γ} denotes the $100(1-\gamma)$ percentile of a standard normal random variable.

Asymptotic normality of the maximum likelihood estimates holds only under certain regularity conditions. These conditions are not easy to check analytically for our models. Section 2.7 performs a simulation study to see if the usual asymptotes of the maximum likelihood estimates hold. Simulations have been used in many papers to check the asymptotic behavior of maximum likelihood estimates, especially when an analytical investigation is not trivial.

2.7. Simulation Studies

Here, we assess the performance of the maximum likelihood estimates with respect to sample size to show, among other things, that the usual asymptotes of maximum likelihood estimators still hold for defective distributions. The assessment is based on simulations. The description of data generation and details of the distributions simulated from this are described below. All computations were performed in R (R Core Team 2013).

Suppose that the time of occurrence of an event of interest has the cumulative distribution function $F(t)$. We want to simulate a random sample of size n containing real times, censored times and a cured fraction of p. An algorithm for this purpose is:

- Determine the desired parameter values, as well as the value of the cured fraction p;
- For each $i = 1, \ldots, n$, generate a random variable $M_i \sim \text{Bernoulli}(1-p)$;
- If $M_i = 0$ set $t_i' = \infty$. If $M_i = 1$, take t_i' as the root of $F(t) = u$, where $u \sim \text{uniform}(0, 1-p)$;
- Generate $u_i' \sim \text{uniform}(0, \max(t_i'))$, for $i = 1, \ldots, n$, considering only the finite t_i';
- Calculate $t_i = \min(t_i', u_i')$. If $t_i < u_i'$ set $\delta_i = 1$, otherwise set $\delta_i = 0$.

We took the sample size to vary from 100 to 1500 in steps of 200. Each sample was replicated 1000 times. The variance of the cure rate p was estimated using the delta method with first-order Taylor's approximation. In Rocha et al. (2015), we can find a simulation algorithm very similar to this one, but it was used for long duration models that use a defective distribution.

Simulation was performed for several scenarios and it was indicated that a relatively large sample size is required to produce a good interval estimation for the parameters. In some cases, even with a large sample size, standard deviations and bias are still not close to zero. The high number of parameters can explain this fact. Another reason may be the use of the *optim* algorithm which, in very complicated cases, cannot find the values of the global maximum of the likelihood function. One possible solution could be to use some other method of maximization.

The cure rate provides a reasonable point estimation, regardless of the sample size. Similar observations held when the simulations were repeated for a wide range of parameter values. The next section illustrates the proposed methodology in a real health risks data set.

3. Real Data Application

Here, we present an application in a health risk-related data set. The data set contains covariate information and is used to illustrate the model proposed in Section 2.5. A similar approach for the regression was used in the Bernoulli Kumaraswamy Exponential, Poisson Kumaraswamy Exponential and Geometric Kumaraswamy Exponential distributions (BerKumExp, PoiKumExp and GeoKumExp, for short). The following measures of model selection are used to distinguish between the fitted distributions: the Akaike information criterion (AIC) and visual comparison of the fitted survival curves and the Kaplan–Meier (Kaplan and Meier 1958) curve. All the computations were performed using the R software (R Core Team 2013). `optim` was used to maximize the log-likelihood function. The algorithm "BFGS" was chosen for maximization. For computational stability, the observed times in each data set were divided by their maximum value. As the simulations results shows large values for deviation in small sample sizes, we are going to use 1000 bootstrap estimates for the deviations of the parameters.

The data set is supposed to contain observations that are not susceptible to the event of interest. In practice, it is unknown whether the event of interest could be observed if enough time was given.

Evidence of the existence of cured individuals is given in cases where the Kaplan–Meier curve reaches a plateau between zero and one. In some cases, this is clearer than others, as one can see in our examples. We can assume that some of the censored observations at the end of the study belong to the cured group. If everyone censored at the end were indeed cured, then the plateau reached by the Kaplan–Meier curve is a good estimate of the cured fraction. In general, a lower value of this plateau or a value close to it is an acceptable estimate.

This data set collected in the period 1991–1998 is related to a clinical study in which patients were observed for recurrence after the removal of a malignant melanoma. Melanoma is a type of cancer that develops in melanocytes, responsible for skin pigmentation. It is a potentially serious malignant tumor that may arise in the skin, mucous membranes, eyes and the central nervous system, with a great risk of producing metastases and high mortality rates in the latter stages. In total, 417 cases were observed, of which 232 were censored (55.63 percent). The overall survival is 3.18 years. This data set has covariate information, which is used to illustrate the generalized linear model proposed in Section 2.5. The covariates taken represent the nodule category ($n_1 = 82$, $n_2 = 87$, $n_3 = 137$, $n_4 = 111$) and age (continuous covariate). The overall survival times for the categories are 3.60, 3.27, 3.07, 2.55 years. For more details on this data, see Ibrahim et al. (2001).

Tables 3–6 show the results for the Bernoulli, Poisson, Geometric and Negative Binomial Kumaraswamy Exponential models. The estimated cure rates $\widehat{p}_1$, $\widehat{p}_2$, $\widehat{p}_3$ and $\widehat{p}_4$ for groups 1, 2, 3 and 4, respectively, are calculated by (5). The age covariate is taken as their average, 48, for the necessary computations.

Table 3. MLEs of the Bernoulli Kumaraswamy Exponential model for the melanoma data set.

Parameters	Estimates	Std. Dev.	Inf 95% CI	Sup 95% CI
α	1.8052	0.7308	0.6052	3.8146
λ	3.5177	1.2003	2.2506	6.6982
ϕ	0.4774	0.3695	0.1361	1.5992
β_0	−1.4788	0.2245	−1.9330	−1.0434
β_1	0.2288	0.0505	0.1281	0.3251
β_2	0.0045	0.0039	−0.0025	0.0121
p_1	0.6412	0.0420	0.5508	0.7171
p_2	0.5506	0.0360	0.4769	0.6185
p_3	0.4357	0.0364	0.3607	0.5040
p_4	0.2896	0.0590	0.1780	0.3991

Table 4. MLEs of the Poisson Kumaraswamy Exponential model for the melanoma data set.

Parameters	Estimates	Std. Dev.	Inf 95% CI	Sup 95% CI
α	1.0735	0.7308	0.2507	2.8913
λ	3.0298	1.0019	2.0155	5.6100
ϕ	1.2187	1.8100	0.1268	5.2827
β_0	−1.7046	0.3675	−2.4282	−1.0042
β_1	0.3640	0.0724	0.2164	0.5122
β_2	0.0103	0.0060	−0.0012	0.0225
p_1	0.6490	0.0464	0.5486	0.7349
p_2	0.5384	0.0412	0.4506	0.6141
p_3	0.4110	0.0424	0.3269	0.4906
p_4	0.2796	0.0525	0.1798	0.3827

Table 5. MLEs of the Geometric Kumaraswamy Exponential model for the melanoma data set.

Parameters	Estimates	Std. Dev.	Inf 95% CI	Sup 95% CI
α	0.7298	0.5598	0.1084	2.1395
λ	2.8893	0.8340	2.0228	4.7584
ϕ	2.4622	4.8243	0.1135	16.4430
β_0	−1.7930	0.4827	−2.7416	−0.8808
β_1	0.5083	0.0902	0.3292	0.6860
β_2	0.0144	0.0079	−0.0001	0.0300
p_1	0.6421	0.0543	0.5212	0.7303
p_2	0.5207	0.0486	0.4147	0.5995
p_3	0.3963	0.0457	0.2976	0.4788
p_4	0.2846	0.0462	0.1905	0.3772

Table 6. MLEs of the Negative Binomial Kumaraswamy Exponential model for the melanoma data set.

Parameters	Estimates	Std. Dev.	Inf 95% CI	Sup 95% CI
α	0.3499	0.3798	0.0533	1.3675
λ	2.8630	0.5271	2.1450	4.1202
ϕ	9.7127	15.0785	0.0946	56.0397
η	3.1508	1.6134	0.7643	7.0171
β_0	−1.4374	1.1867	−3.0628	1.6385
β_1	0.7673	0.2003	0.4468	1.2376
β_2	0.0211	0.0123	−0.0014	0.0480
p_1	0.6073	0.0865	0.3520	0.7217
p_2	0.4956	0.0703	0.2981	0.5906
p_3	0.3931	0.0577	0.2470	0.4778
p_4	0.3065	0.0533	0.1883	0.3937

The estimates of β_0, β_1 and β_2 are in agreement in all models. For β_0, the value is around −1.50, for β_1, the value is around 0.50 and for β_2, the value is around 0.01.

In Figure 1, the fitted survival curves for each nodule category and each proposed model are given. We can see that the one that best captures the Kaplan–Meier curve is the Negative Binomial Kumaraswamy Exponential distribution. This result is also sustained by the AIC values. The values obtained for the Bernoulli, Poisson, Geometric and Negative Binomial Kumaraswamy Exponential models are 1029.53, 1022.77, 1017.64 and 1016.27. The Negative Binomial Kumaraswamy Exponential achieves a better AIC value even with one extra parameter than the others.

Considering the Negative Binomial Kumaraswamy Exponential model and given the average age of 48 in this study, the estimated cure rate for nodule category 1 is around 0.65. For nodule category 2, it is around 0.54. For nodule category 3, it is around 0.41. For nodule category 4, it is around 0.28.

The standard deviations of p_1, p_2, p_3 and p_4 are 0.0464, 0.0412, 0.0424 and 0.0525, respectively. The bootstrap 95 percent confidence intervals are (0.55, 0.73), (0.45, 0.61), (0.33, 0.49) and (0.18, 0.38), respectively. These indicate a significant difference between nodule categories 1 and 3, 1 and 4 and 2 and 4. These results agree with the results found in (Rodrigues et al. 2009, Balakrishnan and Pal 2013a, 2013b).

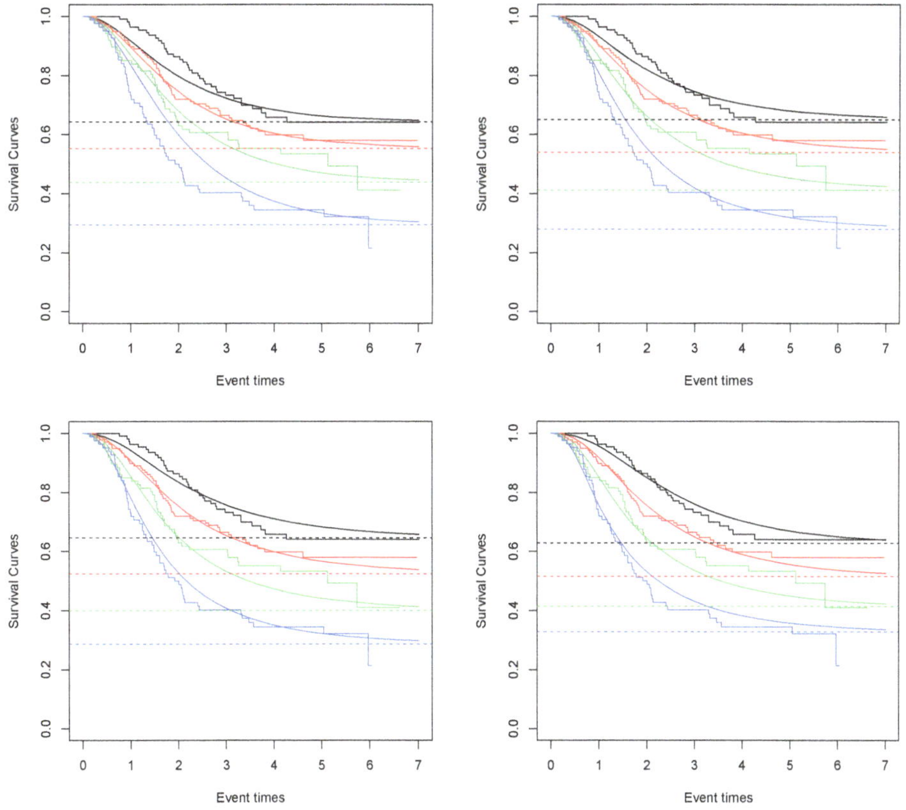

Figure 1. From the left to the right, top to bottom, the BerKumExp, PoiKumExp, GeoKumExp and NegBinKumExp distributions. The colors black, red, green and blue represent the nodule categories 1, 2, 3 and 4, respectively.

4. Conclusions

We have presented the Kumaraswamy generalized family using the Negative Binomial as the distribution of the latent causes, in a survival analysis context. We exemplified the unified family using the exponential distribution as the baseline distribution. This model has several special cases, such as the standard and promotion time cure rate models. In addition, we consider covariates in a long-term model in order to identify factors that influence the survival function and the cured fraction. A simulation study was performed and showed us that, in addition to the interval estimation that takes relatively large sample sizes to converge, a reasonable point estimate of the cure rate is given even in small sample sizes. We thus have a model that is applicable in many practical cases. Through its application, it was found that the models proposed in this work can be useful in the analysis of health risk data.

Acknowledgments: The authors would like to thank CAPES, CNPq and FAPESP for financial support during the course of this project. The authors would also like to thank the two referees and the editors for their comments which greatly improved this paper.

Author Contributions: All authors contributed to the design and implementation of the research, to the analysis of the results and to the writing of the manuscript.

Conflicts of Interest: No conflict of interest to declare.

References

Anscombe, Francis John. 1961. Estimating a mixed-exponential response law. *Journal of the American Statistical Association* 56: 493–502.

Balakrishnan, N., and S. Pal. 2012. EM algorithm-based likelihood estimation for some cure rate models. *Journal of Statistical Theory and Practice* 6: 698–724.

Balakrishnan, Narayanaswamy, and Suvra Pal. 2013a. Lognormal lifetimes and likelihood-based inference for flexible cure rate models based on COM-Poisson family. *Computational Statistics & Data Analysis* 67: 41–67.

Balakrishnan, Narayanaswamy, and Suvra Pal. 2013b. Expectation maximization-based likelihood inference for flexible cure rate models with Weibull lifetimes. *Statistical Methods in Medical Research* 25: 1535–63.

Balakrishnan, Narayanaswamy, and Suvra Pal. 2015. An EM algorithm for the estimation of parameters of a flexible cure rate model with generalized gamma lifetime and model discrimination using likelihood-and information-based methods. *Computational Statistics* 30: 151–89.

Berkson, Joseph, and Robert P. Gage. 1952. Survival Curve for Cancer Patients Following Treatment. *Journal of the American Statistical Association* 47: 501–15.

Boag, John W. 1949. Maximum Likelihood Estimates of the Proportion of Patients Cured by Cancer Therapy. *Journal of the Royal Statistical Society. Series B (Methodological)* 11: 15–53.

Bourguignon, Marcelo, Rodrigo B. Silva, Luz M. Zea, and Gauss M. Cordeiro. 2013. The Kumaraswamy Pareto distribution. *Journal of Statistical Theory and Applications* 12: 129–44.

Broadhurst, Roderic G., and R. A. Maller. 1991. Estimating the numbers of prison terms in criminal careers from one-step probabilities of recidivism. *Journal of Quantitative Criminology* 7: 275–90.

Calderín-Ojeda, Enrique, and Chun Fung Kwok. 2016. Modeling claims data with composite Stoppa models. *Scandinavian Actuarial Journal* 2016: 817–36.

Cancho, Vicente G., Edwin M. Ortega, and Heleno Bolfarine. 2009. The log-exponentiated-Weibull regression models with cure rate: Local influence and residual analysis. *Journal of Data Science* 7: 433–58.

Cancho, Vicente G., Josemar Rodrigues, and Mario de Castro. 2011. A flexible model for survival data with a cure rate: A Bayesian approach. *Journal of Applied Statistics* 38: 57–70.

Castro, Mário de, Vicente G. Cancho, and Josemar Rodrigues. 2009. A Bayesian Long-term Survival Model Parametrized in the Cured Fraction. *Biometrical Journal* 51: 443–55.

Chen, Ming-Hui, Joseph G. Ibrahim, and Debajyoti Sinha. 1999. A new Bayesian model for survival data with a surviving fraction. *Journal of the American Statistical Association* 94: 909–19.

Cooner, Freda, Sudipto Banerjee, Bradley P. Carlin, and Debajyoti Sinha. 2007. Flexible cure rate modeling under latent activation schemes. *Journal of the American Statistical Association* 102: 560–72.

Cordeiro, Gauss M., and Mario de Castro. 2011. A new family of generalized distributions. *Journal of Statistical Computation and Simulation* 81: 883–98.

Cordeiro, Gauss M., Rodrigo R. Pescim, and Edwin M. M. Ortega. 2012. The Kumaraswamy generalized half-normal distribution for skewed positive data. *Journal of Data Science* 10: 195–224.

Cordeiro, Gauss M., Vicente G. Cancho, Edwin M. Ortega, and Gladys D. Barriga. 2015. A model with long-term survivors: Negative binomial Birnbaum-Saunders. *Communications in Statistics-Theory and Methods* 45: 1370–87.

Correa, Michelle A., Denismar Alves Nogueira, and Eric Batista Ferreira. 2012. Kumaraswamy Normal and Azzalini's skew Normal modeling asymmetry. *Sigmae* 1: 65–83.

De Pascoa, Marcelino A. R., Edwin M. M. Ortega, and Gauss M. Cordeiro. 2011. The Kumaraswamy generalized gamma distribution with application in survival analysis. *Statistical Methodology* 8: 411–33.

De Santana, Tiago Viana Flor, Edwin M. Ortega, Gauss M. Cordeiro, and Giovana O. Silva. 2012. The Kumaraswamy -log-logistic distribution. *Journal of Statistical Theory and Applications* 11: 265–91.

Farewell, Vernon T. 1977. A model for a binary variable with time-censored observations. *Biometrika* 64: 43–46.

Goldman, Anne I. 1984. Survivorship analysis when cure is a possibility: A Monte Carlo study. *Statistics in Medicine* 3: 153–63.

Gu, Yu, Debajyoti Sinha, and Sudipto Banerjee. 2011. Analysis of cure rate survival data under proportional odds model. *Lifetime Data Analysis* 17: 123–34.

Gupta, Rameshwar D., and Debasis Kundu. 1999. Theory & methods: Generalized exponential distributions. *Australian & New Zealand Journal of Statistics* 41: 173–88.

Hussian, Mohamed, and Essam A. Amin. 2014. Estimation and prediction for the Kumaraswamy-inverse Rayleigh distribution based on records. *International Journal of Advanced Statistics and Probability* 2: 21–27.

Ibrahim, Joseph G., Ming-Hui Chen, and Debajyoti Sinha. 2001. Bayesian semiparametric models for survival data with a cure fraction. *Biometrics* 57: 383–88.

Ibrahim, Joseph G., Ming-Hui Chen, and Debajyoti Sinha. 2005. *Bayesian Survival Analysis*. Hoboken: John Wiley & Sons, Ltd.

Kaplan, Edward L., and Paul Meier. 1958. Nonparametric estimation from incomplete observations. *Journal of the American Statistical Association* 53: 457–81.

Kumaraswamy, Ponnambalam. 1980. A generalized probability density function for double-bounded random processes. *Journal of Hydrology* 46: 79–88.

Meeker, William Q., and Luis A. Escobar. 1998. *Statistical Methods for Reliability Data*. Hoboken: John Wiley & Sons, vol. 314.

Nadarajah, Saralees, and Sumaya Eljabri. 2013. The Kumaraswamy GP distribution. *Journal of Data Science* 11: 739–66.

Ortega, Edwin M. M., Vicente G. Cancho, and Victor Hugo Lachos. 2008. Assessing influence in survival data with a cure fraction and covariates. *Sort-Statistics and Operations Research Transactions* 32: 115–40.

Ortega, Edwin M. M., Vicente G. Cancho, and Gilberto A. Paula. 2009. Generalized log-gamma regression models with cure fraction. *Lifetime Data Analysis* 15: 79–106.

Peng, Yingwei, and Jianfeng Xu. 2012. An extended cure model and model selection. *Lifetime Data Analysis* 18: 215–33.

R Core Team. 2013. *R: A Language and Environment for Statistical Computing*. Vienna: R Foundation for Statistical Computing.

Rocha, Ricardo, Saralees Nadarajah, Vera Tomazella, Francisco Louzada, and Amanda Eudes. 2015. New defective models based on the Kumaraswamy family of distributions with application to cancer data sets. *Statistical Methods in Medical Research* 26: 1737–55.

Rodrigues, Josemar, Vicente G. Cancho, Mário de Castro, and Francisco Louzada-Neto. 2009. On the unification of long-term survival models. *Statistics & Probability Letters* 79: 753–59.

Rodrigues, Josemar, Mário de Castro, Vicente G. Cancho, and N. Balakrishnan. 2009. COM–Poisson cure rate survival models and an application to a cutaneous melanoma data. *Journal of Statistical Planning and Inference* 139: 3605–11.

Shahbaz, Muhammad Qaiser, Shahbaz Shahbaz, and Nadeem Shafique Butt. 2012. The Kumaraswamy-inverse Weibull distribution. *Pakistan Journal of Statistics and Operation Research* 8: 479–89.

Stoppa, Gabriele. 1990. Proprietà campionarie di un nuovo modello Pareto generalizzato. In *Atti XXXV Riunione Scientifica della Società Italiana di Statistica*. Padova: Cedam, pp. 137–44.

Sy, Judy P., and Jeremy M. G. Taylor. 2000. Estimation in a Cox proportional hazards cure model. *Biometrics* 56: 227–36.

Yakovlev, A. Yu, and Alexander D. Tsodikov. 1996. *Stochastic Models of Tumor Latency and Their Biostatistical Applications*. Singapore: World Scientific, vol. 1.

Journal of
Risk and Financial Management

MDPI

Article

Modified Stieltjes Transform and Generalized Convolutions of Probability Distributions

Lev B. Klebanov [1] and **Rasool Roozegar** [2,*]

[1] Department of Probability and Mathematical Statistics, MFF, Charles University, Prague 1, 116 36, Czech Republic; levbkl@gmail.com
[2] Department of Statistics, Yazd University, Yazd 89195-741, Iran
* Correspondence: rroozegar@yazd.ac.ir

Received: 3 November 2017; Accepted: 11 January 2018; Published: 14 January 2018

Abstract: The classical Stieltjes transform is modified in such a way as to generalize both Stieltjes and Fourier transforms. This transform allows the introduction of new classes of commutative and non-commutative generalized convolutions. A particular case of such a convolution for degenerate distributions appears to be the Wigner semicircle distribution.

Keywords: Stieltjes transform; characteristic function; generalized convolution; beta distribution

1. Introduction

Let us begin with definitions of classical and generalized Stieltjes transforms. Although these are usual transforms given on a set of functions, we will consider more convenient for us a case of probability measures or for cumulative distribution functions. Namely, let μ be a probability measure of Borel subsets of real line $\mathbb{R}^1$. Its Stieltjes transform is defined as[1]

$$S(z) = S(z;\mu) = \int_{-\infty}^{\infty} \frac{d\mu(x)}{x-z},$$

where $\mathtt{Im}(z) \neq 0$. Surely, the integral converges in this case. The generalized Stieltjes transform is represented by

$$S_\gamma(z) = S_\gamma(z;\mu) = \int_{-\infty}^{\infty} \frac{d\mu(x)}{(x-z)^\gamma}$$

for real $\gamma > 0$. For more examples of the generalized Stieltjes transforms of some probability distributions, see Demni (2016) and references therein.

A modification of generalized Stieltjes transform was proposed in Roozegar and Bazyari (2017). Our aim in this paper is to use this modification of the Stieltjes transform to define a class of generalized stochastic convolutions and give their probability interpretation (see Theorem 1 below) in lines of preprint Klebanov and Roozegar (2016).

2. Preliminary Results

Now we prefer to switch to the modified form, and define the following form of transform:

$$R_\gamma(u) = R_\gamma(u;\mu) = \int_{-\infty}^{\infty} \frac{d\mu(x)}{(1-iux)^\gamma}. \tag{1}$$

[1] Sometimes with opposite sign.

Connection to the generalized Stieltjes transform is obvious. It is convenient for us to use this transform for real values of u. It is clear that the limit

$$\lim_{\gamma\to\infty} R_\gamma(u/\gamma) = \int_{-\infty}^{\infty} \exp\{iux\} d\mu(x) \tag{2}$$

represents the Fourier transform (characteristic function) of the measure μ (we used the dominated convergence theorem here to change the order of integration and limit). The uniqueness of a measure recovering from its modified Stieltjes transform follows from the corresponding result for generalized Stieltjes transform.

Relation (2) gives us the limit behavior of the modified Stieltjes transform as $\gamma \to \infty$. Another possibility ($\gamma \to 0$) without any normalization gives trivial limit equal to 1. However, a more proper approach is to calculate the limit $(R_\gamma(u) - 1)/\gamma$ as $\gamma \to 0$. It is easy to see that

$$\lim_{\gamma\to 0}(R_\gamma(u) - 1)/\gamma = \int_{-\infty}^{\infty} \log\frac{1}{1 - iux} d\mu(x). \tag{3}$$

If the measure μ has compact support, it is possible to write series expansion for modified Stieltjes transform:

$$R_\gamma(u) = \int_{-\infty}^{\infty} \frac{d\mu(x)}{(1 - iux)^\gamma} = \sum_{k=0}^{\infty} (-1)^k i^k \binom{-\gamma}{k} m_k(\mu) x^k,$$

where $m_k(\mu) = \int_{-\infty}^{\infty} x^k d\mu(x)$ is the kth moment of the measure μ.

The modified Stieltjes transform may be interpreted in terms of characteristic functions. Namely, let us consider a gamma distribution with probability density function

$$p(x) = \frac{1}{\lambda^\gamma \Gamma(\gamma)} x^{\gamma-1} \exp(-x/\lambda), \tag{4}$$

for $x > 0$, $\lambda > 0$, and zero in other cases. Note that this distribution is an ordinary gamma distribution for positive λ, and its "mirror reflection" on negative semi-axes for negative λ. Let us now consider λ as a random variable with cumulative distribution function μ. In this case, Relation (1) gives the characteristic function of gamma distribution with such random parameter:

$$f(t) = \int_{-\infty}^{\infty} \frac{d\mu(\lambda)}{(1 - it\lambda)^\gamma}. \tag{5}$$

The Gauss-hypergeometric function ${}_2F_1$, which is defined by the series

$${}_2F_1(c, a; b; z) = \sum_{n=0}^{\infty} \frac{(c)_n (a)_n}{(b)_n n!} z^n,$$

where $(a)_0 = 1$ and $(a)_n = a(a+1)(a+2)\cdots(a+n-1)$, $n \geq 1$, denotes the rising factorial. Gauss-hypergeometric function ${}_2F_1$ has Euler's integral representation of the form

$${}_2F_1(c, a; b; z) = \frac{\Gamma(b)}{\Gamma(a)\Gamma(b-a)} \int_0^1 \frac{t^{a-1}(1-t)^{b-a-1}}{(1-zt)^c} dt. \tag{6}$$

For more details on Gauss-hypergeometric function and its properties, see Abramowitz and Stegun (2012) and also Andrews et al. (1999).

3. A Family of Commutative Generalized Convolutions

Using the modified Stieltjes transform, we can introduce a family of commutative generalized convolutions. The main idea for this is the following. Let μ_1 and μ_2 be two probability measures. Take positive γ and consider the product of the modified Stieltjes transforms of these measures $R_\gamma(u, \mu_1)R_\gamma(u, \mu_2)$. We would like to represent this product as a modified Stieltjes transform of a measure. Typically, the product is not a modified Stieltjes transform with the same index γ. However, it can be represented as a modified Stieltjes transform with index $\rho > \gamma$ of a measure ν, which is called a generalized (more precisely "(γ, ρ)") convolution of the measures μ_1 and μ_2. Let us mention that the indexes ρ and γ are not arbitrary, but there are infinitely many suitable pairs of indexes. Clearly, the measure ν—if it exists—depends on μ_1, μ_2, and on indexes γ, ρ.

Unfortunately, we cannot describe all pairs γ, ρ for which corresponding generalized convolution ν of measures μ_1 and μ_2 exists. However, we shall show that the pairs of the form $c, 2c$ (where c is positive, but not necessarily integer number) possess this property.

Theorem 1. *Let μ_1, μ_2 be two probability measures on σ-field Borel subsets of a real line. For arbitrary real $c > 0$ there exists "$(c, 2c)$" convolution ν of μ_1 and μ_2. In other words, for real $c > 0$ and measures μ_1 and μ_2, there exists a measure ν such that*

$$R_{2c}(u; \nu) = R_c(u; \mu_1)R_c(u; \mu_2). \tag{7}$$

Proof. Because convex combination of probability measures is a probability measure again, and each probability on real line can be considered as a limit in weak-$*$ topology of sequence of measures concentrated in finite number of points each, it is sufficient to prove the statement for Dirac δ-measures only.

Suppose now that the measures μ_1 and μ_2 are concentrated in points a and b correspondingly. We have to prove that there is a measure ν depending on a, b and c such that

$$\int_{-\infty}^{\infty} \frac{d\nu(x)}{(1-iux)^{2c}} = \frac{1}{(1-iua)^c} \cdot \frac{1}{(1-iub)^c}. \tag{8}$$

Of course, it is enough to find the measure ν with compact support[2]. Therefore, we must have for $a > 0$ and $b > 0$

$$m_k =$$

$$\sum_{j=0}^{k} \frac{c(c+1)\cdots(c+j-1)}{j!} \cdot \frac{c(c+1)\cdots(c+k-j-1)}{(k-j)!} a^j b^{k-j} / \binom{-2c}{k}, \tag{9}$$

where $m_k = m_k(\nu)$ is the kth moment of ν. It remains to be shown that the left hand side of (9) really defines for $k = 0, 1, \ldots$ moments of a distribution.

Let us denote $\lambda = a/b$ and suppose that $|\lambda| < 1$ (the case $|\lambda| = 1$ may be obtained as a limit case). Then, k_m can be rewritten in the form

$$k_m = (-1)^m b^m \sum_{k=0}^{m} \binom{m}{k} \frac{(c)_k (c)_{m-k}}{(2c)_m} \lambda^k,$$

[2] Another approach may be based on the expression of the right hand side of (8) thought the Lauricella's fourth function and its integral representation (for close results see Van Laarhoven and Kalker (1988)). However, it is out of the scope of this paper.

where $(s)_j = s \cdots (s+j-1)$ is the Pochhammer symbol. Simple calculations allow us to obtain from previous equality that

$$k_m = \frac{b^m (c)_m \, {}_2F_1(-m, c, 1-m-c, a/b)}{(2c)_m}. \tag{10}$$

Let us consider a random variable X having Beta distribution with equal parameters c and c; that is, with probability density function

$$p_X(x) = (1-x)^{c-1} x^{c-1} 2^{2c-1} \Gamma(c+1/2)/(\sqrt{\pi}\,\Gamma(c)),$$

for $x \in (0,1)$, and zero for $x \notin (0,1)$. It is not difficult to calculate that

$$\mathbb{E}\Big(aX + b(1-X)\Big)^m = b^m \, {}_2F_1(-m, c, 2c, 1-a/b),$$

which coincides with (10) for non-negative integer m and real $c > 0$. □

Theorem 1 allows us to define a family of generalized convolutions $\nu = \mu_1 \star_c \mu_2$ depending on c, which is equivalent to the relation (7). Obviously, this operation is commutative. However, it is not associative, which can be easily verified by comparing the convolutions $(\delta_1 \star_c \delta_2) \star_c \delta_3$ and $\delta_1 \star_c (\delta_2 \star_c \delta_3)$, where δ_a denotes Dirac measure at point a. It is easy to verify that $\mu_1 \star_c \mu_2(2A) \underset{c\to\infty}{\longrightarrow} \mu_1 * \mu_2(A)$, where $*$ denotes ordinary convolution of measures. We have $2A$ in the left hand side because $\mathbb{E}X = 1/2$. This generalized convolution may be written through independent random variables U and V in the form

$$W = UX + V(1-X),$$

where X is a random variable independent of (U, V) and having Beta distribution with parameters (n, n), and the distribution of W is exactly a generalized convolution of distributions of U and V.

Let us note that the $\star_{3/2}$-convolution of Dirac measures concentrated at points -1 and 1 gives the well-known Wigner semicircle distribution.

In view of the non-associativity of $\star_c$-convolution, it does not coincide with K. Urbanik's generalized convolution (see Urbanik (1964)). At the same time, its non-associativity shows that the expression $\mu_1 \star_c \mu_2 \star_c \mu_3$ has no sense. However, one can define this 3-argument operation by using stochastic linear combinations; that is, linear forms of random variables with random coefficients. Now we define such k-arguments operation. Namely, let $U_1, \ldots, U_k$ be independent random variables, and $X_1, \ldots, X_{n-1}$ be a random vector having Dirichlet distribution with parameters $(a_1, \ldots, a_k) = (c, \ldots, c)$. Define

$$W = X_1 U_1 + \ldots + X_{k-1} U_{k-1} + (1 - \sum_{j=1}^{k-1} X_j)\, U_k. \tag{11}$$

The map from vector U of marginal distributions of $(U_1, \ldots, U_k)$ to the distribution of random variable W call k-tuple generalized convolution of the components of U. Clearly, this operation is symmetric with respect to the permutations of coordinates of the vector U. Let us mention that it is probably possible to use Lauricella's fourth function and its integral representation for the definition of k-tuple generalized convolution. However, we prefer this approach in view of its probabilistic interpretation.

4. Connected Family of Non-Commutative Generalized Convolutions

Let now $U_1, \ldots, U_k$ be independent random variables, and $X_1, \ldots, X_{n-1}$ be a random vector having Dirichlet distribution with parameters $(a_1, \ldots, a_k)$, possibly different from each other. Using the relation (11), define random variable W. Its distribution will be called a non-commutative generalized convolution of marginal distributions of the vector U. In the particular case of $k = 2$, we obtain a non-commutative variant of two-tuple generalized convolution, which represents the more general case of (1).

Let us give a property of this generalized convolution. To do so, let us define $\tilde{beta}_{A,B}$ distribution over interval (A, B) by its probability density function

$$p_{\alpha,\beta}(x) = \begin{cases} \frac{1}{B(\alpha,\beta)(B-A)^{\alpha+\beta-1}}(x-A)^{\alpha-1}(B-x)^{\beta-1}, & \text{if } A < x < B, \\ 0 & \text{otherwise,} \end{cases}$$

for positive α, β. Here $B(\alpha, \beta)$ is beta function.

Theorem 2. *Let W_1, W_2 be two independent identical distributed random variables having $\tilde{beta}_{A,B}(n, n)$ distribution, and μ_1, μ_2 be corresponding probability distributions. Then the measure $\nu = \mu_1 \star_n \mu_2$ corresponds to $\tilde{beta}_{A,B}(2n, 2n)$ distribution.*

Proof. From the proof of Theorem 1 that $W_j \stackrel{d}{=} AX_j + B(1 - X_j)$, where X_1, X_2 are independent identically distributed random variables having $B(n, n)$ distribution. The rest of the proof is just simple calculation. □

The property given by Theorem 2 is very similar to classical stability definition.

Theorem 3. *Let $U_j, j = 1, \ldots, k$ be independent random variables having $\tilde{b}eta$ distribution with parameters $\alpha_j = r_j + 1/2$, $\beta_j = r_j + 1/2$. Let $X_1, \ldots, X_{k-1}$ be a random vector having Dirichlet distribution with parameters $(r_1, \ldots, r_k)$. Then, random variable*

$$W = X_1 U_1 + \ldots + X_{k-1} U_{k-1} + (1 - \sum_{j=1}^{k-1} X_j)\, U_k$$

has $\tilde{b}eta$ distribution with parameters $\left(\sum_{j=1}^{k} r_j + 1/2,\ \sum_{j=1}^{k} r_j + 1/2\right)$.

Proof. It is sufficient to calculate the modified Stieltjes transform of the distribution of W using some properties of Gauss-hypergeometric function. □

This property is also similar to the classical stability property, but for the case of k-tuple operation.

Acknowledgments: Authors are grateful to the anonymous referees for useful remarks and for drawing our attention to the connection with the Lauricella's fourth function. The work was partially supported by Grant GACR 16-03708S.

Author Contributions: The first author suggested and designed the new subject. The second author contributed analysis tools and wrote the paper with the first author.

Conflicts of Interest: The authors declare no conflicts of interest.

References

Abramowitz, Milton, and Irene A. Stegun, eds. 2012. *Handbook of Mathematical Functions: with Formulas, Graphs, and Mathematical Tables.* Mineola: Courier Dover Publications.

Andrews, George E., Richard Askey, and Ranjan Roy. 1999. *Special Functions.* Cambridge: Cambridge University Press.

Demni, Nizar. 2016. Generalized Stieltjes Transforms of Compactly-Supported Probability Distributions: Further Examples. *Symmetry, Integrability and Geometry: Methods and Applications* 12: 035.

Klebanov, Lev B., and Rasool Roozegar. 2016. Modified Stieltjes Transform and Generalized Convolutions. *arXiv* 1–7. arXiv:1605.02943v1.

Roozegar, Rasool, and Abouzar Bazyari. 2017. Exact Distribution of Random Weighted Convolution of Some Beta Distributions Through an Integral Transform. *Pakistan Journal of Statistics and Operation Research* 13: 799–808.
Urbanik, Kazimierz. 1964. Generalized convolutions. *Studia Math* 23: 217–45.
Van Laarhoven, Peter J. M., and Ton A.C.M. Kalker. 1988. On the computation of Lauricella functions of the fourth kind. *Journal of Computational and Applied Mathematics* 21: 369–75.

Journal of
Risk and Financial Management

MDPI

Article

The Burr X Pareto Distribution: Properties, Applications and VaR Estimation

Mustafa Ç. Korkmaz [1,*], Emrah Altun [2], Haitham M. Yousof [3], Ahmed Z. Afify [3] and Saralees Nadarajah [4]

1. Department of Measurement and Evaluation, Artvin Çoruh University, Artvin 08000, Turkey
2. Department of Statistics, Hacettepe University, Ankara 06800, Turkey; emrahaltun@hacettepe.edu.tr
3. Department of Statistics, Mathematics and Insurance, Benha University, Benha 13511, Egypt; haitham.yousof@fcom.bu.edu.eg (H.M.Y.); AHMED.AFIFY@fcom.bu.edu.eg (A.Z.A.)
4. School of Mathematics, University of Manchester, Manchester M13 9PL, UK; Saralees.Nadarajah@manchester.ac.uk

* Correspondence: mcagatay@artvin.edu.tr

Received: 31 October 2017; Accepted: 18 December 2017; Published: 21 December 2017

Abstract: In this paper, a new three-parameter Pareto distribution is introduced and studied. We discuss various mathematical and statistical properties of the new model. Some estimation methods of the model parameters are performed. Moreover, the peaks-over-threshold method is used to estimate Value-at-Risk (VaR) by means of the proposed distribution. We compare the distribution with a few other models to show its versatility in modelling data with heavy tails. VaR estimation with the Burr X Pareto distribution is presented using time series data, and the new model could be considered as an alternative VaR model against the generalized Pareto model for financial institutions.

Keywords: Burr X distribution; Pareto distribution; maximum likelihood estimation; heavy tail distribution; value-at-risk

1. Introduction

The Pareto (P) distribution is very versatile, and a variety of uncertainties can be usefully modelled by it. It has several applications in actuarial science, economics, finance, life testing, survival analysis and telecommunications because of its heavy tail properties. The probability density function (pdf) and cumulative distribution function (cdf) of the P distribution are given (for $x > \beta$) by:

$$g(x;\alpha,\beta) = \frac{\alpha}{x}\left(\frac{x}{\beta}\right)^{-\alpha} \text{ and } G(x;\alpha,\beta) = 1 - \left(\frac{x}{\beta}\right)^{-\alpha},$$

where $\beta > 0$ is a scale parameter and $\alpha > 0$ is a shape parameter. This distribution is a special form of the Pearson Type VI distribution. Since the P distribution has a reversed-J pdf shape and a decreasing hazard rate function (hrf), it may sometimes be insufficient to model data. Generally, practical problems require a wider range of possibilities for the medium risk, for example when the lifetime data present a bathtub-shaped hrf, such as human mortality and machine life cycles. For this reason, researchers developed various extensions and modified forms of the P distribution to obtain a more flexible model with different numbers of parameters. Some of them can be cited as follows: Exponentiated P (EP) (Stoppa 1990; Gupta et al. 1998), Beta P (BP) (Akinsete et al. 2008), Kumaraswamy P (KwP) (Bourguignon et al. 2013), Kumaraswamy generalized P (Nadarajah and Eljabri 2013), P ArcTan (PAT) (Gómez-Déniz and Calderín-Ojeda 2015), exponentiated Weibull P (Afify et al. 2016) and Weibull P

(WP) distributions (Tahir et al. 2016). On the other hand, Yousof et al. (2016) defined the cdf of the Burr X-G(BX-G) family (for $x \in \Re$) by:

$$F(x;\delta,\xi) = \left(1 - \exp\left\{-\left[\frac{G(x;\xi)}{\overline{G}(x;\xi)}\right]^2\right\}\right)^\delta, \tag{1}$$

where $\delta > 0$ is the shape parameter and $\xi = \xi_k = (\xi_1, \xi_2, \ldots)$ is a parameter vector. The BX-G density function becomes:

$$f(x;\delta,\xi) = \frac{2\delta g(x;\xi)G(x;\xi)}{\overline{G}(x;\xi)^3}\exp\left\{-\left[\frac{G(x;\xi)}{\overline{G}(x;\xi)}\right]^2\right\}\left(1 - \exp\left\{-\left[\frac{G(x;\xi)}{\overline{G}(x;\xi)}\right]^2\right\}\right)^{\delta-1}. \tag{2}$$

This generator can supply the flexibility of pdf and hrf to any baseline distribution model (Yousof et al. 2016).

In this paper, we introduce a new extended P distribution, called the Burr X Pareto (BXP) model, based on the BX-G family. With this idea, we construct the new BXP distribution as more flexible than the P distribution and provide a comprehensive description of some of its mathematical properties. We prove empirically that the BXP model provides better fits than some extensions and generalizations of the P, some of which have one extra model parameter, and the others have the same number of parameters, by means of two applications to real data. We hope that the new distribution will attract wider applications in reliability, engineering and other areas of research.

The rest of the paper is organized as follows. In Section 2, we define the BXP model. In Section 3, we provide a useful mixture representation for its pdf. In Section 4, we derive some of its general mathematical properties. Some estimation methods of the model parameters are performed in Section 5. In Section 6, simulation results to assess the performance of the proposed maximum likelihood estimation procedure are discussed. In Section 7, we provide two applications to real data to illustrate the importance and flexibility of the new family. Value-at-Risk estimation with the BXP distribution is presented in Section 8. Finally, some concluding remarks are presented in Section 9.

2. The New Model

In this section, we define the BXP model and provide some plots for its pdf and hrf. The BXP cdf is given by:

$$F(x;\delta,\alpha,\beta) = \left(1 - \exp\left\{-\left[\left(\frac{x}{\beta}\right)^\alpha - 1\right]^2\right\}\right)^\delta, \; x > \beta > 0, \; \alpha,\delta > 0. \tag{3}$$

The pdf corresponding to (3) is given by:

$$\begin{aligned} f(x;\delta,\alpha,\beta) = 2\delta\frac{\alpha}{x}\left(\tfrac{x}{\beta}\right)^{2\alpha}\left[1 - \left(\tfrac{x}{\beta}\right)^{-\alpha}\right]\exp\left\{-\left[\left(\tfrac{x}{\beta}\right)^\alpha - 1\right]^2\right\} \\ \times\left(1 - \exp\left\{-\left[\left(\tfrac{x}{\beta}\right)^\alpha - 1\right]^2\right\}\right)^{\delta-1}. \end{aligned} \tag{4}$$

Lemma 1 provides random number generations from the BXP and some relations and of the BXP distribution with the well-known Burr X and uniform distributions.

Lemma 1. *(a) If a random variable Y follows the Burr X distribution with shape parameter δ and scale parameter one, then the random variable $X = \beta(1+Y)^{(1/\alpha)}$ follows the BXP(δ,α,β) distribution.*
(b) If a random variable Y follows the uniform distribution on [0,1], then the random variable:

$$X = \beta\left(1 + \sqrt{-\log(1 - Y^{1/\delta})}\right)^{1/\alpha}$$

follows the BXP(δ,α,β) distribution.

Proof. The proofs of (a) and (b) are obtained by the transformation method. □

The hrf, reversed hazard rate function and cumulative hazard rate function of X are given, respectively, by:

$$h(x;\delta,\alpha,\beta)=\frac{2\delta\frac{\alpha}{x}\left(\frac{x}{\beta}\right)^{2\alpha}\left[1-\left(\frac{x}{\beta}\right)^{-\alpha}\right]\exp\left\{-\left[\left(\frac{x}{\beta}\right)^{\alpha}-1\right]^{2}\right\}\left(1-\exp\left\{-\left[\left(\frac{x}{\beta}\right)^{\alpha}-1\right]^{2}\right\}\right)^{\delta-1}}{1-\left(1-\exp\left\{-\left[\left(\frac{x}{\beta}\right)^{\alpha}-1\right]^{2}\right\}\right)^{\delta}},$$

$$r(x;\delta,\alpha,\beta)=\frac{2\delta\frac{\alpha}{x}\left(\frac{x}{\beta}\right)^{2\alpha}\left[1-\left(\frac{x}{\beta}\right)^{-\alpha}\right]\exp\left\{-\left[\left(\frac{x}{\beta}\right)^{\alpha}-1\right]^{2}\right\}}{\left(1-\exp\left\{-\left[\left(\frac{x}{\beta}\right)^{\alpha}-1\right]^{2}\right\}\right)}$$

and:

$$H(x;\delta,\alpha,\beta)=-\left[\log\left(1-\exp\left\{-\left[\left(\frac{x}{\beta}\right)^{\alpha}-1\right]^{2}\right\}\right)^{\delta}\right].$$

In Figure 1, we sketched the possible pdf and hrf shapes of the BXP distribution for some selected parameter values. Figure 1 shows that the BXP distribution has various pdf and hrf shapes.

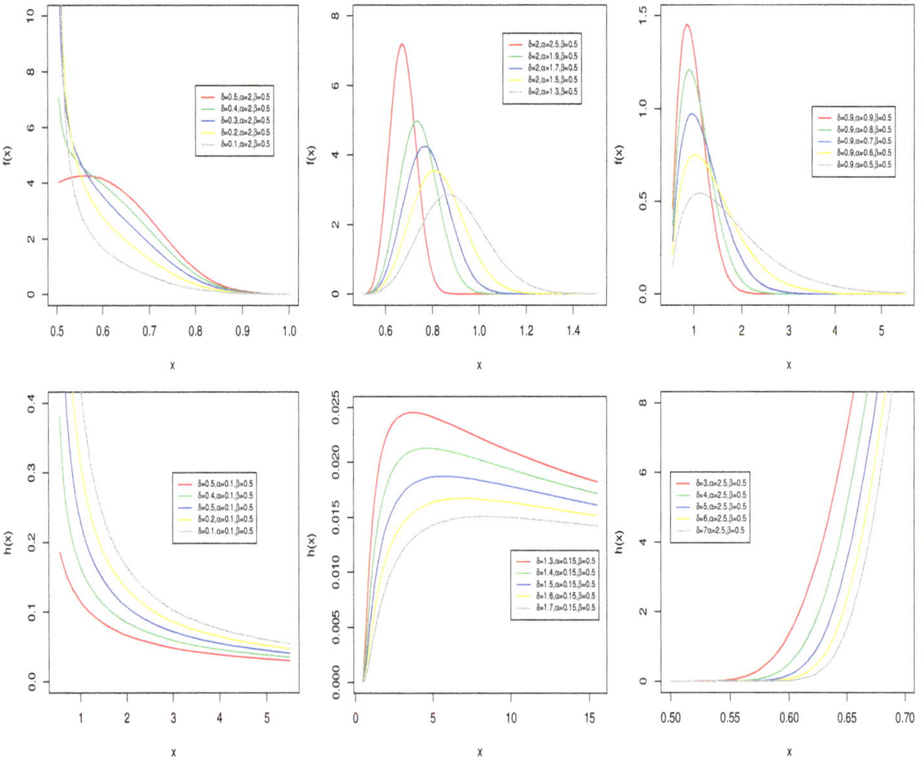

Figure 1. Plots of the Burr XPareto (BXP) pdf (**top**) and plots of the BXP hazard rate function (hrf) (**bottom**).

3. Expansions of pdf and cdf

In this section, we provide a very useful linear representation for the BXP density function. If $|z| < 1$ and $b > 0$ is a real non-integer, the power series holds:

$$(1-z)^{b-1} = \sum_{i=0}^{\infty} \frac{(-1)^i \, \Gamma(b)}{i! \, \Gamma(b-i)} \, z^i. \tag{5}$$

For simplicity, ignoring the dependence of $G(x)$ and $g(x)$ on ξ and applying (5) to (4), we have:

$$f(x) = 2\delta \frac{\alpha}{x} \left(\frac{x}{\beta}\right)^{2\alpha} \left[1 - \left(\frac{x}{\beta}\right)^{-\alpha}\right] \sum_{i=0}^{\infty} \frac{(-1)^i \, \Gamma(\delta)}{i! \, \Gamma(\delta - i)} \exp\left\{-(i+1)\left[\left(\frac{x}{\beta}\right)^{\alpha} - 1\right]^2\right\}. \tag{6}$$

Applying the power series to the term $\exp\left\{-(i+1)\left[\left(\frac{x}{\beta}\right)^{\alpha} - 1\right]^2\right\}$, Equation (6) becomes:

$$f(x) = 2\delta \frac{\alpha}{x} \left(\frac{x}{\beta}\right)^{-\alpha} \sum_{i,j=0}^{\infty} \frac{(-1)^{i+j} \, (i+1)^j \Gamma(\delta)}{i! \, j! \Gamma(\delta - i)} \frac{\left[1 - \left(\frac{x}{\beta}\right)^{-\alpha}\right]^{2j+1}}{\left(\frac{x}{\beta}\right)^{-\alpha(2j+3)}}. \tag{7}$$

Consider the series expansion:

$$(1-z)^{-b} = \sum_{k=0}^{\infty} \frac{\Gamma(b+k)}{k! \Gamma(b)} z^k, \; |z| < 1, \; b > 0. \tag{8}$$

Applying the expansion in (8) to (7) for the term $\left(\frac{x}{\beta}\right)^{-\alpha(2j+3)}$, Equation (7) becomes:

$$f(x) = \sum_{j,k=0}^{\infty} \Omega_{j,k} \, \pi_{2(j+1)+k}(x; \alpha, \beta), \tag{9}$$

where:

$$\Omega_{j,k} = \frac{2\delta(-1)^j \Gamma(\delta) \Gamma(2j+k+3)}{j! k! \Gamma(2j+3)(2j+k+2)} \sum_{i=0}^{\infty} \frac{(-1)^i \, (i+1)^j}{i! \, \Gamma(\delta - i)}$$

and:

$$\pi_{2(j+1)+k}(x; \alpha, \beta) = [2(j+1) + k] g(x; \alpha, \beta) G(x; \alpha, \beta)^{2j+k+1}.$$

Equation (9) reveals that the density of X can be expressed as expansions of the EP densities. Therefore, several mathematical properties of the new family can be obtained by knowing those of the EP distribution. Similarly, the cdf of the BXP family can also be expressed as a mixture of EP cdfs given by:

$$F(x) = \sum_{j,k=0}^{\infty} \Omega_{j,k} \, \Pi_{2(j+1)+k}(x; \alpha, \beta) \tag{10}$$

where:

$$\Pi_{2(j+1)+k}(x) = G(x; \alpha, \beta)^{2(j+1)+k}$$

is the cdf of the EP family with power parameter $2(j+1)+k$.

4. Properties

In this section, we will provide some mathematical properties of the BXP distribution.

4.1. Moments

The r-th ordinary moment of X is given by $\mu'_r = E(X^r) = \int_{-\infty}^{\infty} x^r f(x)dx$. By using Equation (9), we obtain:

$$\mu'_r = \sum_{j,k=0}^{\infty} \Omega_{j,k} E(Y^r_{2(j+1)+k}),$$

$E(Y^r_{2(j+1)+k})$ is the r-th ordinary moment of EP distribution with power parameter $2(j+1)+k$. The j-th order central moment can be obtained by the following relationship:

$$\mu_j = E[(X-\mu)^j] = \sum_{r=0}^{j} \binom{j}{r} \mu_r{}'(-\mu)^{j-r} \text{ for } j = 2,3,\ldots,$$

where $\mu = E(X)$.

For the skewness and kurtosis coefficients, we have:

$$\sqrt{\beta_1} = \sqrt{\frac{\mu_3^2}{\mu_2^3}} \quad \text{and} \quad \beta_2 = \frac{\mu_4}{\mu_2^2}.$$

The values for mean, variance, $\sqrt{\beta_1}$ and β_2 for selected values of δ, α and β are shown in Table 1. We can say that the BXP model can be useful for various data modelling in terms of skewness and kurtosis.

Table 1. Mean, variance, coefficients of skewness and kurtosis for different values of parameters.

(δ, α, β)	μ	$Var(X)$	$\sqrt{\beta_1}$	β_2
(0.5, 0.5, 0.5)	1.2801	1.1395	0.7311	4.4238
(1, 1, 1)	1.6330	0.9671	−1.2539	3.2132
(2, 2, 2)	2.5365	1.7311	−1.9644	4.3986
(1, 2, 3)	2.9606	5.9323	−0.8355	1.3785
(4, 2, 0.5)	0.7411	0.0415	−4.1218	17.7934
(10, 2, 0.25)	0.4074	0.0011	−6.3710	97.4674
(0.25, 5, 2)	0.4962	1.2671	1.4287	2.6058
(0.9, 5, 1.8)	1.0633	1.5440	0.0255	0.7191

4.2. Residual and Reversed Residual Life

The n-th moment of the residual life, say $m_n(t) = E[(X-t)^n \mid X > t]$, $n = 1,2,\ldots$, uniquely determines $F(x)$. The n-th moment of the residual life of X is given by:

$$m_n(t) = \frac{1}{1-F(t)} \int_t^{\infty} (x-t)^n dF(x).$$

Therefore,

$$m_n(t) = \frac{1}{1-F(t)} \sum_{j,k=0}^{\infty} \sum_{r=0}^{n} \Omega_{j,k} \binom{n}{r} (-t)^{n-r} \beta^n [2(j+1)+k] \mathbf{B}_t\Big(1-\frac{n}{\alpha}, 2(j+1)+k\Big), \forall\, n \le \alpha.$$

where:

$$\mathbf{B}_z(a,b) = \int_0^z w^{a-1}(1-w)^{b-1} dw$$

is the incomplete beta function.

The Mean Residual Life (MRL) function or the life expectation at age t defined by $m_1(t) = E[(X-t) \mid X > t]$ follows by setting $n = 1$ in the last equation.

The n-th moment of the reversed residual life, say $M_n(t) = E[(t-X)^n \mid X \leq t]$ for $t > 0$ and $n = 1, 2, \ldots$ uniquely determines $F(x)$. We obtain:

$$M_n(t) = \frac{1}{F(t)} \int_0^t (t-x)^n dF(x).$$

Then, the n-th moment of the reversed residual life of X becomes:

$$M_n(t) = \frac{1}{F(t)} \sum_{j,k=0}^{\infty} \sum_{r=0}^{n} \Omega_{j,k} (-1)^r \binom{n}{r} t^{n-r} \beta^n [2(j+1)+k] \mathbf{B}_t\left(1-\frac{n}{\alpha}, 2(j+1)+k\right), \forall\, n \leq \alpha.$$

The mean inactivity time (MIT) or mean waiting time is given by $M_1(t) = E[(t-X) \mid X \leq t]$, and it can be obtained easily by setting $n = 1$ in the above equation.

4.3. Order Statistics

Order statistics make their appearance in many areas of statistical theory and practice. Let $X_1, \ldots, X_n$ be a random sample from the BXP of distributions, and let $X_{(1)}, \ldots, X_{(n)}$ be the corresponding order statistics. The pdf of the i-th order statistic, say $X_{i:n}$, can be written as:

$$f_{i:n}(x) = \frac{f(x;\delta,\alpha,\beta)}{\mathrm{B}(i, n-i+1)} \sum_{j=0}^{n-i} (-1)^j \binom{n-i}{j} F^{j+i-1}(x). \tag{11}$$

Using (3), (4) and (10), we get:

$$f(x)\, F(x)^{j+i-1} = \sum_{w,k=0}^{\infty} t_{w,k} \pi_{2(w+1)+k}(x),$$

where:

$$t_{w,k} = \frac{2\delta(-1)^w \Gamma(2w+k+3)}{w!k!\Gamma(2w+3)(2w+k+2)} \sum_{m=0}^{\infty} (-1)^m (m+1)^w \binom{\delta(j+i)-1}{m}.$$

The pdf of $X_{i:n}$ can be expressed as:

$$f_{i:n}(x) = \sum_{w,k=0}^{\infty} \sum_{j=0}^{n-i} \frac{(-1)^j \binom{n-i}{j} b_{w,k}}{\mathrm{B}(i, n-i+1)} \pi_{2(w+1)+k}(x).$$

Then, the density function of the BXP order statistics is a mixture of EP densities. Based on the last equation, we note that the properties of $X_{i:n}$ follow from those properties of Y_{2w+k+2}. For example, the moments of $X_{i:n}$ can be expressed as:

$$E\left(X_{i:n}^q\right) = \sum_{w,k=0}^{\infty} \sum_{j=0}^{n-i} \frac{(-1)^j \binom{n-i}{j} t_{w,k}}{\mathrm{B}(i, n-i+1)} \beta^q [2(w+1)+k] \mathbf{B}\left(1-\frac{q}{\alpha}, 2(w+1)+k\right), \forall\, q \leq \alpha. \tag{12}$$

5. Estimation Methods

In this section, we consider the maximum likelihood, least square and weighted least square estimation of the parameters of the BXP distribution.

5.1. Maximum Likelihood Estimation

We consider the estimation of the unknown parameters of the BXP model from complete samples by the maximum likelihood method. The maximum likelihood estimators (MLEs) of the parameters of the BXP (δ, α, β) model are now discussed. Let $x_1, \ldots, x_n$ be a random sample of this distribution with parameter vector $\Theta = (\delta, \alpha, \beta)^\intercal$. The log-likelihood function for δ is given by:

$$\begin{aligned} \ell &= n\log 2 + n\log\delta + n\log\alpha - 2\alpha\log\beta + \sum_{i=1}^{n}\log(1-\beta^{\alpha}x_i^{-\alpha}) \\ &\quad +(2\alpha-1)\sum_{i=1}^{n}\log x_i + \sum_{i=1}^{n}\log s_i + (\delta-1)\sum_{i=1}^{n}\log(1-s_i), \end{aligned}$$

where $s_i = \exp\left\{-\left[\left(\frac{x_i}{\beta}\right)^{\alpha}-1\right]^2\right\}$.

The last equation can be also maximized either by using the different programs such as R (`optim function`), SAS (`PROC NLMIXED`) or by solving the nonlinear likelihood equations obtained by differentiating ℓ. We note that since $x \in (\beta, \infty)$, the MLE of the β parameter cannot be obtained in the usual way. Hence, the MLE of β is the first order statistic $X_{(1)}$ (Johnson et al. 1994).

The components of the score vector, $\mathbf{U}(\Theta) = \frac{\partial\ell}{\partial\Theta} = \left(\frac{\partial\ell}{\partial\delta}, \frac{\partial\ell}{\partial\alpha}\right)^\intercal$, are:

$$U_\delta = \frac{n}{\delta} + \sum_{i=1}^{n}\log\left(1-\exp\left\{-\left[\left(\frac{x_i}{\beta}\right)^{\alpha}-1\right]^2\right\}\right),$$

and:

$$U_\alpha = \frac{n}{\alpha} - 2\log\beta - \sum_{i=1}^{n}\frac{\left(\frac{x}{\beta}\right)^{-\alpha}\log\left(\frac{x}{\beta}\right)}{1-\beta^{\alpha}x_i^{-\alpha}} + 2\sum_{i=1}^{n}\log x_i + \sum_{i=1}^{n}\frac{m_i}{s_i} - (\delta-1)\sum_{i=1}^{n}\frac{m_i}{1-s_i}$$

where:

$$m_i = -2s_i\left[\left(\frac{x_i}{\beta}\right)^{\alpha}-1\right]\left(\frac{x_i}{\beta}\right)^{\alpha}\log\left(\frac{x_i}{\beta}\right).$$

For fixed β, the interval estimation of the model parameters requires the 2×2 observed information matrix $J(\Theta) = \{J_{ij}\}$ for $i, j = \delta, \alpha$. The multivariate normal $N_2(0, J(\widehat{\Theta})^{-1})$ distribution, under standard regularity conditions, can be used to provide approximate confidence intervals for the unknown parameters, where $J(\widehat{\Theta})$ is the total observed information matrix evaluated at $\widehat{\Theta}$. Then, approximate $100(1-\delta)\%$ confidence intervals for δ and α can be determined by:

$\widehat{\delta} \pm z_{\zeta/2}\sqrt{\widehat{J}_{\delta\delta}}$ and $\widehat{\alpha} \pm z_{\zeta/2}\sqrt{\widehat{J}_{\alpha\alpha}}$, where $z_{\zeta/2}$ is the upper ζ-th percentile of the standard normal model.

5.2. Ordinary and Weighted Least Squares

In this section, we use the least square (LS) and weighted least square (WLS) estimators (Swain et al. 1988) to estimate the parameters of the BXP distribution. Let $X_{(1)}, \ldots, X_{(n)}$ be the order statistics of a random sample of size n from the BXP defined in (4), then the least square estimators (LSEs) of the unknown parameters δ, α and β of the BXP distribution can be obtained by minimizing:

$$\sum_{i=1}^{n}\left[\left(1-\exp\left\{-\left[\left(\frac{x_{(i)}}{\beta}\right)^{\alpha}-1\right]^2\right\}\right)^{\delta} - \frac{i}{n+1}\right]^2,$$

with respect to unknown parameters δ, α and β.

The weighted least square estimators (WLSEs) of the unknown parameters δ, α and β follow by minimizing:

$$\sum_{i=1}^{n} \frac{(n+1)^2(n+2)}{n-i+1} \left[\left(1 - \exp\left\{ - \left[\left(\frac{x_{(i)}}{\beta} \right)^{\alpha} - 1 \right]^2 \right\} \right)^{\delta} - \frac{i}{n+1} \right]^2,$$

with respect to unknown parameters δ, α and β.

6. Simulation Study

Here, we perform the simulation study for MLEs of the BXP distribution. We generate $N = 1000$ samples of sizes $n = 50, 100, 200$ from selected BXP distributions. The random numbers generation is simulated by:

$$x = \beta \left(1 + \sqrt{-\log(1 - u^{1/\delta})} \right)^{1/\alpha},$$

where u is a uniform random number on [0,1]. We also calculate the empirical mean, standard deviations (sd), bias and mean square error (MSE) of the MLEs. The empirical bias and MSE are calculated by:

$$Bias_{\hat{h}} = \frac{1}{N} \sum_{i=1}^{N} \left(h - \hat{h}_i \right)$$

and:

$$MSE_{\hat{h}} = \frac{1}{N} \sum_{i=1}^{N} \left(h - \hat{h}_i \right)^2$$

respectively, where $h = (\delta, \alpha, \beta)$. All results of MLEs were obtained using the optim-CG routine in the R programme. The empirical results of this simulation study are reported in Table 2. Table 2 shows that when the sample size increases, the empirical means approach the true parameter value. For the same case, the standard deviations, biases and MSEs decrease in all the cases as expected. Therefore, the MLE method works very well to estimate the model parameters of the BXP distribution.

Table 2. The empirical means, sds (given in $(\cdot)$), biases (given in $[\cdot]$) and MSEs (given in $\{\cdot\}$) for the special BXP distributions.

Parameters	$n = 50$			$n = 100$			$n = 200$		
δ, α, β	$\hat{\delta}$	$\hat{\alpha}$	$\hat{\beta}$	$\hat{\delta}$	$\hat{\alpha}$	$\hat{\beta}$	$\hat{\delta}$	$\hat{\alpha}$	$\hat{\beta}$
3, 1.5, 2	3.0144	1.5495	2.0286	2.9995	1.5247	2.0159	3.0001	1.5125	2.0060
	(0.1831)	(0.1585)	(0.1155)	(0.0399)	(0.1059)	(0.0757)	(0.0400)	(0.0648)	(0.0485)
	[0.0144]	[0.0494]	[0.0286]	[−0.0005]	[0.0247]	[0.0160]	[0.0001]	[0.0125]	[0.0059]
	{0.0330}	{0.0270}	{0.0140}	{0.0016}	{0.0117}	{0.0060}	{0.0016}	{0.0043}	{0.0023}
3, 2, 1	3.0772	2.0550	1.0040	3.0019	2.0093	1.0021	3.0016	2.0073	1.0013
	(0.2928)	(0.2053)	(0.0443)	(0.0212)	(0.0976)	(0.0211)	(0.0203)	(0.0851)	(0.0182)
	[0.0772]	[0.0550]	[0.0040]	[0.0019]	[0.0093]	[0.0021]	[0.0016]	[0.0073]	[0.0013]
	{0.0900}	{0.0443}	{0.0020}	{0.0004}	{0.0095}	{0.0004}	{0.0004}	{0.0072}	{0.0003}
5, 0.5, 5	5.0863	0.5111	5.1216	5.0044	0.5012	5.0065	4.9954	0.4996	4.9970
	(0.2792)	(0.0290)	(0.3641)	(0.0404)	(0.0095)	(0.0490)	(0.0400)	(0.0084)	(0.0439)
	[0.0863]	[0.0111]	[0.1216]	[0.0044]	[0.0012]	[0.0065]	[−0.0046]	[−0.0004]	[−0.0030]
	{0.0838}	{0.0010}	{0.1447}	{0.0072}	{0.00008}	{0.0071}	{0.0054}	{0.00007}	{0.0070}
10, 30, 20	10.0407	30.0438	20.0024	10.0009	30.0013	19.9998	9.9984	29.9980	20.0001
	(0.2318)	(0.2809)	(0.0101)	(0.0110)	(0.0130)	(0.0086)	(0.0101)	(0.0120)	(0.0059)
	[0.0406]	[0.0438]	[0.0024]	[0.0009]	[0.0013]	[−0.0002]	[−0.0016]	[−0.0020]	[0.0001]
	{0.0543}	{0.0793}	{0.0001}	{0.0001}	{0.0001}	{0.00007}	{0.0001}	{0.0001}	{0.00004}
4, 0.5, 0.5	3.9077	0.5147	0.5265	4.0179	0.5121	0.5203	4.0012	0.5052	0.5079
	(0.1261)	(0.0532)	(0.0926)	(0.1010)	(0.0411)	(0.0711)	(0.0878)	(0.0246)	(0.0440)
	[−0.0923]	[0.0147]	[0.0265]	[0.0179]	[0.0121]	[0.0203]	[0.0012]	[0.0052]	[0.0079]
	{0.0356}	{0.0030}	{0.0100}	{0.0164}	{0.0018}	{0.0054}	{0.0076}	{0.0006}	{0.0019}

7. Real Data Modelling

In this section, we present two applications based on the real datasets to show the flexibility of the BXP distribution. The BXP model is compared with the WP, BP, KwP, PAT and P distributions. The cdfs of the above distributions are given (for $x > \beta$ and $a, \alpha, \delta > 0$) by:

$$F_{WP}(x) = 1 - \exp\Big\{ -[(x/\beta)^{\alpha} - 1]^{\delta}\Big\},$$

$$F_{KwP}(x) = 1 - \Big\{1 - \Big[1 - (x/\beta)^{-\alpha}\Big]^{a}\Big\}^{\delta},$$

$$F_{EP}(x) = \Big[1 - (x/\beta)^{-\alpha}\Big]^{\delta},$$

$$F_{PAT}(x) = 1 - \tan^{-1}\Big[\alpha(\beta/x)^{\delta}\Big]\Big[\tan^{-1}\alpha\Big]^{-1}$$

and:

$$F_{BP}(x) = \frac{1}{\mathrm{B}(a,\delta)} \int_0^{1-(\beta x^{-1})^{\alpha}} w^{a-1}(1-w)^{\delta-1}dw.$$

In order to see the best model, we obtain the Akaike Information Criteria (AIC), Corrected Akaike Information Criterion (CAIC), Bayesian Information Criterion (BIC), Hannan–Quinn Information Criterion (HQIC) and Kolmogorov–Smirnov (KS) goodness of-fit statistic to see the fitting of the models to dataset. In general, the best model can be chose as the one that has the smallest values of the AIC, CAIC, BIC, HQIC and KS statistics. All computations of the MLEs are performed by the maxLik routine in the R program.

The first dataset gives the survival times, in weeks, of 33 patients suffering from acute myelogenous leukaemia. These data have been introduced by Feigl and Zelen (1965) and analysed by Mead et al. (2017). The data are: 65, 156, 100, 134, 16, 108, 121, 4, 39, 143, 56, 26, 22, 1, 1, 5, 65, 56, 65, 17, 7, 16, 22, 3, 4, 2, 3, 8, 4, 3, 30, 4, 43. This dataset is well known as being bathtub hrf-shaped.

The second data-set shows the time intervals of the successive earthquakes in the last century in the North Anatolia fault zone between 39.00° to 42.00° north latitude and 39.00° to 40.00° east longitude. This dataset was introduced and analysed by Kuş (2007). This dataset is well known as being decreasing hrf-shaped.

For both datasets, the estimated parameters based on the MLE method are given in Table 3, whereas the values of the information criteria and goodness-of-fit statistics are given in Table 4. Since MLE of the β equals the minimum order statistics, we suppose it as known to be the minimum value the dataset. Table 4 shows that the BXP distribution has the lowest values of these statistics among all the fitted models. Hence, it could be chosen as the best model under these criteria for both datasets.

The histogram of these datasets and the estimated pdfs and cdfs of the application models are displayed in Figures 2 and 3. From the this figure, we show that the BXP model provides the best fit to these datasets as compared to other models.

Table 3. MLEs and their standard errors (in parentheses) for both datasets. P, Pareto; PAT, P ArcTan; KwP, Kumaraswamy P; WP, Weibull P; BP, Beta P; EP, Exponentiated P.

Model	$\widehat{\delta}$	$\widehat{\alpha}$	$\widehat{a}$	$\widehat{\beta}$
Leukaemia Data				
BXP	0.8505 (0.1785)	0.1900 (0.0146)		1
PAT	0.8603 (0.1428)	12.6124 (6.6619)		1
KwP	2.3992 (0.0291)	0.0007 (0.0001)	1,828,015 (5.9317)	1
WP	1.8274 (0.2846)	0.1994 (0.0145)		1
BP	51.9800 (0.1240)	0.0239 (0.0048)	3.8540 (0.6551)	1
EP	4.3606 (1.3221)	0.7089 (0.1192)		1
P		0.3319 (0.0596)		1
Earthquake Data				
BXP	1.9916 (0.5622)	0.1678 (0.0117)		9
PAT	1.1704 (0.0667)	168.1574 (5.9619)		9
WP	2.9843 (0.4949)	0.1408 (0.0074)		9
BP	60.8341 (1.0981)	0.0428 (0.0053)	12.5592 (0.9570)	9
EP	26.9837 (5.7196)	0.8707 (0.0770)		9
P		0.2264 (0.0472)		9

Table 4. Goodness-of-fit statistics for both datasets. CAIC, Corrected Akaike Information Criterion; HQIC, Hannan–Quinn Information Criterion.

Model	AIC	CAIC	BIC	HQIC	KS
Leukaemia Data					
BXP	295.0115	295.4401	297.8795	295.9464	0.1328
PAT	301.1477	301.5763	304.0157	302.0826	0.1398
KwP	298.9148	299.8037	303.2167	300.3171	0.1486
WP	295.2830	295.7116	298.1510	296.2179	0.1418
BP	301.5970	302.4859	305.8990	302.9994	0.1494
EP	300.9643	301.3929	303.8323	301.8992	0.1630
P	319.1294	319.2673	320.5634	319.5968	0.2733
Earthquake Data					
BXP	381.9004	382.5004	384.1714	382.4715	0.0817
PAT	383.7187	384.3187	385.9897	384.2899	0.0971
WP	382.3901	382.9901	384.6610	382.9612	0.0962
BP	384.5029	385.7661	387.9094	385.3597	0.0819
EP	384.3233	384.9233	386.5943	384.8944	0.1038
P	420.6338	420.8243	421.7693	420.9194	0.4218

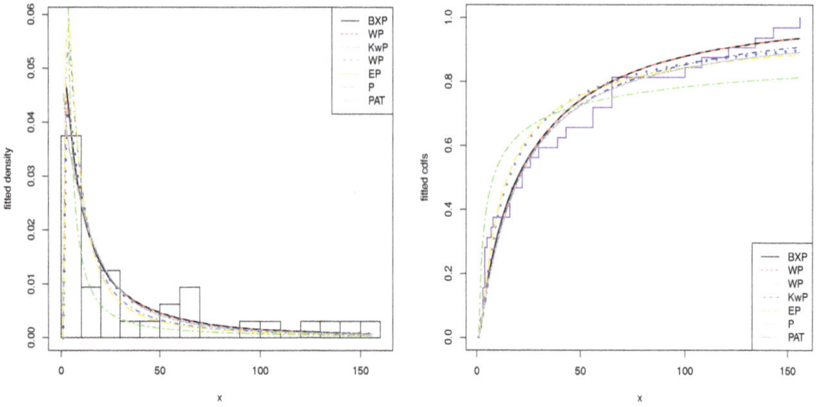

Figure 2. Fitted pdfs (**left panel**) and cdfs (**right panel**) of leukaemia data.

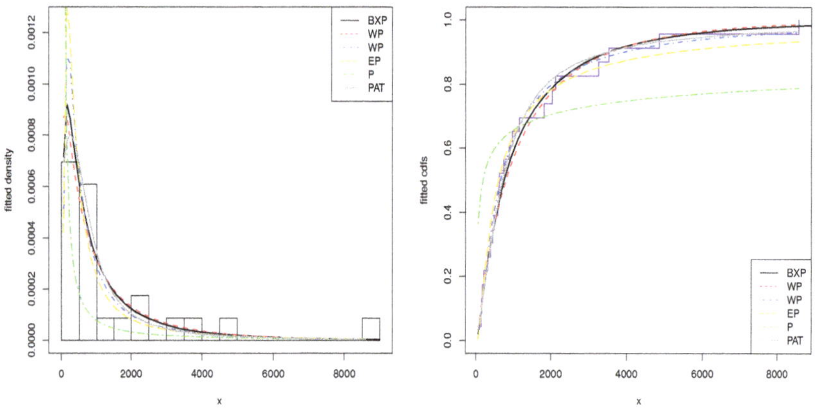

Figure 3. Fitted pdfs (**left panel**) and cdfs (**right panel**) of earthquake data.

8. Value-at-Risk Estimation with the BXP Distribution

In this section, the performance of BXP distribution in estimating Value-at-Risk (VaR) is discussed and compared with the Generalized P (GP) distribution. GP is a widely-used distribution in actuarial sciences, economics and statistics to model the tail of the distribution that contains extreme events. VaR is one of the most popular approaches to measure market risk. From a statistical point of view, the VaR entails the estimation of the quantile of the distribution of returns. The VaR for a long position (left tail of the distribution function) over a given time horizon tis defined as:

$$VaR_p = F^{-1}(p),$$

where F is the distribution function of financial losses, F^{-1} denotes the inverse of F and p is the quantile at which VaR is calculated.

The Peaks-Over-Threshold (POT) method is used to model the tail of the distribution. POT is based on the distribution of exceedances over a given threshold. The conditional excess distribution, F_u, can be defined as follows:

$$F_u(y) = P(X - u \leq y / X > u),\ 0 \leq y \leq x_F - u, \tag{13}$$

where random variable X represents the financial losses, u is the threshold, $y = X - u$ are the excesses and $x_F \leq \infty$ is the right endpoint of F. $F_u(y)$ can be re-defined as follows:

$$F_u(y) = \frac{\Pr\{X-u \leq y, X>u\}}{\Pr(X>u)} = \frac{F(y+u)-F(u)}{1-F(u)} = \frac{F(x)-F(u)}{1-F(u)}. \tag{14}$$

The Balkema and De Haan (1974) and Pickands (1975) theorem shows that for a sufficiently high threshold u, the excess distribution function F_u can be approximated by the GP distribution:

$$F_u(y) \approx G_{\xi,\sigma}(y),\ \mathrm{u} \to \infty$$
$$G_{\xi,\sigma}(y) = \begin{cases} 1-(1+\xi\frac{y}{\sigma})^{-1/\xi}, \xi \neq 0 \\ 1-e^{-y/\sigma}, \xi = 0 \end{cases}, \tag{15}$$

where $y \geq 0$ for $\xi \geq 0$ and $0 \leq y \leq \frac{\sigma}{\xi}$ for $\xi < 0$ and ξ and σ are shape and scale parameters of the GP distribution, respectively. Isolating $F(x)$ from (14), we get:

$$F(x) = (1-F(u))F_u(y) + F(u), \tag{16}$$

where $F_u(y)$ is the GP distribution and $F(u) = (n - N_u)/n$. Then, substituting (14) in (16), the following estimate for $F(x)$ is obtained:

$$\hat{F}(x) = 1 - \frac{N_u}{n}(1 + \frac{\hat{\xi}}{\hat{\sigma}}(x - \hat{u}))^{-1/\hat{\xi}}, \tag{17}$$

where $\hat{\xi}$ and $\hat{\sigma}$ are maximum likelihood estimates of ξ and σ, respectively. Inverting (17) for a given probability p, VaR_p can be obtained as:

$$VaR_p = \hat{u} + \frac{\hat{\sigma}}{\hat{\xi}}\left[\left(\frac{n}{N_u}(1-p)\right)^{-\hat{\xi}} - 1\right]. \tag{18}$$

Threshold selection is a difficult task and an essential part for tail modelling with the GP distribution. The most used method is the Mean Excess (ME) plot for the determination of the threshold. The ME function can be defined as follows:

$$e_n(u) = \frac{\sum\limits_{i=1}^{n}(X_i - u)}{\sum\limits_{i=1}^{n} I_{\{X_i > u\}}}, \tag{19}$$

where I is the indicator function. When the empirical ME function is a positively sloped straight line above a certain threshold u, it is evidence that the used dataset follows the GP distribution with a positive ξ parameter.

Here, the BXP distribution is adopted in the POT method. It is assumed that BXP provides a good approximation to $F_u(y)$ for a sufficiently high threshold u. Then, substituting the cdf of BXP in (16), the new estimate for $F(x)$ can be obtained as:

$$\hat{F}(x) = \left(1 - \frac{n-N_u}{n}\right)\left(1 - \exp\left(-\left[\left(\frac{x}{\hat{\beta}}\right)^{\hat{\alpha}} - 1\right]^2\right)\right)^{\hat{\delta}} + \frac{n-N_u}{n}. \tag{20}$$

The VaR_p can be obtained by inverting (20) for a given probability p, as follows:

$$VaR_p = \hat{u} + \hat{\beta}\left\{1 + \left[-\log\left(1 - \left(\frac{n(p-1)}{N_u}\right)^{\frac{1}{\hat{\delta}}}\right)\right]^{\frac{1}{2}}\right\}^{\frac{1}{\hat{\alpha}}}, \tag{21}$$

where $\hat{\beta}, \hat{\delta}$ and $\hat{\alpha}$ are the maximum likelihood estimates of β, δ and α, respectively.

8.1. S&P-500

To evaluate and compare the performance of the BXP with GP distribution in terms of VaR accuracy, the S&P-500 index is used. The used time series data contain 1465 daily log returns from 4 January 2012 to 27 October 2017. The descriptive statistics of S&P-500 are given in Table 4.

Table 5 shows that the mean returns are closed to zero. The Jarque–Bera statistics in Table 5 also show that the null hypothesis of normality is rejected at any level of significance, as evidenced by the high excess kurtosis and negative skewness. Thus, it is clear that log returns of S&P-500 indexes have non-normal characteristics, excess kurtosis and fat tails. The result of the Ljung–Box test indicates that the raw returns are free from autocorrelation. Therefore, BXP and GP distributions could be applied to the independent and identically distributed observations.

Table 5. Summary statistics for the S&P-500 index.

Descriptive Statistics	S&P-500
Number of observations	1465
Minimum	−0.0402
Maximum	0.0383
Mean	0.0004
Median	0.0004
Std.Deviation	0.007
Skewness	−0.322
Kurtosis	5.403
Jarque–Bera	377.839 (<0.001)
Ljung–Box	28.516 (0.098)

The ME plot is used to determine the optimal threshold value for the POT method. Figure 4 displays the ME plot of the S&P-500 dataset. The optimal threshold could be chosen as 0.02 for the used dataset. It is near the 90% quantile value of the S&P-500.

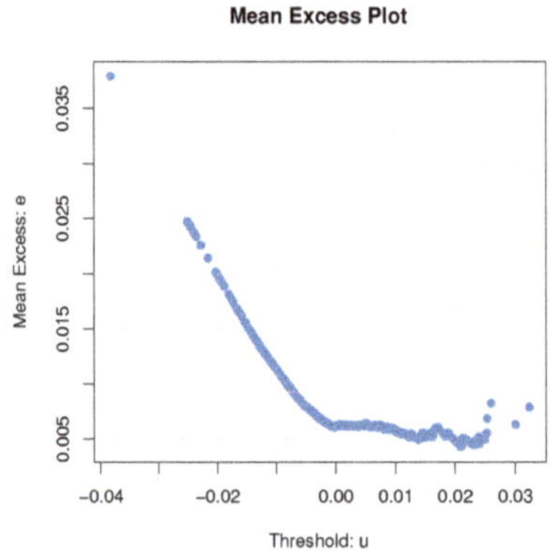

Figure 4. Mean excess plot of the S&P-500 dataset.

Table 6 shows the estimated parameters of BXP distribution and GP distribution using the POT method for the S&P-500 dataset. Based on the figures in Table 6, we conclude that since the BXP distribution has the lowest values of these statistics, BXP provides better fits than the GP distribution for tail modelling of S&P-500 indexes. Figure 5 displays the fitted pdf and cdfs of the BXP and GP distributions. Figure 5 reveals that the BXP distribution provides superior fits to the used dataset.

Table 6. MLEs, corresponding standard errors (in second line) and goodness-of-fit statistics for the S&P-500.

Models	Parameters					Goodness-of-Fit			
	ξ	δ	σ	α	β	$-\ell$	KS	A^*	W^*
BXP		3.2480		0.1893	4.89818×10^{-5}	−93.4016	0.1427	0.3809	0.0556
		1.0266		0.0120	-				
GP	0.0847		0.0057			−88.7171	0.1498	0.4039	0.0661
	0.1996		0.0015						

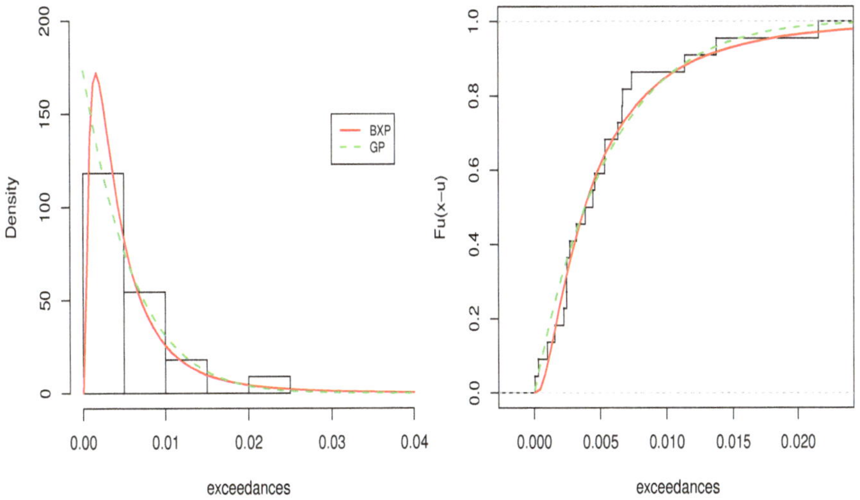

Figure 5. Fitted pdfs (**left**) and cdfs (**right**) of the BXP and GP distribution for the S&P-500 dataset.

Here, VaR is estimated with the GP and BXP distribution using the POT method for values of $p = 0.95, 0.975$ and 0.99. The rolling window estimation method is used to evaluate the out-of-sample performance of the GP and BXP models. The first 1064 daily returns are used as the window length, and the next 400 data points are considered as out-of-sample period. Figure 6 displays daily VaR estimates of the BXP and GP models. Based on Figure 6, it is clear that the BXP and GP models produce similar VaR estimates. Therefore, the BXP model could be considered as an alternative VaR model against to GP model for financial institutions.

In VaR estimation, using the POT method is applied to raw return data assuming the distribution to be stationary or unconditional without considering the time-varying volatility. The POT method can also be considered as a dynamic model, where the conditional distribution of F is taken into account and the volatility of returns is captured. The dynamic POT method based on the BXP distribution, combined with the generalized autoregressive conditional heteroscedasticity type process, introduced by Bollerslev (1986), could be considered as future work of this study.

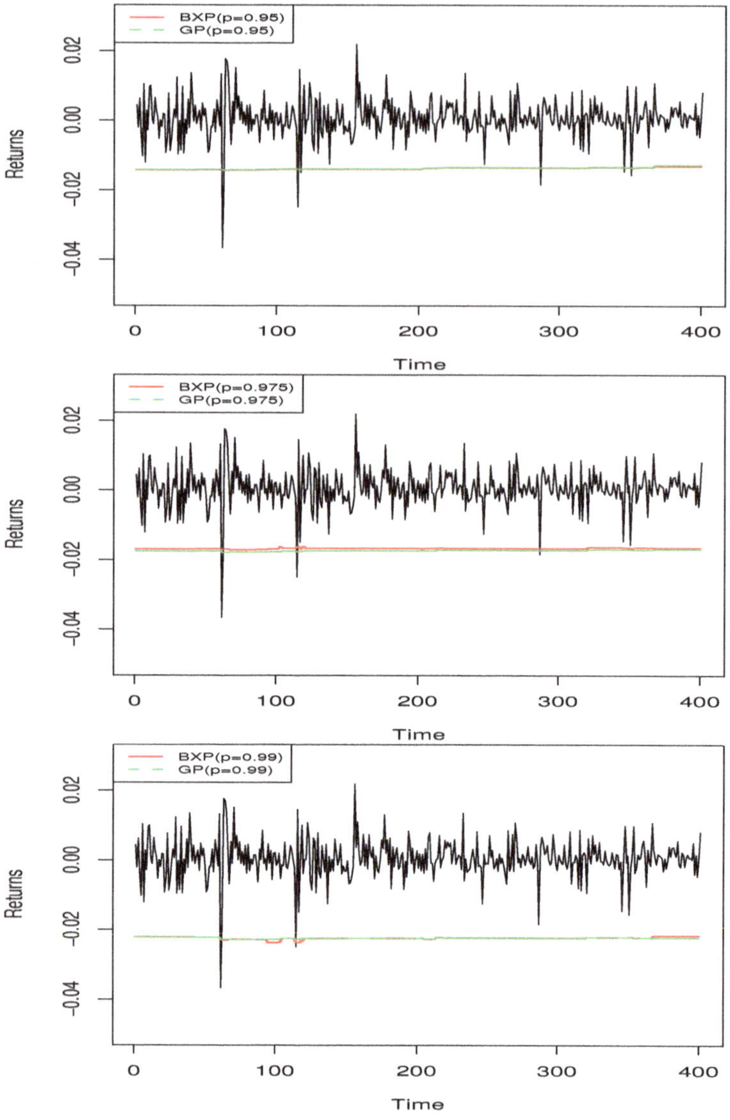

Figure 6. Daily VaR estimates of the BXP and GP models.

9. Conclusions

In this study, we proposed a new distribution that was referred to as the Burr X Pareto (BXP) using the Burr X generator. Some mathematical properties were obtained. The estimation of the model parameters is performed by the MLE, LS and WLS methods. We compare the distribution with a few other models using two real datasets. It is expected that the BXP distribution will serve as a better alternative in modelling real-life datasets. Value-at-Risk estimation with the BXP distribution is presented using time series data, we showed that the new model could be considered as an alternative VaR model against the generalized Pareto model for financial institutions.

Author Contributions: Mustafa Ç. Korkmaz, Emrah Altun, Haitham M. Yousof, Ahmed Z. Afify and Saralees Nadarajah have contributed jointly to all of the sections of the paper.

Conflicts of Interest: The authors declare no conflict of interest.

References

Afify, Ahmed Z., Haitham M. Yousof, Gholamhossein Hamedani, and Gokarna Aryal. 2016. The exponentiated Weibull-Pareto distribution with Application. *Journal of Statistical Theory and Applications* 15: 326–44.

Akinsete, Alfred, Felix Famoye, and Carl Lee. 2008. The beta-Pareto distribution. *Statistics* 42: 547–63.

Balkema, August Aimé, and Laurens De Haan. 1974. Residual life time at great age. *The Annals of Probability* 2: 792–804.

Bourguignon, Marcelo, Rodrigo B. Silva, Luz M. Zea, and Gauss M. Cordeiro. 2013. The Kumaraswamy Pareto distribution. *Journal of Statistical Theory and Applications* 12: 129–44.

Bollerslev, Tim. 1986. Generalized autoregressive conditional heteroskedasticity. *Journal of Econometrics* 31: 307–27.

Feigl, Polly, and Marvin Zelen. 1965. Estimation of exponential survival probabilities with concomitant information. *Biometrics* 21: 826–38.

Gómez-Déniz, Emilio, and Enrique Calderín-Ojeda. 2015. Modelling insurance data with the Pareto ArcTan distribution. *ASTIN Bulletin The Journal of the International Actuarial Association* 45: 639–60.

Gupta, Ramesh C., Pushpa Gupta, and Rameshwar Gupta. 1998. Modeling failure time data by Lehmann alternatives. *Communications in Statistics-Theory and Methods* 27: 887–904.

Johnson, Norman L., Samuel Kotz, and Narayanaswamy Balakrishnan. 1994. *Continuous Univariate Distributions*. New York: Wiley, vol. 1.

Kuş, Coşkun. 2007. A new lifetime distribution. *Computational Statistics & Data Analysis* 51: 4497–509.

Mead, Mohamed E., Ahmed Z. Afify, Gholamhossein Hamedani, and Indranil Ghosh. 2017. The beta exponential Frechet distribution with applications. *Austrian Journal of Statistics* 46: 41–63.

Nadarajah, Saralees, and Sumaya Eljabri. 2013. The Kumaraswamy GP distribution. *Journal of Data Science* 11: 739–66.

Pickands III, James. 1975. Statistical inference using extreme order statistics. *The Annals of Statistics* 3: 119–31.

Stoppa, Gabriele. 1990. A new model for income size distribution. In *Income and Wealth Distribution, Inequality and Poverty*. Berlin: Springer, pp. 33–41.

Swain, James J., Sekhar Venkatraman, and James R. Wilson. 1988. Least squares estimation of distribution function in Johnsons translation system. *Journal of Statistical Computation and Simulation* 29: 271–97.

Tahir, Muhammad H., Gauss M. Cordeiro, Ayman Alzaatreh, M. Mansoor, and M. Zubair. 2016. A New Weibull-Pareto Distribution: Properties and Applications. *Communications in Statistics-Simulation and Computation* 45: 3548–67.

Yousof, Haitham M., Ahmed Z. Afify, Gholamhossein Hamedani, and Gokarna Aryal. 2016. The Burr X generator of distributions for lifetime data. *Journal of Statistical Theory and Applications* 16: 1–19.

Journal of
Risk and Financial Management

MDPI

Article

Bivariate Kumaraswamy Models via Modified FGM Copulas: Properties and Applications

Indranil Ghosh

Department of Mathematics and Statistics, University of North Carolina, Wilmington, NC 28403, USA; ghoshi@uncw.edu

Received: 13 September 2017; Accepted: 26 October 2017; Published: 1 November 2017

Abstract: A copula is a useful tool for constructing bivariate and/or multivariate distributions. In this article, we consider a new modified class of FGM (Farlie–Gumbel–Morgenstern) bivariate copula for constructing several different bivariate Kumaraswamy type copulas and discuss their structural properties, including dependence structures. It is established that construction of bivariate distributions by this method allows for greater flexibility in the values of Spearman's correlation coefficient, ρ and Kendall's τ.

Keywords: bivariate Kumaraswamy distribution; copula based construction; Kendall's tau; dependence structures

1. Introduction

Over the last decade or so, there has been a growing interest in constructing various bivariate distributions and study their dependence structure. For an excellent survey on this, an interested reader is suggested to see Balakrishnan and Lai (2009) and the references therein. Of late, copula based methods of construction have also gained a considerable amount of attention, mainly due to their analytical tractability in the sense of discussing dependence structure between two dependent random variables. A copula is a multivariate distribution function whose marginals are uniform on $[0,1]$ (see Sklar (1959), Nelsen (2006) for further details). It couples or links the marginal distributions to their joint distribution. In order to obtain a bivariate/multivariate distribution function, one needs to simply combine two (in the bivariate case) and/or several marginal distribution functions with any copula function. Consequently, for the purpose of statistical modeling, it is desirable to have a plethora of copulas at one's disposal. One of the most important parametric family of copulas is the Farlie–Gumbel–Morgenstern (FGM, henceforth) family defined as $C(u,v) = uv[1 + \theta(1-u)(1-v)]$, $(u,v) \in (0,1)$, where $\theta \in [-1,1]$. This family of copulas have the following properties. Such family is derived from so called Farlie–Gumbel–Morgenstern distributions considered by Morgenstern (1956) and Gumbel (1960) and further developed by Farlie (1960).

- Symmetry: $C(u,v) = C(v,u)$, $\forall (u,v) \in [0,1]^2$, and have the lower and upper tail dependence coefficients equal to zero.
- It is positive quadrant dependent (PQD) for $\theta \in (0,1]$ and negative quadrant dependent (NQD) for $\theta \in [-1,0)$.

However, the major drawback of FGM copula is that the range of values of Spearman's correlation coefficient (ρ) and Kendal's (τ) is $[-1/3, 1/3]$ and $[-2/9, 2/9]$, respectively. To overcome this limited nature of dependence, several authors proposed extensions of this family (for example, Bairamov and Kotz (2000), Rodriguez-Lallena and Ubeda-Flores (2004)). It is to be noted here that a good number of literary works are available for the FGM family and the associated dependence parameter. Huang and Kotz (1999) studied a polynomial type parameter extensions of the FGM bivariate distribution and have shown that the positive correlation between the marginal distributions can be increased up to 0.39, while the maximal negative correlation remains at $-1/3$. Lai and Xie (2000) used uniform representation of the FGM bivariate distributions having positive quadrant dependence (henceforth, PQD) with the association parameter between 0 and 1. Bairamov and Kotz (2000) showed that, for such a bivariate family, the related association parameter has a much wider range. In another article, Bairamov et al. (2001) developed a new generalization of the bivariate FGM distribution by introducing additional parameters. In their representation, with some specific choice of the functions $A(x) = 1 - x$, and $B(y) = 1 - y$ (see Equation (1) of Bairamov et al. (2001), they have shown that the admissible range for the association parameter is between $[-1, 1]$, while the Pearson correlation coefficient ρ between X and Y will never exceed $1/3$.

This fuels working in this direction in the sense of considering a modified FGM class and using it as a pivot for constructing bivariate Kumaraswamy models.

The Kumaraswamy distribution (Kumaraswamy 1980) is a two parameter absolutely continuous distribution useful for double bounded random processes with hydrological applications. The Kumaraswamy distribution (hereafter the KW distribution) on the interval $(0, 1)$ has its probability density function (pdf) and its cumulative distribution function (cdf) with two shape parameters $a > 0$ and $b > 0$ defined by

$$f(x) = abx^{a-1}(1 - x^a)^{b-1}, \quad (0 < x < 1), \quad \text{and} \quad F(x) = 1 - (1 - x^a)^b. \tag{1}$$

If a random variable X has Equation (1) as its density, then we will write $X \sim KW(\delta, \beta)$ (for details, see Jones (2009)). The density function in Equation (1) has similar properties to those of the beta distribution. The KW pdf is unimodal, uniantimodal, increasing, decreasing or constant depending (similar to the beta distribution) on the values of the parameters. However, the construction of bivariate KW distributions has received limited attention. Barreto-Souza and Lemonte (2013) introduced a bivariate KW distribution related to a Marshall–Olkin survival copula and discussed some structural properties of their bivariate KW distributions. Arnold and Ghosh (2017) discussed some different strategies for constructing legitimate bivariate KW models via Arnold–Ng type copula approach. Recently, Ghosh and Ray (2016) discussed some copula based approach to construct several bivariate KW type models along with an application to a real life data set focusing on financial risk assessment. This article is a follow up paper to Ghosh and Ray (2016), in which we examine in detail the utility of a well-known bivariate FGM copula by a slight modification to allow greater flexibility in modeling various types of data sets. In this article, we start with a standard KW quantile function from two independent KW distributions (with two different sets of shape parameters) and construct the corresponding bivariate copula with different shape parameters. The rest of the article is organized as follows: in Section 2, we define the modified FGM copula and discuss some structural properties. In Section 3, we consider four special classes of modified bivariate KW FGM type copulas for constructing bivariate KW distributions. In Section 4, we establish some dependence structures for those developed bivariate KW FGM type copulas. In Section 5, an outline of simulation from the proposed copula model is provided. In Section 6, some applications of the four bivariate KW-FGM type copula models on two real-life data insurance data sets are considered for illustrative purposes. In Section 7, some concluding remarks are presented.

2. Modified Bivariate FGM Copula

We consider the following modified version of the bivariate FGM copula defined as

$$C(u, v) = uv\left[1 + \theta\Phi(u)\Psi(v)\right] = uv + \theta\widetilde{\Phi(u)}\widetilde{\Psi(v)}, \tag{2}$$

where $\widetilde{\Phi(u)} = u\Phi(u)$, and $\widetilde{\Psi(v)} = v\Psi(v)$, and $\theta \in [-1, 1]$.
For a detailed study on this family of bivariate copula, see Rodriguez-Lallena and Ubeda-Flores (2004), where $\Phi(u)$ and $\Psi(v)$ are two absolutely continuous functions on $(0, 1)$ with the following conditions.

- $\Phi(0) = \Psi(0) = \Phi(1) = \Psi(1) = 0$. This is known as a boundary condition.
- $\min\{\alpha\beta, \xi\eta\} \geq 1$, where $\alpha = inf\{\frac{\partial\widetilde{\Phi(u)}}{\partial u} : u \in A_1\} < 0$,

  where $\frac{\partial\widetilde{\Phi(u)}}{\partial u} = \Phi(u) + u\frac{\partial\Phi(u)}{\partial u}$,

  $\beta = sup\{\frac{\partial\widetilde{\Phi(u)}}{\partial u} : u \in A_1\} > 0$.

  Again, $\xi = inf\{\frac{\partial\widetilde{\Psi(v)}}{\partial v} : v \in A_2\} < 0$, and

  $\eta = sup\{\frac{\partial\widetilde{\Psi(v)}}{\partial v} : v \in A_2\} > 0$, where

$$A_1 = \{u \in (0,1) : \frac{\partial\widetilde{\Phi(u)}}{\partial u} exists\},$$

$$A_2 = \{v \in (0,1) : \frac{\partial\widetilde{\Psi(v)}}{\partial v} exists\}.$$

Theorem 1. *The function in Equation (2) is a valid copula provided, the functions $\widetilde{\Phi(u)}$, $\widetilde{\Psi(v)}$ satisfy all the conditions stated above. In addition, provided all the conditions are satisfied, the bivariate copula in Equation (2) is absolutely continuous.*

Proof. The proof immediately follows, since it matches with the form of bivariate copula (Equation (3), p. 316) in Rodriguez-Lallena and Ubeda-Flores (2004). □

First, we make a note of the following:

- The associated bivariate copula density from Equation (2) will be

$$c(u,v) = \frac{\partial C(u,v)}{\partial u \partial v} = 1 + \theta\Phi(u)\Psi(v)\left\{\left[1 + u\frac{\partial\Phi(u)}{\partial u}\right]\left[1 + v\frac{\partial\Phi(v)}{\partial v}\right]\right\}. \quad (3)$$

- The conditional copula density of U given $V = v$, from Equation (3), will be

$$c(u|v) = \frac{\partial C(u,v)}{\partial v} = u\left\{1 + \theta\Phi(u)\Psi(v)\left(1 + v\right)\right\}. \quad (4)$$

Similarly, one can find the conditional copula density of V given $U = u$.

It is noteworthy to mention that copulas are instrumental for understanding the dependence between random variables. With them, we can separate the underlying dependence from the marginal distributions. It is well known that a copula that characterizes dependence is invariant under strictly monotone transformations. Subsequently, a better global measure of dependence would also be invariant under such transformations. Among other dependence measures, Kendall's and Spearman's are invariant under strictly monotone transformations of the random variables, and, as we will see in the next section, they can be expressed in terms of the associated copula.

- Kendall's τ: This measures the amount of concordance present in a bivariate distribution. Suppose that (X,Y) and $(\tilde{X},\tilde{Y})$ are two independent pairs of random variables from a joint distribution function. We say that these pairs are concordant if "large values of one tend to be associated" with "large values of the other", and "small values of one" tend to be associated with "small values of the other". The pairs are called discordant if large goes with small or vice versa. Algebraically we have concordant pairs if $(X - \tilde{X})(Y - \tilde{Y}) > 0$ and discordant pairs if we reverse the inequality. Let X and Y be continuous random variables with copula C. Then, Kendall's τ is given by

$$\tau_s(X,Y) = 4\iint_{[0,1]^2} C(u,v)dC(u,v) - 1. \tag{5}$$

- Spearman's ρ: For two random variables, X and Y are equal to the linear correlation coefficient between $F_1(X)$ and $F_2(Y)$, where F_1 and F_2 are the marginal distributions of X and Y, respectively. Then, Spearman's ρ_s is given by

$$\rho_s(X,Y) = \rho\left(U = F_1(X), V = F_2(Y)\right) = 12\iint_{[0,1]^2} uvdC(u,v) - 3, \tag{6}$$

where ρ is the linear correlation coefficient.

Alternatively, $\rho_s(X,Y)$ can be written as $\rho_s = 12\int_0^1\int_0^1 [C(u,v) - uv]\, dudv$. Also, as mentioned earlier, one can equivalently show that $\rho_s(U,V) = \rho\left(F_1(X), F_2(V)\right)$. For details on such copula based measures of dependence, see Nelsen (2006).

Proposition 1. *Let (X,Y) be a random pair with copula $C(u,v)$ given by Equation (2). Then, the expressions for Kendall's tau and Spearman's rho are*

- $\rho_s(X,Y) = \theta A(u,v)$, *where* $A(u,v) = 12\left[\int_0^1 u\Phi(u)du\right]\left[\int_0^1 v\Psi(v)dv\right]$,
- $$\begin{aligned}\tau_s(X,Y) &= \frac{2}{3}\rho_\theta + \int_0^1 v^2\frac{\Psi'(v)}{\Psi(v)}dv\left\{2 + \int_0^1 u^2\frac{\Phi'(u)}{\Phi(u)}du\right\} \\ &\quad +\theta^2\left\{\left(\int_0^1 u\Phi'(u)\Phi(u)du\right)\left(\int_0^1 v\Psi'(v)\Psi(v)dv\right)\right\},\end{aligned}$$

respectively.

Proof. The proofs are almost similar in approach for the two coefficients. First, consider for the Spearman's $\rho_s(X,Y)$. For our copula model in Equation (2), the corresponding $\rho_s(X,Y)$ will be

$$\begin{aligned}\rho_s(X,Y) &= 12\int_0^1\int_0^1 C(u,v)dudv - 3 \\ &= 12\left[\int_0^1 v\left(\int_0^1 u(1+\theta\Phi(u)\Psi(v))du\right)dv\right] - 3.\end{aligned} \tag{7}$$

Next, consider the integral in parenthesis, which, after some simplification, reduces to

$$\int_0^1 u(1+\theta\Phi(u)\Psi(v))du = \frac{1}{2} + \theta\Psi(v)\int_0^1 u\Phi(u)du. \tag{8}$$

Substituting Equation (8) in Equation (7), we get

$$\begin{aligned}\rho_s(X,Y) &= 12\left[\int_0^1 v\left(\frac{1}{2} + \theta\Psi(v)\int_0^1 u\Phi(u)du\right)\right]dv - 3 \\ &= \theta A(u,v),\end{aligned}$$

after simple algebraic operation—hence the result.

□

Next, for the proof of $\tau_s(X,Y)$, note that from Equations (2) and (3), one may write (by taking their product)

$$\begin{aligned} C(u,v)c(u,v) &= uv + \theta uv\Phi(u)\Psi(v) + (\theta\Phi(u)\Psi(v))\left\{u\left[1+u\frac{\partial\Phi(u)}{\partial u}\right]\right\}\left\{v\left[1+v\frac{\partial\Phi(v)}{\partial v}\right]\right\} \\ &+ \left(\theta^2 uv\Phi^2(u)\Psi^2(v)\right)\Phi(u)\Psi(v)\left\{u\left[1+u\frac{\partial\Phi(u)}{\partial u}\right]\right\}\left\{v\left[1+v\frac{\partial\Phi(v)}{\partial v}\right]\right\}. \end{aligned} \tag{9}$$

Our result in the expression for $\tau_s(X,Y)$ immediately follows by substituting Equation (9) in Equation (5), and after some simple algebra—hence the result. In the next section, we will consider some specific choices of $\Phi(u)$ and $\Psi(v)$ to construct bivariate Kumaraswamy type copulas.

3. Bivariate KW-FGM Type Models

In this section, we discuss in detail two different types of bivariate FGM type copula models to construct bivariate KW-type distribution.

Bivariate KW-FGM (Type I) Model:

Here, we consider the following functional form for both $\Phi(u)$ and $\Psi(v)$:

- $\Phi(u) = u(1-u^{a_1})^{b_1}$, for $(a_1, b_1) > 0$,
- $\Psi(v) = v(1-v^{a_2})^{b_2}$, for $(a_2, b_2) > 0$.

Note that this particular functional form does satisfy all the conditions stated earlier for $\Phi(u)$ and $\Psi(v)$. In that case, the corresponding bivariate copula (obtained from Equation (2)) will be given by

$$C(u,v) = uv\left[1+\theta\left(u(1-u^{a_1})^{b_1}\right)\left(v(1-v^{a_2})^{b_2}\right)\right]. \tag{10}$$

Next, suppose $X_1 \sim KW(\lambda_1, \alpha_1)$ $X_2 \sim KW(\lambda_2, \alpha_2)$ and they are independent. Then, using Equation (10), a bivariate dependent FGM-Kumaraswamy (Type I) distribution will be of the following form (replacing u and v by the quantiles of X_1 and X_2, respectively):

$$\begin{aligned} &F(x_1,x_2) \\ &= \left(1-\left(1-x_1^{\lambda_1}\right)^{\alpha_1}\right)\left(1-\left(1-x_1^{\lambda_2}\right)^{\alpha_2}\right) \\ &\times\left\{1+\theta\left(1-\left(1-x_1^{\lambda_1}\right)^{\alpha_1}\right)\left(1-\left(1-\left(1-x_1^{\lambda_1}\right)^{\alpha_1}\right)^{b_1}\right)\right. \\ &\times\left.\left(1-\left(1-x_2^{\lambda_2}\right)^{\alpha_2}\right)\left(1-\left(1-\left(1-x_2^{\lambda_2}\right)^{\alpha_2}\right)^{b_2}\right)\right\}, \end{aligned}$$

for $(\lambda_1, \lambda_2, \alpha_1, \alpha_2) > 0$ and $0 < (x_1, x_2) < 1$.

Bivariate KW-FGM (Type II) Model:

Here, we consider the following functional form for both $\Phi(u)$ and $\Psi(v)$:

- $\Phi(u) = u^{\delta_1}(1-u)^{1-\delta_1}$, for $\delta_1 > 0$,
- $\Psi(v) = v^{\delta_2}(1-v)^{1-\delta_2}$, for $\delta_2 > 0$.

Note that this particular functional form does satisfy all the conditions stated earlier for $\Phi(u)$ and $\Psi(v)$. In that case, the corresponding bivariate copula (henceforth, BK-FGM(Type II) copula) will be given by

$$C(u,v) = uv\left[1+\theta u^{\delta_1}v^{\delta_2}(1-u)^{1-\delta_1}(1-v)^{1-\delta_2}\right]. \tag{11}$$

In this case, like the previous one, a bivariate dependent KW-FGM (Type II) distribution, arising from two independent KW variables, will be of the following form:

$$
\begin{aligned}
& F(x_1, x_2) \\
& = \left(1-\left(1-x_1^{\lambda_1}\right)^{\alpha_1}\right)^{\delta_1}\left(1-\left(1-x_2^{\lambda_2}\right)^{\alpha_2}\right)^{\delta_2} \\
& \times\left[1+\theta\left(1-\left(1-x_1^{\lambda_1}\right)^{\alpha_1}\right)^{\delta_1}\left(\left(1-x_1^{\lambda_1}\right)^{\alpha_1(1-\delta_1)}\right)\right. \\
& \left.\times\left(1-\left(1-x_2^{\lambda_2}\right)^{\alpha_2}\right)^{\delta_2}\left(\left(1-x_2^{\lambda_2}\right)^{\alpha_2(1-\delta_2)}\right)\right].
\end{aligned}
$$

Bivariate KW-FGM (Type III) Model:

Here, we consider the following functional form for both $\Phi(u)$ and $\Psi(v)$:

- $\Phi(u) = u\left[\log\left(1+(1-u)\right)\right]$,
- $\Psi(v) = v\left[\log\left(1+(1-v)\right)\right]$.

Note that this particular functional form does satisfy all the conditions stated earlier for $\Phi(u)$ and $\Psi(v)$. In that case, the corresponding BK-FGM (Type III) copula will be given by

$$
C(u,v) = uv\left[1+\theta uv\left\{\log\left(1+(1-u)\right)\log\left(1+(1-v)\right)\right\}\right]. \tag{12}
$$

In this case, one can also obtain a closed form expression for the associated distribution function.

Bivariate KW-FGM (Type-IV) Copula:

For the standard KW distribution with parameters (a, b), we have the pdf, cdf and the inverse cdf are given, respectively, by

$f_i(x_i) = abx_i^{a-1}(1-x_i^a)^{b-1}$, $F_i(x_i) = 1-(1-x_i^a)^b$ and $F_i^{-1}(u_i) = 1-(1-u_i^{1/b})^{1/a}$, $a>0$, $b>0$.

Hence, the associated copula for suitable parameters a and b, and having two given marginal distributions that are the standard KW distributions, has the following form:

$$
\begin{aligned}
C(u_1, u_2) &= u_1\left(1-(1-u_2)^{1/b}\right)^{1/a} + u_2\left(1-(1-u_1)^{1/b}\right)^{1/a} \\
&\quad -\left(1-(1-u_1)^{1/b}\right)^{1/a}\left(1-(1-u_2)^{1/b}\right)^{1/a}.
\end{aligned} \tag{13}
$$

For details on this, see Ghosh and Ray (2016).

4. Some Properties of the Bivariate KW-FGM Type Copulas

Next, we have the following:

1. For the BK-FGM (Type I) bivariate copula
   - Closed form expression for Kendall's τ is not available.
   - Spearman's correlation coefficient will be

     $$\rho_\theta = \theta\left(a_1 a_2\right)^{-1},$$

     provided $\max(a_1, a_2) < 3$.
2. For the BK-FGM (Type II) bivariate copula
   - Kendall's τ will be

     $$
     \begin{aligned}
     \tau_s(X,Y) &= B(\delta_1+2, 2-\delta_1)B(\delta_1+3, 2-\delta_1) + (\delta_1-1)[B(\delta_1+2, 2-\delta_1) - B(\delta_1+1, 1-\delta_1)] \\
     &\quad +\delta_1 B(\delta_1+2, 1-\delta_1)\left(\delta_1-\frac{1}{2}\right) - \frac{B(\delta_1+1, 1-\delta_1)}{2},
     \end{aligned}
     $$

     provided $\delta_1 < 1$.

- Corresponding Spearman's correlation coefficient will be

$$\rho_s(X,Y) = \theta\left(B(\delta_1+2, 2-\delta_1)\right)^2,$$

provided $\delta_1 < 2$.

3. For the BK-FGM (Type III) copula, no closed form expressions for Kendall's τ and Spearman's ρ are available. They need to be evaluated numerically.
4. For the BK-FGM (Type III) copula
   - Kendall's τ will be

$$\tau_s(X,Y) = 4\left(1 - \frac{\Gamma(1+1/a)\Gamma(1+b)}{\Gamma(1+1/a+b)} - \left(1 - \frac{\Gamma(1+1/a)\Gamma(1+b)}{\Gamma(1+1/a+b)}\right)^2\right) - 1$$

(by straightforward integration).

   - Spearman's correlation coefficient will be

$$\rho_s(X,Y) = 12\left(1 - \frac{\Gamma(1+1/a)\Gamma(1+b)}{\Gamma(1+1/a+b)} - \left(1 - \frac{\Gamma(1+1/a)\Gamma(1+b)}{\Gamma(1+1/a+b)}\right)^2\right) - 3.$$

Dependence Properties

In this section, we focus on the following properties.

Tail Dependence Property:

Let X and Y be two continuous random variables with $X \sim F$, and $Y \sim G$. The upper tail dependence coefficient (parameter) λ_U is the limit (if it exists) of the conditional probability that Y is greater than 100α th percentile of G given that X is greater than the 100α th percentile of F as α approaches 1:

$$\lambda_U = \lim_{\alpha\uparrow 1} P\left(Y > G^{-1}(\alpha)|X > F^{-1}(\alpha)\right).$$

If $\lambda_U > 0$, then X and Y are upper tail dependent and asymptotically independent otherwise. Similarly, the lower tail dependence coefficient is defined as

$$\lambda_L = \lim_{\alpha\downarrow 0} P\left(Y \le G^{-1}(\alpha)|X \le F^{-1}(\alpha)\right).$$

Let C be the copula of X and Y. Then, equivalently, we can write $\lambda_L = \lim_{u\downarrow 0}\frac{C(u,u)}{u}$ and $\lambda_U = \lim_{u\downarrow 0}\frac{\tilde{C}(u,u)}{u}$, where $\tilde{C}(u,u)$ is the corresponding joint survival copula given by

$$\tilde{C}(u,u) = 1 - 2u + C(u,u).$$

Next, we consider the following.

- In our case (for the bivariate KW-FGM (type I) copula model),

$$\begin{aligned}\lambda_L &= \lim_{u\downarrow 0}\frac{C(u,u)}{u}\\ &= \lim_{u\downarrow 0} u^2\left(1+\theta\left(u^2(1-u^{a_1})^{b_1}(1-u^{a_2})^{b_2}\right)\right) \\ &= 0.\end{aligned} \tag{14}$$

Thus, X and Y are asymptotically independent. The corresponding joint survival copula will be given by

$$\begin{aligned}\tilde{C}(u,u) &= 1-2u+C(u,u)\\ &= 1-2u+u^2\left(1+\theta\left(u^2\left[1-((1-u)^{a_1})\right]^{b_1}\left[1-((1-u)^{a_2})\right]^{b_2}\right)\right).\end{aligned}$$

Again,

$$\begin{aligned}\lambda_U &= \lim_{u\uparrow 1} \frac{1-2u+C(u,u)}{1-u} \\ &= \lim_{u\uparrow 1} \frac{2(1-u)}{1-u} - \lim_{u\to 1} \frac{1-C(u,u)}{1-u} \\ &= 2 - \lim_{u\uparrow 1} \frac{1-u^2\left(1+\theta\left(u^2\left[1-((1-u)^{a_1})\right]^{b_1}\left[1-((1-u)^{a_2})\right]^{b_2}\right)\right)}{1-u} \\ &= 0.\end{aligned}$$

Thus, (X, Y) are asymptotically dependent.

- For the bivariate KW-FGM (type II) copula model,

$$\begin{aligned}\lambda_L &= \lim_{u\downarrow 0} \frac{C(u,u)}{u} \\ &= \lim_{u\downarrow 0} u^2\left(1+\theta\left(u^{\delta_1+\delta_2}(1-u)^{2-(\delta_1+\delta_2)}\right)\right) \\ &= 0,\end{aligned} \tag{15}$$

provided $2 > \delta_1 + \delta_2$. Hence, it is asymptotically independent provided $2 > \delta_1 + \delta_2$.

Again,

$$\begin{aligned}\lambda_U &= \lim_{u\uparrow 1} \frac{1-2u+C(u,u)}{1-u} \\ &= \lim_{u\uparrow 1} \frac{2(1-u)}{1-u} - \lim_{u\to 1} \frac{1-C(u,u)}{1-u} \\ &= 2 - \lim_{u\uparrow 1} \frac{1-u^2\left(1+\theta\left(u^{\delta_1+\delta_2}(1-u)^{2-(\delta_1+\delta_2)}\right)\right)}{1-u} \\ &= 0,\end{aligned}$$

provided $\delta_1 + \delta_2 < 2$, this again implying that (X, Y) are asymptotically dependent.

Similarly, one can establish these properties for the bivariate KW-FGM (type III) and (type IV) copula models.

Positive Quadrant Dependent (PQD) and Left-Tail Decreasing (LTD) Property:

According to Amblard and Girard (2002), (Theorem 3), for $\theta > 0$ and (X, Y) a random pair with copula $C(u, v)$ as defined in equation (2), we have the following result:

- X and Y are PQD if and only if either $\forall\, u \in (0,1)$ and $\forall\, u \in (0,1)$, $\Phi(u)\,[\Psi(v)] \geq 0$ or $\Phi(u)\,[\Psi(v)] \leq 0$,
- X and Y are LTD if and only if $\frac{\Phi(u)}{u}$ and $\frac{\Psi(v)}{v}$ is monotone. Next, consider the following:

Proposition 2. *The BK-FGM (Type I, Type II and Type III) copulas are PQD.*

Proof. For the modified BK-FGM (Type I) copula, we have $\Phi(u) = u^{a_1}(1-u^{a_1})^{b_1}$ and $\Psi(v) = v^{a_2}(1-v^{a_2})^{b_2}$. Note that, for any real $(a_1, a_2, b_1, b_2) > 0$, $\Phi(u) \geq 0$, for all $u \in (0,1)$ as well as $\Psi(v) \geq 0$, for all $v \in (0,1)$. Hence, (X, Y) are PQD. □

Similarly, one can easily check the PQD property for the other two copula models.

Proposition 3. *The BK-FGM (Type I and Type III) copula exhibits LTD properties, while, for the BK-FGM (Type II), it is indeterministic.*

Proof. For the modified BK-FGM (Type I) copula, consider the ratio $\frac{\Phi(u)}{u} = u^{a_1}(1-u^{a_1})^{b_1}$. It is monotonically decreasing provided, $a_1 > 1$ and for any $b_1 > 0$, and it is also true for any $u \in (0,1)$. Similar results hold for the other ratio $\frac{\Psi(v)}{v}$, for any $v \in (0,1)$. Hence, it is LTD for only $a_1 > 1$ and for any $b_1 > 0$, but not for any other possible choices of the constants a_1 and b_1. □

Again, for the modified BK-FGM (Type III)copula, the ratio $\frac{\Phi(u)}{u} = \log(1+(1-u))$. It is monotonically decreasing for any $u \in (0,1)$. Similar results will hold for the other ratio $\frac{\Psi(v)}{v}$, for any $v \in (0,1)$. Hence, it is LTD.

However, for the modified BK-FGM (Type II) copula, these ratios are not uniformly increasing and/or decreasing. This is why it is indeterministic in this sense.

5. Simulation from a Bivariate Copula

There are several different methods (for example, acceptance–rejection sampling for bivariate cases, via transformation to a known bivariate distribution, etc.) that are available to simulate/generate bivariate random samples from a bivariate copula. We can, in principle, use the following result Joe (1997), to simulate random samples from our modified BK-FGM type copula as follows. Let us define the conditional copula distribution function (say, of V given $U = u$), $C_{2|1}(v|u) = \frac{\partial C(u,v)}{\partial u}$. Next, if U and W are independent $U(0,1)$ random variables, then $(U,V) = \left(U, C_{2|1}^{-1}(W|U)\right)$ will have the distribution $C(u,v)$. This method, sometimes known as conditional distribution approach or iterative conditioning, is appealing because it involves only univariate simulation. In our case, we do have closed form expressions of $C_{2|1}(v|u)$ for both types of modified BK-FGM bivariate copula available. For example, for the modified FGM BK (type I) copula, one can write (from Equation (10))

$$
\begin{aligned}
C_{2|1}(v|u) &= \frac{\partial C(u,v)}{\partial u} \\
&= 2\theta u v^2 \left((1-u^{a_1})^{b_1}\right)\left(v(1-v^{a_2})^{b_2}\right) + v\left\{1-\theta b_1 u^{a_1}\left((1-u^{a_1})^{b_1}\right)\left(v(1-v^{a_2})^{b_2}\right)\right\}.
\end{aligned}
$$

Consequently, we can easily apply this method. Needless to say, there are other distinct sampling procedures that are also available (for example, importance sampling, adaptive acceptance–rejection sampling, etc.), which is suitable for other classes of copulas.

6. Applications

6.1. Application in Risk Management

In practice, several risk managers employ VaR (Value at Risk) as a tool of risk measurement. Briefly speaking, VaR is the maximal potential loss of a position or a portfolio on some investment horizon at a given confidence level. Because of the enormous literature, we only provide its definition. Let $\{P_t\}_{t=1}^{n}$ be the market values of an asset or a portfolio of assets over n periods, and $X_t = -\log\left(\frac{P_t}{P_{t-1}}\right)$ be the negative log return (loss) over the t-th period. Next, given a positive value α close to 0, the VaR of X at confidence level $(1-\alpha)$ is given by

$$
VaR = inf\{x \in \mathbb{R} | P(X \leq x) \geq 1-\alpha\}.
$$

For a detailed study on the computation of VaR used in the pure copula method, an interested reader is suggested to see Ouyang et al. (2009). Here, we will propose one idea based on bivariate KW-FGM copula (Type II). We list the steps as follows:

1. Simulate U, V and W independently from standard uniform distribution,
2. If $U \leq \lambda_s$, for the given bivariate KW-FGM (Type II) copula (say, $C_{\rho_s,1}$), take $(X,Y)^T = \left(F_1^{-1}(V), F_2^{-1}(C_{\rho_s,1,U}^{-1}(W))\right)^T$.

3. If $U > \lambda_s$, for the given bivariate KW-FGM (Type II) copula (say, $C_{\rho_s,2}$,), take $(X,Y)^T = \left(F_1^{-1}(V), F_2^{-1}(C_{\rho_s,2,U}^{-1}(W))\right)^T$.

Then, the random vector (X,Y) has the joint distribution

$$\tilde{F}(x,y) = \lambda_s C_{\rho_s,1}(F_1(x), F_2(y)) + (1-\lambda_s) C_{\rho_s,2}(F_1(x), F_2(y)),$$

where $\lambda_s = \frac{\rho_{s,2}-\rho_s}{\rho_{s,2}-\rho_{s,1}}$, and its marginal distributions are F_1 and F_2, and linear correlation is ρ_s. After this, we consider the following formula $R = -\log(\lambda_1 \exp(X_1) + \lambda_2 \exp(X_2))$ to generate the random number of the negative log returns of portfolios. Here, λ_1 and λ_2 are the weights and must satisfy $\lambda_1 + \lambda_2 = 1$. Then, VaR_α will be computed by calculating the $(1-\alpha)$-th quantile of R.

For illustrative purposes, we consider the portfolio composed of Nasdaq and S&P 500 stock indices. The database contains 2972 daily closing prices from 2 January 1992 to 1 October 2003. We denote the log-returns of Nasdaq as variable 1 (X, say) and the log-returns of S&P 500 as variable 2 (Y). For details on this data set, see Palaro and Hotta (2006).

From Table 1, it is evident that the annualized means of both series are positive. Both return series distributions are nearly symmetric and have large kurtosis, with the Nasdaq presenting the larger one. We do not present the autocorrelation functions of the series, but, for the Nasdaq returns, only the autocorrelations of lag 12 and 13 are significant at the 5% level (t statistic equals to 3.68 and 4.48, respectively). There is no significant correlation for the S&P 500 returns at the 5% level. In order to specify the bivariate model for these two returns, and to estimate the associated Var under several bivariate copula models, we will consider some specific Autoregressive integrated moving average-Generalized Autoregressive Conditional Heteroskedastic (or in short, ARMA-GARCH) models, the reason being that return series are usually successfully modeled by ARMA-GARCH models by many authors. As suggested in Palaro and Hotta (2006), we will mainly consider three different ARMA-GARCH models: GARCH-N, GARCH-t, and GARCH-E. In terms of modeling the dependence between the two series, we consider three copula functions that are quite popular among other authors: FGM, Gumbel–Hougaard, Bivariate Gaussian copula along with our bivariate KW-FGM type copulas. In order to asses the accuracy of the VaR estimates at 95%, and 99% confidence level, we followed the procedure as discussed in Palaro and Hotta (2006). In the table below, we present the proportion of observations (in brackets), for $t = 751$ to 2971, where the portfolio loss exceeded the estimated VaR for $\alpha = 0.05$.

Table 1. Descriptive statistics of daily log-returns of Nasdaq and S&P 500 stock indices.

Statistics	Nasdaq	S&P 500
Mean	0.00038	0.00030
Mean (annualized)	10.141%	7.857%
Standard Deviation	0.01694	0.01076
Minimum	−0.10168	−0.07113
Median	0.00122	0.00028
Maximum	0.13255	0.05574
Excess of Kurtosis	4.91481	3.78088
Asymmetry	0.01490	−0.10267

From Table 2, it appears that the Bivariate KW-FGM (Type III) copula model provided a better result in estimating VaR. This is quite expected, since, for the data, the estimated coefficients a_1 and a_2 for the Bivariate KW-FGM (Type III) copula appear to be very close to 1, which then behaves more like a symmetric copula. In addition, for this data, both of the return series are nearly symmetric.

Table 2. Proportion of observations (number of observations in brackets), for t = 751 to 2971, where the portfolio loss exceeded the estimated Value at Risk for $\alpha = 0.05$.

Copula	GARCH-N	GARCH-t	GARCH-E
Nelsen–Ten	0.0675 (167)	0.0698 (122)	0.0322 (63)
Gumbel–Hougaard	0.0666 (128)	0.0207 (46)	0.0312 (69)
Bivariate Gaussian	0.0693 (117)	0.0359 (92)	0.0281 (78)
Bivariate KW-FGM (Type I) copula	0.0828 (82)	0.0244 (42)	0.0206 (46)
Bivariate KW-FGM (Type II) copula	0.2141 (77)	0.0286 (48)	0.0153 (52)
Bivariate KW-FGM (Type III) copula	0.0287 (37)	0.0126 (30)	0.0103 (28)
Bivariate KW-FGM (Type IV) copula	0.1354 (54)	0.0329 (47)	0.0189 (39)

6.2. *An Application to Insurance Data*

Here, we consider one application for the four proposed bivariate KW copula models to a heavily used data set, originally considered by Genest et al. (2009), as well as in Ghosh and Ray (2016). This data set contains two variables:

- X_1: an indemnity payment,
- X_1: an allocated loss adjustment expense (comprising lawyers' fees and claim investigation process).

This data set is comprised of 1500 general liability claims. Several other authors, among others, have used (for e.g., Chen and Fan (2005)) this data set to demonstrate copula-model selection and fitting in an insurance context. We conjecture that this data might well be explained by one or more bivariate Kumaraswamy copula models derived in this paper. For the sake of simplicity, we apply all four bivariate Kumaraswamy copula models to 1466 uncensored claims. As suggested by Genest et al. (2009), based on a comparative study on the numerical estimates of the dependence parameter (θ), this imposed restriction has a very little or no effect on it. For the uncensored sample, the observed value of Kendall's tau is 0.4328. In the table below, we provide results of the goodness-of-fit tests based on the statistics S_n, T_n, and $S_{\xi n}$, with $\xi = 0$. For a detailed description on each of these goodness-of-fit statistics, see Genest et al. (2009).

Here, the dependence parameter θ is estimated in each case through inversion of Kendall's τ. The critical values and p-values reported in Table 1 are based on $N = 30,000$ repetitions of the parametric bootstrap procedure discussed in Genest et al. (2009). From Table 3, it appears that bivariate Kumaraswamy (Type III and Type IV) copula provide a better fit as compared to other BK copula models.

Table 3. Goodness of fit statistics for the insurance data.

Bivariate Copula	θ	S_n	T_n	S_{0n}	p-Value (in %)	Critical Value (c_{2n})
Bivariate KW-FGM (Type I) copula	0.623	3.0755	2.643	1.036	45.3	0.422
Bivariate KW-FGM (Type II) copula	1.233	2.189	3.547	0.427	0.18	0.163
Bivariate KW-FGM (Type III) copula	1.026	0.147	0.564	0.117	78.3	0.795
Bivariate KW-FGM (Type IV) copula	0.342	0.422	0.642	0.137	88.2	0.831
FGM copula	0.589	1.567	2.034	0.493	37.2	0.327
Nelsen-Ten	1.253	2.384	4.031	0.622	43.4	0.285
Gumbel–Hougaard	0.783	1.657	2.842	0.842	18.9	0.638
Bivariate Gaussian	0.732	1.268	2.416	0.715	44.8	0.483

7. Conclusions

In this paper, we consider a modified version of the FGM family of copulas and study some important structural properties including the dependence structure. With this modified version, we consider the construction of bivariate KW distributions and discuss some of their structural properties. It is evident from Equation (2), that, depending on suitable choices of $\Phi()$ and $\Psi()$ functions, satisfying associated boundary conditions as mentioned earlier, one can generate a plethora of such copula models and subsequently develop a wide spectrum of bivariate KW distributions. Our future work would focus on the following:

- Extension to the multivariate case and study several associated properties. It is noteworthy to mention that, albeit complex nature of these type of models (involving several parameters), we expect that multivariate KW distribution construction via such type of copula models will be much more interesting and computationally will be more easy to handle.

- For modeling large losses, asymmetric copulas are more useful as compared to symmetric copulas. Thus, we will consider a family of asymmetric copulas as introduced in Nelsen (2006), Chapter 4, which has the following form:

$$C(u,v) = uv + \theta a(u)b(v), \quad \theta \in [-1,1].$$

Here, a and b are functions defined on the interval $(0,1)$. The associated several types of dependence measures will also be considered. In addition, based on this, bivariate and subsequently multivariate KW distributions construction will be considered and then a comparison study will be made with those bivariate and multivariate KW models constructed under a symmetric class of copulas.

- Since a convex combination of any two (or more) valid copulas is also a copula, we would be interested in studying the role of such a mixture of copula in developing bivariate, and sub- sequently multivariate, Kumaraswamy type distributions. For example, one may start with the following:

$$C^{mixture}(u,v) = \theta_1 C^{symmetric}(u,v) + (1-\theta_1) C^{asymmetric}(u,v)$$

for $\theta_1 \in (0,1]$.

- A natural multivariate extension of the above asymmetric copula would be

$$C(u_1, u_2, \cdots, u_p) = \prod_{i=1}^{p} u_1 + \theta \prod_{i=1}^{p} a_i(u_i),$$

with $(u_1, u_2, \cdots, u_p) \in [0,1]^p, \quad \theta \in [-1,1]$. A natural question would be what judicious choices of the functions $a_i()$, for $i = 1, 2, ..., p$ would result in a tractable model. Associated model inference will be a challenging task due to the involvement of so many parameters. We plan to report all of these findings in a separate article somewhere else.

Acknowledgments: The author would like to thank two anonymous referees for their insightful comments and suggestions, which have greatly helped to improve on an earlier version of this manuscript.

Conflicts of Interest: The author declares no conflict of interest.

References

Amblard, Cécile, and Stéphane Girard. 2002. Symmetry and dependence properties within a semiparametric family of bivariate copulas. *Journal of Nonparametric Statistics* 14: 715–27.

Arnold, Barry C., and Indranil Ghosh. 2017. Bivariate Kumaraswamy models involving use of Arnold–Ng copulas. *Journal of Applied Statistical Science* 22: 227–41.

Bairamov, Ismihan G., and Samuel Kotz. 2000. *On a New Family of Positive Quadrant Dependent Bivariate Distribution*. Technical Report. Washington: The George Washington University.

Bairamov, Ismihan G., Samuel Kotz, and Muhammet Bekci. 2001. New generalized Farlie–Gumbel–Morgenstern distributions and concomitants of order statistics. *Journal of Applied Statistics* 28: 521–36.

Balakrishnan, Narayanaswamy, and Chin-Diew Lai. 2009. *Continuous Bivariate Distributions*, 2nd ed. New York: Springer.

Barreto-Souza, Wagner, and Artur J. Lemonte. 2013. Bivariate Kumaraswamy distribution: Properties and a new method to generate bivariate classes. *Statistics* 47: 1–22.

Chen, Xiaohong, and Yanqin Fan. 2005. Pseudo-likelihood ratio tests for model selection in semiparametric multivariate copula models. *The Canadian Journal of Statistics* 33: 389–414.

Farlie, Dennis J. G. 1960. The performance of some correlation coefficients for a general bivariate distribution. *Biometrika* 47: 307–23.

Ghosh, Indranil, and Samik Ray. 2016. Some alternative bivariate Kumaraswamy type distributions via copula with application in risk management. *Journal of Statistical Theory and Practice* 10: 693–706.

Genest, Christian, Michael Gendron, and Michael Bourdeau-Brien. 2009. The Advent of Copulas in Finance. *The European Journal of Finance* 15: 609–18.

Gumbel, Emil J. 1960. Bivariate exponential distributions. *Journal of American Statistical Association* 55: 698–707.

Huang, Jian Shan, and Samuel Kotz. 1999. Modifications of the Farlie–Gumbel–Morgenstern distributions: A tough hill to climb. *Metrika* 49: 307–23.

Joe, Harry. 1997. *Multivariate Models and Multivariate Dependence Concepts*. New York: Chapman & Hall/ CRC Monographs on Statistics & Applied Probability.

Jones, Chris. 2009. Kumaraswamy's distribution: A beta-type distribution with some tractability advantages. *Statistical Methodology* 6: 70–81.

Kumaraswamy, Poondi. 1980. Generalized probability density-function for double-bounded random-processes. *Journal of Hydrology* 462: 79–88.

Lai, Chin-Diew, and Min Xie. 2000. *Stochastic Ageing and Dependence for Reliability*. New York: Springer.

Morgenstern, David. 1956. Einfache Beispiele zweidimensionaler Verteilungen. *Mitteinlings fu Mathematische Statistik* 8: 234–35.

Nelsen, Roger. 2006. *An Introduction to Copulas*. New York: Springer.

Ouyang, Zi-Sheng, Hui Liao, and Xiang-qun Yang. 2009. Modeling dependence based on mixture copulas and its application in risk management. *Applied Mathematics—A Journal of Chinese Universities* 24: 393–401.

Palaro, Helder P., and Luiz Koodi Hotta. 2006. Using Conditional Copula to Estimate Value at Risk. *Journal of Data Science* 4: 93–115.

Rodriguez-Lallena, Jose Antonio, and Manuel Ubeda-Flores. 2004. A new class of bivariate copulas. *Statistics and Probability Letters* 66: 315–25.

Sklar, Abe. 1959. Fonctions de Repartition 'a n Dimensions et Leurs Marges. *Publications de l'Institut de Statistique de l'Universite de Paris* 8: 229–31.

Journal of
Risk and Financial Management

Article

GARCH Modelling of Cryptocurrencies

Jeffrey Chu [1], Stephen Chan [2], Saralees Nadarajah [1,*] and Joerg Osterrieder [3]

1 School of Mathematics, University of Manchester, Manchester M13 9PL, U.K.; jeffrey.chu@manchester.ac.uk
2 Department of Mathematics and Statistics, American University of Sharjah, Sharjah P.O. Box 26666, UAE; schan@aus.edu
3 School of Engineering, Zurich University of Applied Sciences, 8400 Winterthur, Switzerland; oste@zhaw.ch
* Correspondence: mbbsssn2@manchester.ac.uk

Received: 31 August 2017; Accepted: 28 September 2017; Published: 1 October 2017

Abstract: With the exception of Bitcoin, there appears to be little or no literature on GARCH modelling of cryptocurrencies. This paper provides the first GARCH modelling of the seven most popular cryptocurrencies. Twelve GARCH models are fitted to each cryptocurrency, and their fits are assessed in terms of five criteria. Conclusions are drawn on the best fitting models, forecasts and acceptability of value at risk estimates.

Keywords: exchange rate; maximum likelihood; value at risk

---

1. Introduction

A cryptocurrency can be defined as "a digital asset designed to work as a medium of exchange using cryptography to secure the transactions and to control the creation of additional units of the currency". In recent years, the popularity and use of cryptocurrencies has increased dramatically. For example, the U.K. government is looking at Bitcoin technology (Bitcoin is the first and the most popular cryptocurrency) for tracking taxpayer money. The U.S. government is to sell over 44,000 Bitcoins.

Because of this increasing interest, there is a need to quantify the variation of cryptocurrencies. It is well known that cryptocurrencies are highly volatile compared to traditional currencies. Certainly, their exchange rates cannot be assumed to be independently and identically distributed. Perhaps the most popular models for the exchange rates of traditional currencies are based on Generalized Autoregressive Conditional Heteroskedasticity (GARCH) models. However, there exists little work on fitting of GARCH-type models to the exchange rates of cryptocurrencies. The known work focuses on GARCH modelling of Bitcoin, the first and the most popular cryptocurrency.

Katsiampa (2017) estimated the volatility of Bitcoin through a comparison of GARCH models, and the AR-CGARCH model was shown to give the optimal fit. Urquhart (2017) illustrated that HARmodels are more robust in modelling Bitcoin volatility than traditional GARCH models. Stavroyiannis and Babalos (2017) examined dynamic properties of Bitcoin modelling through univariate and multivariate GARCH models and vector autoregressive specifications. Cermak (2017) used a GARCH (1, 1) to model Bitcoin's volatility with respect to macroeconomic variables, in countries where Bitcoin has the highest volume of trading. The results showed that Bitcoin behaves similarly to fiat currencies in China, the U.S. and Europe, but not in Japan. In particular, Bitcoin appeared to be an attractive asset for investment and store of value in China; Bouoiyour and Selmi (2015, 2016) analysed daily Bitcoin prices using an optimal-GARCH model and showed that the volatility has decreased when comparing data from 2010–2015 with data from the first half of 2015. The asymmetry in the Bitcoin market was still significant, suggesting that Bitcoin prices were driven more by negative than positive shocks; Chen et al. (2016) provided an econometric analysis of the CRIXindex family using data from 2014–2016. Using a variety of GARCH models, they found that the TGARCH (1, 1) model is the best fitting model for all sample data based on discrimination criteria such as the log likelihood, AIC and BIC. In addition, the DCC-GARCH (1, 1) was found to show volatility clustering and time varying covariances between three CRICindices; Letra (2016) used a GARCH (1, 1) model to analyse daily Bitcoin prices and search trends on Google, Wikipedia and tweets on Twitter. They found that Bitcoin prices were influenced by popularity, but also that web content and Bitcoin prices had some predictable power. Dyhrberg (2016a) applied the asymmetric GARCH methodology to explore the hedging capabilities of Bitcoin. It was shown that Bitcoin can be used as a hedge against stocks in the Financial Times Stock Exchange Index and against the American dollar in the short term. Dyhrberg (2016b) used GARCH models to explore the financial asset capabilities of Bitcoin. It was shown that Bitcoin has a place on the financial markets and in portfolio management as it can be classified as something in between gold and the American dollar, on a scale from pure medium of exchange advantages to pure store of value advantages. Bouri et al. (2017) used asymmetric GARCH models to investigate the relationship between price returns and volatility changes in the Bitcoin market around the price crash of 2013.

The aim of this paper is to provide GARCH-type modelling of the seven most popular cryptocurrencies. They are Bitcoin, Dash, Dogecoin, Litecoin, Maidsafecoin, Monero and Ripple. We fit twelve different GARCH-type models to the log returns of the exchange rates of each of these cryptocurrencies. The method of maximum likelihood was used for fitting. The goodness of fit was assessed in terms of five different criteria. Conclusions are drawn on the best fitting GARCH models, forecasts based on them and the ability of the models to estimate value at risk.

The contents of the paper are organized as follows. Section 2 describes the data used and some summary statistics of the data described. Section 3 describes the GARCH-type models fitted and the criteria used to assess their goodness of fit. The results of fitting the models and their discussion are given in Section 4. Finally, some conclusions are noted in Section 5.

2. Data

The data that we used in our analysis were the historical daily global price indices of particular cryptocurrencies and were extracted from the BNC2database from Quandl. In order to obtain the most accurate prices, the global indices were used as they are computed by using a weighted average of the price of each cryptocurrency, using prices from a number of different exchanges, as in Chan et al. (2017). Although our daily data begin only one day earlier than those in Chan et al. (2017), 22 June 2014, the end date is much later, on 17 May 2017. We obtained more up to date data for our analysis so that we could again analyse seven of the top fifteen cryptocurrencies, ranked by market capitalization, in May 2017. The most up to date (daily) market capitalization figures for all cryptocurrencies can be found online; see CoinMarketCap (2017). In May 2017, the top seven cryptocurrencies ranked by market capitalization were the same as those in February 2017 (Chan et al. (2017)) and include Bitcoin, Dash, LiteCoin, MaidSafeCoin, Monero, DogeCoin and Ripple. Other notable cryptocurrencies such as Ethereum, Ethereum Classic, Agur and NEMwere omitted due to the volume of available data. It should be noted that in May 2017, the seven cryptocurrencies represented 90 percent of the total market capitalization. However, due to the volatility of cryptocurrencies, the rankings of the respective cryptocurrencies has since changed. For a brief description of the seven cryptocurrencies, see Chan et al. (2017).

The summary statistics are the largest for Bitcoin, followed by Dash, Litecoin, Monero, Ripple, Maidsafecoin and Dogecoin (Table 1). The log returns for each cryptocurrency are positively skewed. The log returns are heavy tailed with kurtosis greater than that of the normal distribution for Bitcoin, Dash, Litecoin and Ripple. The log returns are light tailed with kurtosis less than that of the normal distribution for Dogecoin, Maidsafecoin and Monero.

Figure 1 shows the histograms of the log returns of the daily market price indices for all exchanges trading in Bitcoin, Dash, Dogecoin, Litecoin, Maidsafecoin, Monero and Ripple. From the plots, we find that the log returns are more or less symmetrically distributed. Some histograms appear more peaked than others.

Table 1. Summary statistics of the exchange rates of Bitcoin, Dash, Dogecoin, Litecoin, Maidsafecoin, Monero and Ripple from 22 June 2014–17 May 2017.

Statistic	Bitcoin	Dash	Dogecoin	Litecoin	Maidsafecoin	Monero	Ripple
Minimum	594.069	9.834	0.000	9.772	0.014	3.984	−0.632
Q1	588.454	9.551	0.000	9.741	0.014	3.224	−0.020
Median	570.611	9.045	0.000	9.241	0.014	3.299	−0.002
Mean	582.795	10.050	0.000	9.134	0.015	2.957	0.004
Q3	605.908	10.147	0.000	9.342	0.015	2.253	0.018
Maximum	598.986	9.518	0.000	9.253	0.014	2.557	1.020
Skewness	603.710	9.267	0.000	9.002	0.015	2.559	2.579
Kurtosis	640.815	8.958	0.000	9.008	0.017	2.517	47.042
SD	642.122	7.936	0.000	8.192	0.016	2.352	0.073
Variance	650.489	6.635	0.000	8.185	0.017	2.309	0.005
CV	643.383	7.757	0.000	8.025	0.017	2.660	17.048
Range	630.412	7.504	0.000	7.303	0.018	2.646	1.651
IQR	629.299	7.006	0.000	7.286	0.020	2.469	0.038

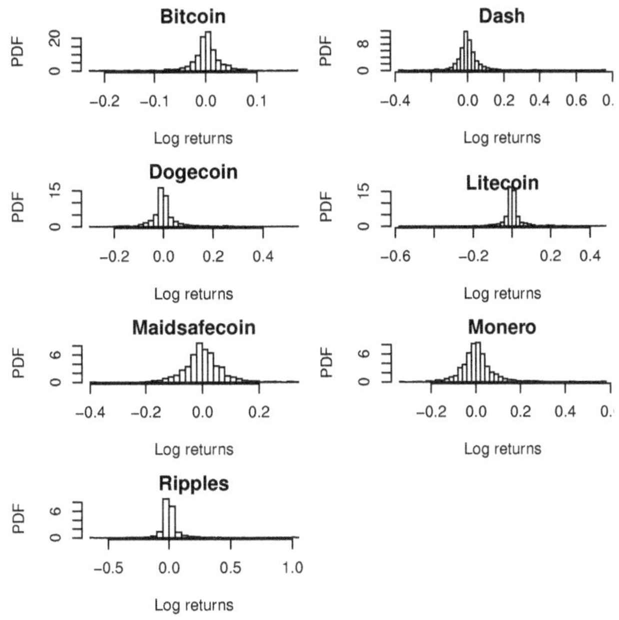

Figure 1. The histogram of the log returns of the exchange rates of Bitcoin, Dash, Dogecoin, Litecoin, Maidsafecoin, Monero and Ripple from 22 June 2014–17 May 2017.

3. Models

First, we provide an introduction to twelve GARCH type models used to analyse our cryptocurrency datasets: SGARCH, EGARCH, GJRGARCH, APARCH, IGARCH, CSGARCH, GARCH, TGARCH, AVGARCH, NGARCH, NAGARCHand ALLGARCH models. Secondly, criteria used to selected the best fitting models are given. Thirdly, formulas are provided for estimating value at risk based on the fitted models.

3.1. GARCH Models

Let X_t denote the observed financial data series; in our case, these are the log returns of the prices of the respective cryptocurrencies. Then, GARCH models can be specified as:

$$X_t = \mu_t + \sigma_t Z_t, \tag{1}$$

where μ_t denotes the conditional mean and σ_t denotes a volatility process. All of the GARCH-type models used follow the above specification in (1); however, in each case, the volatility process σ_t is different. For simplicity, we restrict all of the models to a maximum order of one. In addition, for each GARCH-type model, the innovation process Z_t is allowed to follow one of eight distributions; these are the normal distribution, skew normal distribution (Azzalini (1985)), Student's t distribution (Gosset (1908)), skew Student's distribution (Fernandez and Steel (1998)), skew generalized error distribution (Theodossiou (1998)), generalized hyperbolic distribution Barndorff-Nielsen (1977; 1978) normal inverse Gaussian distribution Barndorff-Nielsen (1977, 1978) and Johnson's SU distribution (Johnson (1949)).

The standard GARCH model (Bollerslev (1986)), denoted by SGARCH (1, 1), has:

$$\sigma_t^2 = \omega + \alpha_1 Z_{t-1}^2 + \beta_1 \sigma_{t-1}^2$$

for $\alpha_1 > 0$, $\beta_1 > 0$ and $\omega > 0$. The main feature of this and other models is that they capture volatility clustering in the data. The "persistence" parameter (which accounts for the amount of volatility clustering captured by the model) for this model is $\alpha_1 + \beta_1$. Weak stationarity holds if $\alpha_1 + \beta_1 < 1$.

The integrated GARCH model (Engle and Bollerslev (1986)), denoted by IGARCH (1, 1), is a particular case of the SGARCH (1, 1) model for $\alpha_1 + \beta_1 = 1$. That is, the persistence parameter is equal to one. This model is strictly stationary.

The exponential GARCH model (Nelson (1991)), denoted by EGARCH (1, 1), has:

$$\log \sigma_t^2 = \omega + \alpha_1 Z_{t-1} + \gamma_1 \left[|Z_{t-1}| - E\left(|Z_{t-1}|\right) \right] + \beta_1 \log \sigma_{t-1}^2$$

for $\alpha_1 > 0$, $\beta_1 > 0$, $\gamma_1 > 0$ and $\omega > 0$. α_1 captures the sign effect, and γ_1 captures the size effect. The persistence parameter for this model is β_1. A difference from SGARCH (1, 1) is that the conditional variance is written as a function of the past standardized innovations, instead of the past innovations. A one line derivation of the EGARCH (1, 1) is described in McAleer and Hafner (2014).

The GJRGARCH (1, 1) model due to Glosten et al. (1993) has:

$$\sigma_t^2 = \omega + \alpha_1 Z_{t-1}^2 + \gamma_1 I_{t-1} Z_{t-1}^2 + \beta_1 \sigma_{t-1}^2$$

for $\alpha_1 > 0$, $\beta_1 > 0$, $\gamma_1 > 0$ and $\omega > 0$, where $I_{t-1} = 1$ if $Z_{t-1} \leq 0$ and $I_{t-1} = 0$ if $Z_{t-1} > 0$. GJRGARCH (1, 1) is an asymmetric version of SGARCH (1, 1), reflects the asymmetric nature of investor response to stock and index returns and leads to positive and negative shocks having different effects on the conditional volatility. γ_1 represents an asymmetry parameter. A positive shock will increase volatility by α_1 at t; a negative shock will increase volatility by $\alpha_1 + \gamma_1$ at t. The persistence depends on this parameter through $\alpha_1 + \beta_1 + \gamma_1 \kappa$, where κ denotes the expected value of the standardized residuals.

In both the EGARCH (1, 1) and GJRGARCH (1, 1) models, asymmetry arises if $\gamma_1 > 0$ (McAleer (2014)), so they both always display asymmetry. Leverage is not possible in either the EGARCH (1, 1) or GJRGARCH (1, 1) model (McAleer (2014); Chang and McAleer (2017)).

The ALL GARCH (1, 1) model due to Hentschel (1995) has:

$$\sigma_t^\delta = \omega + \alpha_1 \sigma_{t-1}^\delta \left[|Z_{t-1} - \eta_1| - \gamma_1 \left(Z_{t-1} - \eta_1\right) \right]^\delta + \beta_1 \sigma_{t-1}^\delta$$

for $\delta > 0$, $\alpha_1 \geq 0$, $\beta_1 \geq 0$, $-1 < \gamma_1 < 1$, $-\infty < \eta_1 < \infty$ and $\omega > 0$. δ is a parameter for the Box–Cox transformation. The persistence parameter is equal to $\beta_1 + \alpha_1\kappa_1$, where κ_1 is the expected value of the standardized residuals under the Box–Cox transformation of the absolute value of the asymmetry term. The ALLGARCH(1, 1) model contains the following as particular cases: the NAGARCH (1, 1) model of Engle and Ng (1993) for $\delta = 2$ and $\gamma_1 = 0$; the GARCH (1, 1) model of Bollerslev (1986) for $\delta = 2$ and $\gamma_1 = \eta_1 = 0$; the GJRARCH (1, 1) model of Glosten et al. (1993) for $\delta = 2$ and $\eta_1 = 0$; the TGARCH (1, 1) model of Zakoian (1994) for $\delta = 1$ and $\eta_1 = 0$; the NGARCH (1, 1) model of Higgins and Bera (1992) for $\gamma_1 = \eta_1 = 0$; the APARCH (1, 1) model of Ding et al. (1993) for $\eta_1 = 0$.

The asymmetric power ARCH model (Ding et al. (1993)), denoted by APARCH (1, 1), has:

$$\sigma_t^\delta = \omega + \alpha_1 \left(|Z_{t-1}| - \gamma_1 Z_{t-1}\right)^\delta + \beta_1 \sigma_{t-1}^\delta$$

for $\delta > 0$, $\alpha_1 \geq 0$, $\beta_1 \geq 0$, $-1 < \gamma_1 < 1$ and $\omega > 0$. APARCH (1, 1) models for both the leverage and the effect that the sample autocorrelation of absolute returns are usually larger than that of squared returns. δ is a parameter for the Box–Cox transformation, and γ_1 is a leverage parameter. The persistence parameter is equal to $\beta_1 + \alpha_1\kappa_1$, where κ_1 is the expected value of the standardized residuals under the Box–Cox transformation of the term, which includes the leverage parameter γ_1. APARCH (1, 1) contains the following as particular cases: the SGARCH (1, 1) model due to Bollerslev (1986) for $\delta = 2$ and $\gamma_1 = 0$; the AVGARCH (1, 1) model due to Taylor (1986) and Schwert (1990) for $\delta = 1$ and $\gamma_1 = 0$; the GJRGARCH (1, 1) model due to Glosten et al. (1993) for $\delta = 2$; the NGARCH (1, 1) model due to Higgins and Bera (1992) for $\beta_1 = 0$ and $\gamma_1 = 0$.

The TGARCH (1, 1) model due to Zakoian (1994) is the particular case of APARCH (1, 1) for $\delta = 1$. Therefore, the specification is one on the conditional standard deviation instead of the conditional variance.

The component standard GARCH model (Lee and Engle (1999)), denoted by CSGARCH (1, 1), has:

$$\sigma_t^2 = q_t + \alpha_1 \left(Z_{t-1}^2 - q_{t-1}\right) + \beta_1 \left(\sigma_{t-1}^2 - q_{t-1}\right),$$

where:

$$q_t = \omega + \rho q_{t-1} + \phi \left(Z_{t-1}^2 - \sigma_{t-1}^2\right)$$

for $\delta > 0$, $\alpha_1 \geq 0$, $\beta_1 \geq 0$, $\phi \geq 0$ and $\omega > 0$. Weak stationarity holds if $\alpha_1 + \beta_1 < 1$ and $\rho < 1$. CSGARCH (1, 1) decomposes the conditional variance into permanent and transitory components so as to investigate the long- and short-run movements of volatility. Compared to SGARCH (1, 1), the intercept parameter is now a time-varying first order autoregressive process.

Detailed conditions for stationarity (weak or strict) for several of the GARCH models can be found in: Nelson (1990) (Theorems 1 and 2, p. 320, 1990) for the SGARCH (1, 1) and IGARCH (1, 1) models; Zakoian (1994) (Propositions 2-3, 1994), Francq and Zakoian (2010) (Theorem 10.3 to 10.5, 2010) and Goncalves et al. (2012) (Theorems 5 and 6, 2012) for the TGARCH (1, 1) model; the Appendix in Hentschel (1995) for the ALL GARCH (1, 1) model; Ling and McAleer (2003) (Theorem 2.1, 2003) for the ARMA-GARCH model; Francq and Zakoian (2010) (Theorem 10.1, 2010) and Francq et al. (2013) (Theorem 2.1, p. 36, 2013) for the EGARCH (1, 1) model; Bardet et al. (2017) (Proposition 2.1, p. 456, 2017) for the APARCH (1, 1) model.

Estimators, their consistency and their asymptotic normality have been established for several of the known GARCH models. The estimators include a Gaussian quasi-maximum likelihood estimator for the GARCH (1, 1) model (Theorem 3, p. 580, Lumsdaine (1996)); a quasi-maximum likelihood estimator for the ARMA-GARCH model (Theorems 4.1 and 5.1, Ling and McAleer (2003)); a stable quasi-maximum likelihood estimator for the EGARCH (1, 1) model (Theorem 6, p. 859, Wintenberger (2013)); a restricted normal mixture quasi-maximum likelihood estimator for the TGARCH (1, 1) model (Theorem 2.4, p. 1346, Wang and Pan (2014)); a Laplacian quasi-maximum likelihood estimator for the APARCH (1, 1) model (Theorem 3.3, pp. 457–458, Bardet et al. (2017)). Propositions 4.1 and 4.2 in Martinet and McAleer (2017) derive conditions of invertibility of quasi-maximum likelihood estimators of the EGARCH (p, q) model.

Explicit expressions for moments of GARCH models have been derived in: Bollerslev (1986) (Theorem 2, 1986) for the SGARCH (1, 1) model; Nelson (1990) (Theorem 6, p. 326, 1990) for the SGARCH (1, 1) and IGARCH (1, 1) models; Zakoian (1994) (Proposition 7, 1994) for the TGARCH (1, 1) model; Karanasos and Kim (2003) (Theorem 1, pp. 149–150, 2003) and Francq and Zakoian (2010) (Theorem 10.2, 2010) for the EGARCH (1, 1) model.

3.2. Model Selection

All of the GARCH-type models were fitted by the method of maximum likelihood. Many of the fitted models are not nested. Discrimination among them was performed using various criteria:

- the Akaike information criterion due to Akaike (1974) defined by:

$$\mathrm{AIC} = 2k - 2\ln L\left(\widehat{\boldsymbol{\Theta}}\right),$$

  where k denotes the number of unknown parameters, $\boldsymbol{\Theta}$ the vector of the unknown parameters and $\widehat{\boldsymbol{\Theta}}$ their maximum likelihood estimates;
- the Bayesian information criterion due to Schwarz (1978) defined by:

$$\mathrm{BIC} = k\ln n - 2\ln L\left(\widehat{\boldsymbol{\Theta}}\right),$$

  where n denotes the number of observations;
- the Consistent Akaike Information Criterion (CAIC) due to Bozdogan (1987) defined by:

$$\mathrm{CAIC} = -2\ln L\left(\widehat{\boldsymbol{\Theta}}\right) + k\left(\ln n + 1\right);$$

- the corrected Akaike Information Criterion (AICc) due to Hurvich and Tsai (1989) defined by:

$$\mathrm{AICc} = \mathrm{AIC} + \frac{2k(k+1)}{n-k-1};$$

- the Hannan–Quinn criterion due to Hannan and Quinn (1979) defined by:

$$\mathrm{HQC} = -2\ln L\left(\widehat{\boldsymbol{\Theta}}\right) + 2k\ln\ln n.$$

The smaller the values of these criteria, the better the fit. For more discussion on these criteria, see Burnham and Anderson (2004) and Fang (2011).

3.3. Estimation of Value at Risk

Here, we provide formulas for estimating the one day-ahead value at risk (see, for example, Equation (6) in Kinateder and Wagner (2014)) for the eight innovation distributions considered in Section 3.1.

For the normal distribution,

$$\widehat{\mathrm{VaR}}_p = \widehat{\mu}_{t+1} + \widehat{\sigma}_{t+1}\Phi^{-1}(p),$$

where $\Phi(\cdot)$ denotes the cumulative distribution function of the standard normal distribution.

For the skew normal distribution (Azzalini (1985)),

$$\widehat{\mathrm{VaR}}_p = \widehat{\mu}_{t+1} + \widehat{\sigma}_{t+1}F^{-1}(p),$$

where:

$$F(x) = \Phi(x) - 2T(x, \widehat{\alpha})$$

for $-\infty < x < \infty$ and $-\infty < \alpha < \infty$, where $T(\cdot,\cdot)$ denotes Owen's T function (Owen (1956)).

For the Student's t distribution (Gosset (1908)),

$$\widehat{\text{VaR}}_p = \widehat{\mu}_{t+1} + \widehat{\sigma}_{t+1} F^{-1}(p),$$

where:

$$F(x) = \int_{-\infty}^{x} f(y)dy$$

for $-\infty < x < \infty$, where

$$f(x) = \frac{2\Gamma\left(\frac{\widehat{\nu}+1}{2}\right)}{\sqrt{\widehat{\nu}(\widehat{\nu}-2)}\Gamma\left(\frac{\widehat{\nu}}{2}\right)} \left(1 + \frac{x^2}{\widehat{\nu}-2}\right)^{-\frac{\widehat{\nu}+1}{2}}$$

for $-\infty < x < \infty$ and $\nu > 0$.

For the skew Student's distribution (Fernandez and Steel (1998)),

$$\widehat{\text{VaR}}_p = \widehat{\mu}_{t+1} + \widehat{\sigma}_{t+1} F^{-1}(p),$$

where:

$$F(x) = \int_{-\infty}^{x} f(y)dy$$

for $-\infty < x < \infty$, where:

$$f(x) = \frac{2\Gamma\left(\frac{\widehat{\nu}+1}{2}\right)}{\sqrt{\widehat{\nu}(\widehat{\nu}-2)}\left(\widehat{\xi}+\widehat{\xi}^{-1}\right)\Gamma\left(\frac{\widehat{\nu}}{2}\right)} \begin{cases} \left(1 + \frac{\widehat{\xi}^2 x^2}{\widehat{\nu}-2}\right)^{-\frac{\widehat{\nu}+1}{2}}, & \text{if } x < 0, \\ \left[1 + \frac{x^2}{\widehat{\xi}^2(\widehat{\nu}-2)}\right]^{-\frac{\widehat{\nu}+1}{2}}, & \text{if } x \geq 0 \end{cases}$$

for $-\infty < x < \infty$, $\nu > 0$ and $\xi > 0$.

For the skew generalized error distribution (Theodossiou (1998)),

$$\widehat{\text{VaR}}_p = \widehat{\mu}_{t+1} + \widehat{\sigma}_{t+1} F^{-1}(p),$$

where:

$$F(x) = \int_{-\infty}^{x} f(y)dy$$

for $-\infty < x < \infty$, where:

$$f(x) = C \begin{cases} \left[1 + \dfrac{\widehat{k}\widehat{\theta}^{-\widehat{k}} \left(1 - \widehat{\lambda}\right)^{-\widehat{k}}}{\widehat{n} - 2} |x|^{\widehat{k}} \right]^{-\frac{\widehat{n}+1}{\widehat{k}}}, & \text{for } x < 0, \\ \left[1 + \dfrac{\widehat{k}\widehat{\theta}^{-\widehat{k}} \left(1 + \widehat{\lambda}\right)^{-\widehat{k}}}{\widehat{n} - 2} |x|^{\widehat{k}} \right]^{-\frac{\widehat{n}+1}{\widehat{k}}}, & \text{for } x \geq 0 \end{cases}$$

for $-\infty < x < \infty, k > 0, n > 2$ and $-1 < \lambda < 1$.

For the generalized hyperbolic distribution Barndorff-Nielsen (1977, 1978),

$$\widehat{\text{VaR}}_p = \widehat{\mu}_{t+1} + \widehat{\sigma}_{t+1} F^{-1}(p),$$

where:

$$F(x) = \int_{-\infty}^{x} f(y) dy$$

for $-\infty < x < \infty$, where

$$f(x) = C\sqrt{1+x^2}^{\widehat{\lambda}-\frac{1}{2}} K_{\widehat{\lambda}-\frac{1}{2}} \left(\widehat{\alpha}\sqrt{1+x^2} \right) \exp\left(\widehat{\beta} x \right) \tag{2}$$

for $-\infty < x < \infty, -\infty < \lambda < \infty, -\infty < \alpha < \infty, -\infty < \beta < \infty, \mid \beta \mid < \alpha$ if $\lambda > 0, \mid \beta \mid < \alpha$ if $\lambda = 0$ and $\mid \beta \mid \leq \alpha$ if $\lambda < 0$, where C is a normalizing constant and $K_\nu(\cdot)$ denotes the modified Bessel function of the second kind defined by:

$$K_\nu(x) = \begin{cases} \dfrac{\pi \csc(\pi\nu)}{2} \left[I_{-\nu}(x) - I_\nu(x) \right], & \text{if } \nu \notin \mathbb{Z}, \\ \lim\limits_{\mu \to \nu} K_\mu(x), & \text{if } \nu \in \mathbb{Z}, \end{cases}$$

where $I_\nu(\cdot)$ denotes the modified Bessel function of the first kind of order ν defined by:

$$I_\nu(x) = \sum_{k=0}^{\infty} \frac{1}{\Gamma(k+\nu+1)k!} \left(\frac{x}{2} \right)^{2k+\nu}.$$

For the normal inverse Gaussian distribution Barndorff-Nielsen (1977, 1978),

$$\widehat{\text{VaR}}_p = \widehat{\mu}_{t+1} + \widehat{\sigma}_{t+1} F^{-1}(p),$$

where:

$$F(x) = \int_{-\infty}^{x} f(y) dy$$

for $-\infty < x < \infty$, where

$$f(x) = C\sqrt{1+x^2}^{\widehat{\lambda}-\frac{1}{2}} K_{-1} \left(\widehat{\alpha}\sqrt{1+x^2} \right) \exp\left(\widehat{\beta} x \right) \tag{3}$$

for $-\infty < x < \infty, -\infty < \alpha < \infty, -\infty < \beta < \infty$, and $\mid \beta \mid \leq \alpha$, where C is a normalizing constant.

For Johnson's SU distribution (Johnson (1949)),

$$\widehat{\text{VaR}}_p = \widehat{\mu}_{t+1} + \widehat{\sigma}_{t+1} F^{-1}(p),$$

where:

$$F(x) = \Phi\left(\widehat{\alpha} + \widehat{\beta}\text{arcsinh}(x)\right)$$

for $-\infty < x < \infty$, $\alpha > 0$ and $\beta > 0$.

4. Results

We fitted SGARCH (1, 1), EGARCH (1, 1), GJRGARCH (1, 1), APARCH (1, 1), IGARCH (1, 1), CSGARCH (1, 1), GARCH (1, 1), TGARCH (1, 1), AVGARCH (1, 1), NGARCH (1, 1), NAGARCH (1, 1) and ALL GARCH (1, 1) models to the log returns of the exchange rates of Bitcoin, Dash, Dogecoin, Litecoin, Maidsafecoin, Monero and Ripple. The distribution of the innovation process were taken to be one of normal distribution, skew normal distribution, Student's t distribution, skew Student's t distribution, skew generalized error distribution, normal inverse Gaussian distribution, generalized hyperbolic distribution or Johnson's SU distribution. The values of AIC, AICc, BIC, HQCand CAICare given in Tables 3–14 in Chu et al. (2017) for the fitted models.

The normal distribution gives the smallest values of AIC, AICc, BIC, HQC and CAIC for each cryptocurrency and each GARCH-type model. There are two exceptions however: for the TGARCH (1, 1) models fitted to Ripple, the skew normal distribution gives the smallest values of AIC, AICc, BIC, HQC and CAIC; for the AVGARCH (1, 1) models fitted to Ripple, the skew normal distribution gives the smallest values of AIC, AICc, BIC, HQC and CAIC.

Hence, the best fitting GARCH-type models are the ones with the innovation process following the normal distribution. The two exceptions are: the best of the TGARCH (1, 1) models fitted to Ripple is the one with the innovation process following the skew normal distribution; the best of the AVGARCH (1, 1) models fitted to Ripple is the one with the innovation process following the skew normal distribution.

Among the twelve best fitting GARCH type models, the IGARCH (1, 1) model with normal innovations gives the smallest values of AIC, AICc, BIC, HQC and CAIC for Bitcoin, Dash, Litecoin, Maidsafecoin and Monero. The GJRGARCH (1, 1) model with normal innovations gives the smallest values of AIC, AICc, BIC, HQC and CAIC for Dogecoin. The GARCH (1, 1) model with normal innovations gives the smallest values of AIC, AICc, BIC, HQC and CAIC for Ripple.

Hence, among all of the GARCH type models fitted, the IGARCH (1, 1) model gives the best fit for Bitcoin, Dash, Litecoin, Maidsafecoin and Monero; the GJRGARCH (1, 1) model gives the best fit for Dogecoin; the GARCH (1, 1) model gives the best fit for Ripple.

Figures 2–13 in Chu et al. (2017) show predicted values for the twenty five days following the end of each dataset. The predictions are given for each of the best fitting GARCH-type model. The predictions given are those based on the fitted model (red) and bootstrapping (black). The curves formed by the blue dots are the 5 percentiles, 25 percentiles, 75 percentiles and 95 percentiles of the bootstrap samples.

We see that the predictions based on the best fitting model and bootstrapping agree well. This is a sign of the goodness of fit of the models. The variation of the bootstrap-based percentile appears largest for Ripple for each GARCH-type model. The variation appears smallest for Bitcoin for each GARCH-type model.

We further checked the goodness of fit of the models by the one-sample Kolmogorov–Smirnov test. The p-values of this test for the seven best fitting SGARCH models were 0.238, 0.107, 0.290, 0.207, 0.228, 0.124 and 0.058. The corresponding p-values for the seven best fitting EGARCH models were 0.148, 0.333, 0.338, 0.116, 0.337, 0.369 and 0.229. The corresponding p-values for the seven best fitting GJRGARCH models were 0.345, 0.306, 0.352, 0.314, 0.286, 0.153 and 0.258. The corresponding p-values for the seven best fitting APARCH models were 0.091, 0.241, 0.109, 0.300, 0.394, 0.364 and 0.115. The corresponding p-values for the seven best fitting IGARCH models were 0.197, 0.118, 0.166, 0.207, 0.377, 0.238 and 0.370. The corresponding p-values for the seven best fitting CSGARCH models were

0.136, 0.298, 0.100, 0.073, 0.366, 0.167 and 0.279. The corresponding p-values for the seven best fitting GARCH models were 0.183, 0.217, 0.103, 0.236, 0.142, 0.392 and 0.129. The corresponding p-values for the seven best fitting TGARCH models were 0.087, 0.214, 0.280, 0.317, 0.219, 0.080 and 0.297. The corresponding p-values for the seven best fitting AVGARCH models were 0.071, 0.377, 0.210, 0.136, 0.120, 0.050 and 0.240. The corresponding p-values for the seven best fitting NGARCH models were 0.375, 0.231, 0.207, 0.139, 0.118, 0.236 and 0.341. The corresponding p-values for the seven best fitting NAGARCH models were 0.053, 0.267, 0.312, 0.281, 0.211, 0.051 and 0.335. The corresponding p-values for the seven best fitting ALLGARCH models were 0.241, 0.067, 0.304, 0.078, 0.155, 0.184 and 0.072. Hence, all of the best fitting models provide adequate fits at least at the five percent significance level.

Finally, we perform the unconditional and conditional coverage value at risk exceedances tests (Christoffersen (1998); Christoffersen et al. (2001)). The p-values of the unconditional test for the best fitting models and various exceedance probabilities are given in Tables 2–8. The corresponding p-values of the conditional test are given in the same tables. All of the p-values are significant at the five percent level of significance. Hence, the best fitting models can be used to provide acceptable estimates of value at risk.

Table 2. p-values of the unconditional (conditional) coverage value at risk exceedance test for the log returns of the exchange rates of Bitcoin from 22 June 2014–17 May 2017.

	Exceedance Probability					
	0.05	**0.025**	**0.01**	**0.005**	**0.001**	**0.0001**
SGARCH	0.078 (0.312)	0.099 (0.238)	0.263 (0.173)	0.284 (0.266)	0.264 (0.104)	0.350 (0.138)
EGARCH	0.287 (0.125)	0.238 (0.349)	0.227 (0.127)	0.319 (0.385)	0.231 (0.094)	0.094 (0.091)
GJRGARCH	0.242 (0.120)	0.356 (0.394)	0.384 (0.393)	0.198 (0.297)	0.299 (0.118)	0.341 (0.300)
APARCH	0.398 (0.334)	0.280 (0.331)	0.071 (0.344)	0.088 (0.193)	0.267 (0.137)	0.284 (0.184)
IGARCH	0.128 (0.086)	0.301 (0.356)	0.144 (0.053)	0.302 (0.115)	0.398 (0.249)	0.145 (0.261)
CSGARCH	0.256 (0.243)	0.179 (0.149)	0.115 (0.175)	0.384 (0.140)	0.137 (0.109)	0.261 (0.319)
GARCH	0.323 (0.336)	0.387 (0.347)	0.100 (0.242)	0.069 (0.396)	0.334 (0.238)	0.097 (0.092)
TGARCH	0.253 (0.189)	0.358 (0.165)	0.259 (0.286)	0.089 (0.126)	0.213 (0.102)	0.143 (0.143)
AVGARCH	0.203 (0.347)	0.348 (0.079)	0.277 (0.376)	0.082 (0.082)	0.371 (0.052)	0.208 (0.240)
NGARCH	0.097 (0.194)	0.064 (0.290)	0.199 (0.240)	0.064 (0.204)	0.100 (0.127)	0.266 (0.186)
NAGARCH	0.199 (0.069)	0.072 (0.149)	0.185 (0.061)	0.216 (0.167)	0.285 (0.121)	0.062 (0.099)
ALLGARCH	0.271 (0.327)	0.201 (0.072)	0.262 (0.097)	0.114 (0.320)	0.162 (0.180)	0.167 (0.249)

Table 3. p-values of the unconditional (conditional) coverage value at risk exceedance test for the log returns of the exchange rates of Dash from 22 June 2014–17 May 2017.

	Exceedance Probability					
	0.05	**0.025**	**0.01**	**0.005**	**0.001**	**0.0001**
SGARCH	0.358 (0.383)	0.051 (0.231)	0.357 (0.129)	0.122 (0.167)	0.150 (0.234)	0.146 (0.162)
EGARCH	0.396 (0.340)	0.333 (0.225)	0.374 (0.157)	0.216 (0.170)	0.220 (0.138)	0.132 (0.196)
GJRGARCH	0.282 (0.254)	0.115 (0.196)	0.218 (0.280)	0.141 (0.262)	0.069 (0.358)	0.211 (0.328)
APARCH	0.257 (0.304)	0.290 (0.194)	0.087 (0.204)	0.238 (0.212)	0.304 (0.182)	0.314 (0.240)
IGARCH	0.222 (0.241)	0.110 (0.262)	0.305 (0.297)	0.206 (0.364)	0.068 (0.374)	0.390 (0.100)
CSGARCH	0.268 (0.055)	0.378 (0.391)	0.352 (0.276)	0.286 (0.302)	0.100 (0.368)	0.134 (0.081)
GARCH	0.200 (0.145)	0.165 (0.080)	0.186 (0.293)	0.272 (0.077)	0.323 (0.243)	0.265 (0.298)
TGARCH	0.304 (0.121)	0.299 (0.155)	0.231 (0.173)	0.264 (0.385)	0.092 (0.337)	0.376 (0.305)
AVGARCH	0.227 (0.335)	0.261 (0.303)	0.151 (0.214)	0.179 (0.101)	0.359 (0.052)	0.364 (0.392)
NGARCH	0.069 (0.212)	0.054 (0.246)	0.216 (0.259)	0.222 (0.119)	0.138 (0.145)	0.162 (0.240)
NAGARCH	0.116 (0.180)	0.129 (0.302)	0.332 (0.183)	0.179 (0.354)	0.344 (0.397)	0.196 (0.339)
ALLGARCH	0.069 (0.195)	0.380 (0.378)	0.350 (0.075)	0.152 (0.263)	0.243 (0.256)	0.172 (0.243)

Table 4. *p*-values of the unconditional (conditional) coverage value at risk exceedance test for the log returns of the exchange rates of Dogecoin from 22 June 2014–17 May 2017.

	Exceedance Probability					
	0.05	**0.025**	**0.01**	**0.005**	**0.001**	**0.0001**
SGARCH	0.063 (0.109)	0.178 (0.264)	0.297 (0.230)	0.101 (0.256)	0.178 (0.280)	0.246 (0.393)
EGARCH	0.398 (0.069)	0.077 (0.107)	0.370 (0.214)	0.079 (0.339)	0.347 (0.274)	0.340 (0.210)
GJRGARCH	0.215 (0.095)	0.178 (0.114)	0.061 (0.073)	0.298 (0.266)	0.116 (0.302)	0.342 (0.380)
APARCH	0.368 (0.178)	0.264 (0.359)	0.381 (0.103)	0.221 (0.326)	0.225 (0.100)	0.222 (0.361)
IGARCH	0.098 (0.073)	0.164 (0.070)	0.172 (0.115)	0.187 (0.136)	0.375 (0.227)	0.382 (0.380)
CSGARCH	0.096 (0.267)	0.063 (0.181)	0.324 (0.069)	0.200 (0.354)	0.223 (0.237)	0.264 (0.292)
GARCH	0.132 (0.377)	0.342 (0.133)	0.332 (0.054)	0.137 (0.388)	0.137 (0.084)	0.386 (0.197)
TGARCH	0.178 (0.346)	0.329 (0.211)	0.250 (0.329)	0.141 (0.181)	0.186 (0.205)	0.137 (0.276)
AVGARCH	0.254 (0.218)	0.181 (0.122)	0.394 (0.280)	0.150 (0.385)	0.118 (0.369)	0.208 (0.106)
NGARCH	0.086 (0.118)	0.396 (0.314)	0.144 (0.244)	0.120 (0.242)	0.169 (0.318)	0.341 (0.303)
NAGARCH	0.282 (0.284)	0.106 (0.127)	0.342 (0.234)	0.342 (0.321)	0.309 (0.288)	0.308 (0.105)
ALLGARCH	0.252 (0.267)	0.223 (0.189)	0.242 (0.201)	0.290 (0.249)	0.319 (0.317)	0.178 (0.226)

Table 5. *p*-values of the unconditional (conditional) coverage value at risk exceedance test for the log returns of the exchange rates of Litecoin from 22 June 2014–17 May 2017.

	Exceedance Probability					
	0.05	**0.025**	**0.01**	**0.005**	**0.001**	**0.0001**
SGARCH	0.056 (0.092)	0.166 (0.267)	0.383 (0.156)	0.134 (0.187)	0.231 (0.099)	0.352 (0.261)
EGARCH	0.134 (0.139)	0.209 (0.370)	0.062 (0.390)	0.297 (0.215)	0.256 (0.200)	0.127 (0.074)
GJRGARCH	0.052 (0.245)	0.091 (0.153)	0.204 (0.275)	0.081 (0.194)	0.211 (0.089)	0.187 (0.055)
APARCH	0.362 (0.180)	0.292 (0.229)	0.280 (0.294)	0.322 (0.161)	0.391 (0.170)	0.095 (0.138)
IGARCH	0.358 (0.242)	0.106 (0.391)	0.068 (0.087)	0.117 (0.051)	0.298 (0.053)	0.108 (0.310)
CSGARCH	0.092 (0.117)	0.267 (0.129)	0.102 (0.318)	0.379 (0.234)	0.241 (0.345)	0.261 (0.371)
GARCH	0.158 (0.114)	0.109 (0.307)	0.350 (0.265)	0.399 (0.339)	0.309 (0.354)	0.337 (0.361)
TGARCH	0.326 (0.268)	0.207 (0.397)	0.090 (0.179)	0.392 (0.223)	0.148 (0.144)	0.158 (0.192)
AVGARCH	0.108 (0.098)	0.131 (0.167)	0.178 (0.069)	0.054 (0.287)	0.374 (0.286)	0.171 (0.104)
NGARCH	0.259 (0.072)	0.297 (0.097)	0.085 (0.219)	0.344 (0.085)	0.227 (0.185)	0.386 (0.295)
NAGARCH	0.313 (0.338)	0.053 (0.274)	0.390 (0.148)	0.251 (0.276)	0.251 (0.106)	0.230 (0.094)
ALLGARCH	0.080 (0.236)	0.357 (0.299)	0.184 (0.202)	0.115 (0.154)	0.065 (0.209)	0.116 (0.199)

Table 6. *p*-values of the unconditional (conditional) coverage value at risk exceedance test for the log returns of the exchange rates of Maidsafecoin from 22 June 2014–17 May 2017.

	Exceedance Probability					
	0.05	**0.025**	**0.01**	**0.005**	**0.001**	**0.0001**
SGARCH	0.304 (0.218)	0.099 (0.128)	0.318 (0.080)	0.072 (0.287)	0.271 (0.192)	0.351 (0.310)
EGARCH	0.337 (0.315)	0.308 (0.128)	0.229 (0.152)	0.178 (0.051)	0.139 (0.324)	0.382 (0.091)
GJRGARCH	0.181 (0.215)	0.054 (0.353)	0.375 (0.144)	0.173 (0.262)	0.342 (0.378)	0.090 (0.252)
APARCH	0.386 (0.067)	0.387 (0.343)	0.116 (0.165)	0.108 (0.272)	0.198 (0.197)	0.374 (0.092)
IGARCH	0.385 (0.280)	0.308 (0.189)	0.184 (0.177)	0.096 (0.225)	0.259 (0.241)	0.155 (0.284)
CSGARCH	0.379 (0.190)	0.175 (0.158)	0.315 (0.246)	0.148 (0.125)	0.133 (0.054)	0.379 (0.356)
GARCH	0.316 (0.130)	0.172 (0.083)	0.388 (0.183)	0.385 (0.298)	0.198 (0.104)	0.239 (0.228)
TGARCH	0.397 (0.351)	0.372 (0.069)	0.377 (0.305)	0.243 (0.255)	0.142 (0.195)	0.081 (0.150)
AVGARCH	0.087 (0.227)	0.136 (0.278)	0.397 (0.228)	0.195 (0.348)	0.260 (0.308)	0.124 (0.153)
NGARCH	0.077 (0.177)	0.314 (0.398)	0.214 (0.247)	0.384 (0.147)	0.265 (0.063)	0.320 (0.135)
NAGARCH	0.369 (0.292)	0.115 (0.205)	0.058 (0.180)	0.100 (0.258)	0.226 (0.144)	0.330 (0.249)
ALLGARCH	0.077 (0.266)	0.074 (0.207)	0.244 (0.302)	0.335 (0.287)	0.275 (0.352)	0.091 (0.389)

Table 7. p-values of the unconditional (conditional) coverage value at risk exceedance test for the log returns of the exchange rates of Monero from 22 June 2014–17 May 2017.

	Exceedance Probability					
	0.05	**0.025**	**0.01**	**0.005**	**0.001**	**0.0001**
SGARCH	0.251 (0.095)	0.105 (0.294)	0.158 (0.136)	0.081 (0.388)	0.386 (0.077)	0.382 (0.397)
EGARCH	0.098 (0.077)	0.302 (0.319)	0.364 (0.118)	0.398 (0.385)	0.186 (0.198)	0.326 (0.300)
GJRGARCH	0.317 (0.140)	0.234 (0.124)	0.088 (0.350)	0.174 (0.092)	0.122 (0.240)	0.072 (0.262)
APARCH	0.077 (0.311)	0.298 (0.260)	0.149 (0.179)	0.211 (0.264)	0.381 (0.090)	0.232 (0.287)
IGARCH	0.275 (0.179)	0.057 (0.087)	0.060 (0.398)	0.379 (0.310)	0.288 (0.254)	0.247 (0.133)
CSGARCH	0.350 (0.123)	0.109 (0.330)	0.331 (0.343)	0.372 (0.174)	0.241 (0.051)	0.238 (0.091)
GARCH	0.198 (0.093)	0.162 (0.380)	0.316 (0.395)	0.249 (0.309)	0.388 (0.097)	0.224 (0.053)
TGARCH	0.228 (0.060)	0.233 (0.158)	0.170 (0.156)	0.148 (0.150)	0.236 (0.135)	0.162 (0.333)
AVGARCH	0.079 (0.233)	0.399 (0.293)	0.376 (0.259)	0.224 (0.229)	0.216 (0.240)	0.371 (0.235)
NGARCH	0.233 (0.228)	0.215 (0.266)	0.326 (0.385)	0.231 (0.056)	0.312 (0.193)	0.258 (0.370)
NAGARCH	0.395 (0.102)	0.105 (0.130)	0.292 (0.242)	0.354 (0.116)	0.170 (0.207)	0.121 (0.114)
ALLGARCH	0.337 (0.245)	0.275 (0.131)	0.221 (0.223)	0.169 (0.304)	0.170 (0.197)	0.086 (0.181)

Table 8. p-values of the unconditional (conditional) coverage value at risk exceedance test for the log returns of the exchange rates of Ripple from 22 June 2014–17 May 2017.

	Exceedance Probability					
	0.05	**0.025**	**0.01**	**0.005**	**0.001**	**0.0001**
SGARCH	0.249 (0.368)	0.318 (0.256)	0.353 (0.249)	0.193 (0.075)	0.199 (0.243)	0.063 (0.131)
EGARCH	0.259 (0.287)	0.281 (0.191)	0.309 (0.157)	0.167 (0.222)	0.086 (0.109)	0.256 (0.084)
GJRGARCH	0.143 (0.303)	0.219 (0.135)	0.394 (0.085)	0.095 (0.319)	0.299 (0.184)	0.308 (0.224)
APARCH	0.312 (0.083)	0.356 (0.162)	0.125 (0.097)	0.216 (0.126)	0.138 (0.075)	0.177 (0.103)
IGARCH	0.288 (0.331)	0.071 (0.246)	0.053 (0.154)	0.113 (0.063)	0.367 (0.234)	0.265 (0.109)
CSGARCH	0.096 (0.386)	0.114 (0.207)	0.065 (0.312)	0.117 (0.398)	0.308 (0.380)	0.069 (0.070)
GARCH	0.305 (0.256)	0.083 (0.332)	0.245 (0.070)	0.333 (0.379)	0.275 (0.258)	0.209 (0.277)
TGARCH	0.149 (0.293)	0.327 (0.342)	0.076 (0.399)	0.176 (0.236)	0.369 (0.289)	0.307 (0.136)
AVGARCH	0.093 (0.084)	0.309 (0.259)	0.222 (0.210)	0.071 (0.327)	0.187 (0.395)	0.109 (0.300)
NGARCH	0.225 (0.143)	0.246 (0.150)	0.317 (0.320)	0.105 (0.099)	0.134 (0.233)	0.210 (0.249)
NAGARCH	0.141 (0.350)	0.050 (0.242)	0.189 (0.207)	0.259 (0.227)	0.379 (0.289)	0.075 (0.205)
ALLGARCH	0.283 (0.253)	0.343 (0.068)	0.081 (0.236)	0.309 (0.298)	0.386 (0.153)	0.162 (0.304)

5. Conclusions

We find that the IGARCH and GJRGARCH models provide the best fits, in terms of modelling of the volatility in the most popular and largest cryptocurrencies. The IGARCH model falls within the standard GARCH framework and contains a conditional volatility process, which is highly persistent (with infinite memory), and this has been shown in the literature (Caporale et al. (2003)). However, although the IGARCH (1, 1) with normal innovations appears to give a good fit for numerous cryptocurrencies, it has been shown that this could stem from a structural change in the data, which may not be accounted for; i.e., a policy change (Caporale et al. (2003)). Therefore, more in depth analysis of the datasets may be required to confirm or deny possible structural change.

Due to the increasing demand and interest in cryptocurrencies, we believe that they should now be treated as more than just a novelty. Some cryptocurrencies have recently seen more growth than others, for example, Bitcoin, Ethereum, Litecoin and Ripple. However, there is still much discussion about whether cryptocurrencies, especially Bitcoin, should be classed as currencies, assets or investment vehicles, and this is a key topic in itself. Our analysis assumes that we are looking at cryptocurrencies in terms of financial assets, where most users are trading them for investment purposes: either as a long-term investment in new technology or looking to make a short-term profit. Investigating the volatility of cryptocurrencies is important in terms of financial investment like hedging or pricing instruments. Therefore, these results would be particularly useful in terms of portfolio and risk management and could help others make better informed decisions with regard to financial investments and the potential benefits and pitfalls of utilizing cryptocurrencies.

Our results show that cryptocurrencies such as Bitcoin, Ethereum, Litecoin and many others exhibit extreme volatility especially when we look at their inter-daily prices. This is suited for risk-seeking investors looking for a way to invest or enter into technology markets. Our results can also assist financial institutions.

Regulations and policies surrounding cryptocurrencies are being gradually tightened up by many countries; most recently, the U.S. Securities and Exchange Commission (SEC) has initiated plans to regulate the cryptocurrency exchange and all digital currencies. With the exponential growth of the initial coin offering to raise funds for start ups, we have seen China and South Korea (the biggest markets for cryptocurrencies) already regulating and banning such products. Overall, we believe in implementing more regulations and policy for cryptocurrencies as people are starting to see them as investment prospects.

A future work is to fit multivariate GARCH-type models to describe the joint behaviour of the exchange rates of Bitcoin, Dash, Dogecoin, Litecoin, Maidsafecoin, Monero and Ripple. This will require methodological, as well as empirical developments. Furthermore, we have used value at risk since it has been the most popular risk measure in finance. However, there is a shift of value at risk to stressed expected shortfall in the new Basel III regulation (see, for example, Kinateder (2016)). Therefore, another future work is to use expected shortfall instead of value at risk.

Acknowledgments: The authors would like to thank the Editor and the three referees for careful reading and comments, which greatly improved the paper.

Conflicts of Interest: The authors declare no conflict of interest.

References

Akaike, Hirotugu. 1974. A new look at the statistical model identification. *IEEE Transactions on Automatic Control* 19: 716–23.

Azzalini, A. 1985. A class of distributions which includes the normal ones. *Scandinavian Journal of Statistics* 12: 171–78.

Bardet, Jean-Marc, Yakoub Boularouk, and Khedidja Djaballah. 2017. Asymptotic behaviour of the Laplacian quasi-maximum likelihood estimator of affine causal processes. *Electronic Journal of Statistics* 11: 452–79.

Barndorff-Nielsen, Ole E. 1977. Exponentially decreasing distributions for the logarithm of particle size. *Proceedings of the Royal Society of London A: Mathematical and Physical Sciences* 353: 401–9.

Barndorff-Nielsen, Ole E. 1978. Hyperbolic distributions and distributions on hyperbolae. *Scandinavian Journal of Statistics* 5: 151–57.

Bollerslev, Tim. 1986. Generalized autoregressive conditional heteroskedasticity. *Journal of Econometrics* 31: 307–27.

Bouoiyour, Jamal, and Refk Selmi. 2015. Bitcoin Price: Is it Really That New Round of Volatility Can Be on Way? MPRA Paper No. 65580, CATT, University of Pau, Pau, France.

Bouoiyour, Jamal, and Refk Selmi. 2016. Bitcoin: A beginning of a new phase? *Economics Bulletin* 36: 1430–40.

Bouri, Elie, Georges Azzi, and Anne Haubo Dyhrberg. 2017. On the return-volatility relationship in the Bitcoin market around the price crash of 2013. *Economics: The Open-Access, Open-Assessment E-Journal* 11: 1–16.

Bozdogan, Hamparsum. 1987. Model selection and Akaike's Information Criterion (AIC): The general theory and its analytical extensions. *Psychometrika* 52: 345–70.

Burnham, Kenneth P., and David R. Anderson. 2004. Multimodel inference: Understanding AIC and BIC in model selection. *Sociological Methods and Research* 33: 261–304.

Caporale, Guglielmo Maria, Nikitas Pittis, and Nicola Spagnolo. 2003. IGARCH models and structural breaks. *Applied Economics Letters* 10: 765–68.

Cermak, Vavrinec. 2017. Can Bitcoin become a viable alternative to fiat currencies? An empirical analysis of Bitcoin's volatility based on a GARCH model. Available online: https://ssrn.com/abstract=2961405 (accessed on 30 September 2017).

Chan, Stephen, Jeffrey Chu, Saralees Nadarajah, and Joerg Osterrieder. 2017. A statistical analysis of cryptocurrencies. *Journal of Risk Financial Management* 10: 12. doi:10.3390/jrfm10020012.

Chang, Chia-Lin, and Michael McAleer. 2017. The Correct Regularity Condition and Interpretation of Asymmetry in EGARCH. Tinbergen Institute Discussion Paper 2017-056/III, Tinbergen Institute, The Netherlands, to appear in Economics Letters.

Chen, Shi, Cathy Yi-Hsuan Chen, Wolfgang K. Hardle, TM Lee, and Bobby Ong. 2016. A first econometric analysis of the CRIX family. Available online: https://ssrn.com/abstract=2832099 (accessed on 30 September 2017).

Christoffersen, Peter F. 1998. Evaluating interval forecasts. *International Economic Review* 39: 841–62.

Christoffersen, Peter, Jinyong Hahn, and Atsushi Inoue. 2001. Testing and comparing Value at Risk measures. *Journal of Empirical Finance* 8: 325–42.

Chu, Jeffrey, Stephen Chan, Saralees Nadarajah, and Joerg Osterrieder. 2017. *GARCH Modeling of Cryptocurrencies*, Technical Report. School of Mathematics, University of Manchester, Manchester, UK.

CoinMarketCap. 2017. Crypto-currency market capitalizations. Available online: https://coinmarketcap.com/ (accessed on 30 September 2017).

Ding, Zhuanxin, Clive W. J. Granger, and Robert F. Engle. 1993. A long memory property of stock market returns and a new model. *Journal of Empirical Finance* 1: 83–106.

Dyhrberg, Anne Haubo. 2016a. Hedging capabilities of Bitcoin. Is it the virtual gold? *Finance Research Letters* 16: 139–44.

Dyhrberg, Anne Haubo. 2016b. Bitcoin, gold and the dollar—A GARCH volatility analysis. *Finance Research Letters* 16: 85–92.

Engle, Robert F., and Tim Bollerslev. 1986. Modelling the persistence of conditional variances. *Econometric Reviews* 5: 1–50.

Engle, Robert F., and Victor K. Ng. 1993. Measuring and testing the impact of news on volatility. *Journal of Finance* 48: 1749–78.

Fang, Yixin. 2011. Asymptotic equivalence between cross-validations and Akaike Information Criteria in mixed-effects models. *Journal of Data Science* 9: 15–21.

Fernandez, Carmen, and Mark F. J. Steel. 1998. On Bayesian modelling of fat tails and skewness. *Journal of the American Statistical Association* 93: 359–71.

Francq, Christian, Olivier Wintenberger, and Jean-Michel Zakoian. 2013. GARCH models without positivity constraints: Exponential or log GARCH? *Journal of Econometrics* 177: 34–46.

Francq, Christian, and Jean-Michel Zakoian. 2010. *GARCH Models: Structure, Statistical Inference and Financial Applications*. New York: John Wiley and Sons.

Glosten, Lawrence R., Ravi Jagannathan, and David E. Runkle. 1993. On the relation between the expected value and the volatility of the nominal excess return on stocks. *Journal of Finance* 48: 1779–801.

Goncalves, Esmeralda, Joana Leite, and Nazaré Mendes-Lopes. 2012. On the probabilistic structure of power threshold generalized arch stochastic processes. *Statistics and Probability Letters* 82: 1597–609.

Gosset, W. S. 1908. The probable error of a mean. *Biometrika* 6: 1–25.

Hannan, E. J., and Barry G. Quinn. 1979. The determination of the order of an autoregression. *Journal of the Royal Statistical Society: Series B* 41: 190–95.

Hentschel, Ludger. 1995. All in the family nesting symmetric and asymmetric GARCH models. *Journal of Financial Economics* 39: 71–104.

Higgins, Matthew L., and Anil. K. Bera. 1992. A class of nonlinear arch models. *International Economic Review* 33: 137–58.

Hurvich, Clifford M., and Chih-Ling Tsai. 1989. Regression and time series model selection in small samples. *Biometrika* 76: 297–307.

Johnson, N. L. 1949. Systems of frequency curves generated by methods of translation. *Biometrika* 36: 149–76.

Karanasos, Menelaos, and J. Kim. 2003. Moments of the ARMA-EGARCH model. *The Econometrics Journal* 6: 146–66.

Katsiampa, Paraskevi. 2017. Volatility estimation for Bitcoin: A comparison of GARCH models. *Economics Letters* 158: 3–6.

Kinateder, Harald. 2016. Basel II versus III—A comparative assessment of minimum capital requirements for internal model approaches. *Journal of Risk* 18: 25–45.

Kinateder, Harald, and Niklas Wagner. 2014. Multiple-period market risk prediction under long memory: When VaR is higher than expected. *Journal of Risk Finance* 15: 4–32.

Lee, Gary J., and Robert F. Engle. 1999. A permanent and transitory component model of stock return volatility. In *Cointegration Causality and Forecasting A Festschrift in Honor of Clive W. J. Granger*. Oxford: Oxford University Press, pp. 475–97.

Letra, Ivo José Santos. 2016. What drives cryptocurrency value? A volatility and predictability analysis. Available online: https://www.repository.utl.pt/handle/10400.5/12556 (accessed on 30 September 2017).

Ling, Shiqing, and Michael McAleer. 2003. Asymptotic theory for a vector ARMA-GARCH model. *Econometric Theory* 19: 278–308.

Lumsdaine, Robin L. 1996. Consistency and asymptotic normality of the quasi-maximum likelihood in IGARCH(1, 1) and covariance stationary GARCH(1, 1) models. *Econometrica* 64: 575–96.

Martinet, Guillaume Gaetan, and Michael McAleer. 2017. On the Invertibility of EGARCH (p, q). Tinbergen Institute Discussion Paper 2015-022/III, Tinbergen Institute, The Netherlands, to appear in Econometric Reviews.

McAleer, Michael. 2014. Asymmetry and leverage in conditional volatility models. *Econometrics* 2: 145–50.

McAleer, Michael, and Christian Hafner. 2014. A one line derivation of EGARCH. *Econometrics* 2: 92–97.

Nelson, Daniel B. 1990. Stationarity and persistence in the GARCH(1,1) model. *Econometric Theory* 6: 318–34.

Nelson, Daniel B. 1991. Conditional heteroskedasticity in asset returns: A new approach. *Econometrica* 59: 347–70.

Owen, Donald B. 1956. Tables for computing bivariate normal probabilities. *Annals of Mathematical Statistics* 27: 1075–90.

Schwarz, Gideon E. 1978. Estimating the dimension of a model. *Annals of Statistics* 6: 461–64.

Schwert, G. William. 1990. Stock volatility and the crash of '87. *Review of Financial Studies* 3: 103–6.

Stavroyiannis, Stavros, and Vassilios Babalos. 2017. Dynamic properties of the Bitcoin and the US market. Available online: https://ssrn.com/abstract=2966998 (accessed on 30 September 2017).

Taylor, Stephen J. 1986. *Modelling Financial Time Series*. New York: John Wiley and Sons.

Theodossiou, Panayiotis. 1998. Financial data and the skewed generalized t distribution. *Management Science* 44: 1650–61.

Urquhart, Andrew. 2017. The volatility of Bitcoin. Available online: https://ssrn.com/abstract=2921082 (accessed on 30 September 2017)

Wang, Hui, and Jiazhu Pan. 2014. Restricted normal mixture QMLE for non-stationary TGARCH(1, 1) models. *Science China Mathematics* 57: 1341–60.

Wintenberger, Olivier. 2013. Continuous invertibility and stable QML estimation of the EGARCH(1, 1) model. *Scandinavian Journal of Statistics* 40: 846–67.

Zakoian, Jean-Michel. 1994. Threshold heteroskedastic models. *Journal of Economic Dynamics and Control* 18: 931–55.

MDPI
St. Alban-Anlage 66
4052 Basel
Switzerland
Tel. +41 61 683 77 34
Fax +41 61 302 89 18
www.mdpi.com

Journal of Risk and Financial Management Editorial Office
E-mail: jrfm@mdpi.com
www.mdpi.com/journal/jrfm

www.ingramcontent.com/pod-product-compliance
Lightning Source LLC
Chambersburg PA
CBHW051914210326
41597CB00033B/6141
* 9 7 8 3 0 3 8 9 7 4 3 9 0 *